Deception
in the Marketplace

Deception

in the Marketplace

*The Psychology of Deceptive Persuasion
and Consumer Self-Protection*

David M. Boush • Marian Friestad • Peter Wright

Routledge
Taylor & Francis Group
New York   London

Routledge
Taylor & Francis Group
270 Madison Avenue
New York, NY 10016

Routledge
Taylor & Francis Group
27 Church Road
Hove, East Sussex BN3 2FA

International Standard Book Number: 978-0-8058-6086-3 (Hardback) 978-0-8058-6087-0 (Paperback)

Library of Congress Cataloging-in-Publication Data

Boush, David M.
    Deception in the marketplace : the psychology of deceptive persuasion and consumer self protection / David M. Boush, Marian Friestad, Peter Wright.
        p. cm.
    Includes bibliographical references.
    ISBN 978-0-8058-6086-3 (hardback : acid-free paper) – ISBN 978-0-8058-6087-0 (pbk. : acid-free paper)
    1. Deceptive advertising--United States. 2. Marketing--United States. 3. Consumer protection--United States. I. Friestad, Marian. II. Wright, Peter. III. Title.

HF5827.8.B68 2009
659.101'9--dc22   2008043548

Visit the Taylor & Francis Web site at
http://www.taylorandfrancis.com

and the Psychology Press Web site at
http://www.psypress.com

Dedication

We dedicate this book to our grandchildren.

Contents

Preface   xi

The Authors   xv

1   Deception in the Marketplace   1

    Deception in the Modern Marketplace   3
        Misleading and Deceptive: Defining Marketplace Deception   6
        Legalistic Definitions   8
        Marketplace Deception Is Persuasion   11
        Deceptions Are Context Bound   13
        A Deception Agent's Definition: It Is Deception if Persuasion Targets
            Perceive It as Such   14
        Ethics and Morality   15
        Marketplace Deception Is a Special Domain of Societal Deception   16
    A Framework for Examining Marketplace Deception   17
        The Scope of This Book   18

2   Theoretical Perspectives on Deceptive Persuasion   21

    Deception Theory   22
    Persuasion Theory   29
        Dual-Process Models of Persuasion   29
        Social Influence and Persuasion Tactics   30
        Resistance to Persuasion   31
        The Persuasion Knowledge Model   32
        Metacognition and Deception Protection   34
        Protection Motivation Theory and Regulatory Focus Theory   35
        Aversion to Feeling Duped   37

3   Marketplace Deception Tactics I   39

    Overview of Marketplace Deception Strategy   40
    Types of Deception Tactics   43
    Distraction and Camouflage   45
    Corrupted and Subverted Persuasion Tactics   49
    Suppressing Deception-Protection Motivation and Opportunity   52

The Run-Around   55
Omissions   56

4   Marketplace Deception Tactics II   59

    Simulation   59
    Deceptive Framings   62
    Impersonation   64
    Language That Misleads and Avoids Responsibility   65
    Exploiting Automatized Inferencing Tendencies   67
    Verbal and Visual Misrepresentation   68
    Exploiting Limited Numeracy, Research, and Statistical Understanding   70
    Rhetorical Deception: Visual and Verbal Figures of Speech   73
    Marketing Bullshit   74

5   How Deception-Minded Marketers Think   79

    A Mental Model of a Professional Deception Planner   79
    Social Engineering   86
    The Mind of a Telescammer   88
    Marketing Managers' Deception Decisions   90

6   How People Cope With Deceptiveness: Prior Research   95

    Uncertainty and Suspicion   96
    Suspicion Effects on Processing of Subsequent Persuasion Attempts   100
    Omissions, Misleading Inferences, and Message Tactics   102
    The Heard-It-Before "Truth Effect"   111
    The Use of Marketplace Persuasion Knowledge   114
    Detecting Deceptions   117

7   Marketplace Deception Protection Skills   123

    Deception Protection Skills: Detection, Neutralization, Resistance   124
    Proactive Coping Skills: Preparing for Battle Before It Begins   131
    Resource Management Skills   133
    Marketplace Deception Protection Self-Efficacy   136

8   Developing Deception Protection Skills in Adolescence
    and Adulthood   143

    Growing Up Targeted   145
    Children's Beliefs About Television Advertising   146
    Developing Persuasion Knowledge   149
    Developmental Psychology and Theory of Mind   154
    Domain Specific Skills and Cross-Context Transfers   156
    Adolescence and Marketplace Deception-Protection Skills   160

9   Teaching Marketplace Deception Protection Skills: Prior Research   163

    Coping With Implied Claims   164
    Coaching Consumers to Detect Omitted Information   166
    Coaching Consumers to Detect and Resist Corrupted
     Persuasion Tactics   168
    Coaching Adolescents to Cope With Deceptive
     Alcohol Advertising   175
    Coaching Adolescents to Cope With Deceptive
     Cigarette Advertising   178
    The "Off the Hook" Program to Reduce Participation in
     Telemarketing Fraud   181

10   Societal Perspectives: Regulatory Frontiers, Societal Trust,
    and Deception Protection Education   187

    Changes in Communication Technology   187
    Regulatory Protections   190
    Deception's Effects on Societal and Marketplace Trust   197
    Societal Education on Deception Protection   201

References   209

Author Index   227

Subject Index   233

Preface

This book grew out of conversations among the authors that began about four years ago. When we considered the immense literature on marketplace persuasion, there seemed to be a 500-pound gorilla in the room that no one really wanted to recognize—deception. The more we talked about it, the more we agreed that deception is a more fundamental issue in consumer research and marketing than was reflected in the research literature. After exploring the diverse writings on deception in the social sciences, humanities, marketing, and popular culture literatures, and wrestling with how to integrate and synthesize these perspectives usefully, we crafted this book.

Our goal here is to motivate more research on marketplace deception. We view this as the first research-grounded book to fully address the topics of the psychology of deceptive persuasion in the marketplace and the psychology of consumer self-protection. Deception permeates the American marketplace, harms consumers' health, welfare, and financial resources, and ultimately undermines trust in society. Individual consumers must try to protect themselves from marketers' deceptive communications by acquiring personal marketplace deception protection skills that go beyond reliance on legal protections. Deception protection skill is a critical life skill. Therefore, we believe that understanding the psychology of deceptive persuasion and consumer self-protection should be a central goal for future consumer behavior research.

Marketplace deception is not solely or mainly a legal issue, although that is how current marketing textbooks and writings on marketplace deception treat it. Further, deceptiveness in persuasion is a more important topic than is acknowledged in research and writing on the science of social influence. There is a tremendous opportunity and need for educational interventions that focus directly on teaching people deception protection skills applicable to the marketplace. Our motivation for analyzing the social psychology of deception in the marketplace is not just intellectual curiosity about a fascinating and underresearched topic. Rather, it is a vital step toward designing effective training programs that help youngsters and adults better protect themselves from marketplace deception.

In this book, we explore these questions: What makes persuasive communications misleading and deceptive? How do marketing managers decide to prevent or practice deception in planning their campaigns? What skills must consumers acquire to effectively cope with marketers' deception tactics? What does research tell us about how people detect, neutralize and resist misleading persuasion attempts? What does research suggest about how to teach marketplace deception protection skills to adolescents and adults?

Chapters in the book cover theoretical perspectives on deceptive persuasion; different types of deception tactics; how deception-minded marketers think; prior research on how people cope with deceptiveness; the nature of marketplace deception protection skills; how people develop deception protection skills in adolescence and adulthood; prior research on teaching consumers marketplace deception protection skills; and societal issues such as regulatory frontiers, societal trust, and consumer education practices.

Our primary audience is scholars, researchers, and advanced students in consumer behavior, social psychology, communication, and marketing. Marketing practitioners and marketplace regulators will find it stimulating and authoritative, as will social scientists and educators who are concerned with consumer welfare. We hope it will serve as a mind-stretching text for students in upper division and graduate courses in those areas. We intend the book to be rigorous enough for a scholarly audience but accessible enough for marketing and advertising practitioners. We hope to provide consumer researchers with the outline of a research agenda and, for some, a better appreciation of legal issues in the marketplace. We hope marketing practitioners will gain added perspective on the pressures they may feel to act deceptively, the costs of doing so, and how to effectively prevent consumer deception. For regulators we hope to provide a consumer researcher's perspective on the frontier regulatory and public policy topics they must deal with in the near future.

This book's content and ambition grew substantially as we considered the suggestions of insightful scholars who reviewed early drafts. We thank Meg Campbell, University of Colorado; L. J. Shrum, University of Texas–San Antonio; Kent Grayson, Northwestern University; Esther Thorson, University of Missouri; and David Shulman, Lafayette College, for help in shaping the book's overall structure and directions. We especially thank Dave Schumann, University of Tennessee, and Norbert Schwartz, University of Michigan, for their careful analysis of the semifinal draft and for motivating us to make the book's content as significant as its topic. The generous support of the University of Oregon and the Lundquist College of Business enabled our work, and we thank the Edwin E. and June Woldt Cone family foundation for their support.

David M. Boush
Marian Friestad
Peter Wright

The Authors

David M. Boush is the head of the marketing department and associate professor of marketing at the Lundquist College of Business, University of Oregon. He was previously a visiting professor at ESSEC in Cergy-Pontoise, France, and has taught e-commerce classes in Mexico City, Buenos Aires, Santiago, and Bogota. Professor Boush's research on trust, consumer socialization, and brand equity has been published in the *Journal of Consumer Research, Journal of Marketing Research, Journal of Business Research, Journal of the Academy of Marketing Sciences, Journal of Public Policy & Marketing*, and the *Journal of International Business Studies*. He has served on the editorial board of the *Journal of the Academy of Marketing Sciences*.

Marian Friestad is the vice provost for graduate studies at the University of Oregon, and professor of Marketing in the Lundquist College of Business. She was previously dean of the graduate school and a visiting scholar at Stanford University. Professor Friestad's research on persuasion and social influence has been heavily cited and won a best-paper award from the *Journal of Consumer Research*. Her work has been published in the *Journal of Consumer Research, Journal of Consumer Psychology, Psychology & Marketing, Journal of Public Policy & Marketing*, and *Communication Research*. Professor Friestad is a past president and fellow of the Society for Consumer Psychology.

Peter Wright is the Edwin E. and June Woldt Cone Professor of Marketing at the Lundquist College of Business, University of Oregon. He was previously a professor and head of the marketing department at the Graduate School of Business, Stanford University, and a visiting scholar at the Harvard University School of Business. His work has been published in the *Journal of Consumer Research, Journal of Personality and Social Psychology, Journal of Marketing Research, Journal of Public Policy & Marketing, Management Science, Journal of Marketing*, and the *Journal of Applied Psychology*. Professor Wright is a past president and fellow of the Association for Consumer Research.

consumers evaluate and enjoy the author's skillful deception of the audience in the plot and characters, as well as the drama of the characters themselves who discuss and expose their interpersonal deceptions of one another. Through these experiences the audience learns about how deception is conceived and executed in a character's mind and actions. The marketplace also provides the opportunity to purchase professional services in deception detection (e.g., police interrogators) or deceptive skills (e.g., attorneys, advertising professionals, doctors). In this context there may be difficult issues raised about the level and types of deceptions the buyer wants and does not want versus the provider's views of how to provide the service effectively with or without using some deception. Providing these types of professional services could be thought of as akin to dramatic performances, in that there is tension and negotiation and possible misunderstanding and misalignment between what level and type of deceptions the buyer wants and needs versus those the provider believes are essential to successfully provide the service.

This book is focused on how consumers can detect, neutralize and resist the varied types of deception that face modern consumers on a daily basis. Examples of these include

1. Deceptions that are rooted in the careful choice of words and the construction of prose texts to imply things without stating them
2. The strategic digital alteration of photos, videos, and other visual representations
3. Misrepresentations via numerical information and calculations, statistical information, and research results
4. The artful omission, masking, camouflage, and obfuscation of information
5. Strategic uses of distraction and information overload
6. Using persuasion tactics that depend on deceptiveness to be effective, and using subverted persuasion tactics as accomplices to deception to decrease consumer caution and suspicion
7. Actions designed to build friendship and shared-interests relationships with customers
8. Displaying false emotions in sales and service delivery situations
9. Incomplete and misleading framings of comparisons, risk information and decision problems
10. Inadequate information search and product usage instructions
11. Brand mimicking and artful advertising confusion
12. Fabricated brand personalities and brand images
13. Disguising product placements in movies, television shows, and Web sites

14. Disguising hired laypeople as everyday consumers to execute so-called ambush or guerilla marketing
15. Exaggeration, puffery, and marketing bullshit
16. Blatant outright lying about product attributes and usage consequences

The topic of marketplace deception is important because when people see deceptions and frauds everywhere, even in high-consequence markets such as health care, financial services, and housing, overall levels of societal mistrust may increase. Societal mistrust is further magnified when people perceive an imbalance between the limited skills and resources consumers have to protect themselves from being duped compared to the substantial resources and expertise of modern marketing organizations. We suspect that in the public mind, the perceived threat from marketplace fraud and deception is magnified by other societal happenings, such as the spectacle of lying and deception by national leaders and political candidates, and the dangers of personal privacy invasions opened up recently by the global Internet.

Misleading and Deceptive: Defining Marketplace Deception

The concepts of "deception" and "deceptive" are ambiguous, socio-culturally constructed notions. Conceptions of deception vary across cultures and across generations in a culture. We examine the definitions offered from the perspectives of the community of western academic researchers, the American legal community, and the professional deception planner. First, drawing on the research literatures of the social sciences, Masip, Garrrido, and Herrero (2004) thoroughly reviewed various definitions of deception. They proposed an integrative definition that describes deception as "the deliberate attempt, whether successful or not, to conceal, fabricate, and/or manipulate in any other way factual and/or emotional information, by verbal and/or nonverbal means, in order to create or maintain … [in someone] … a belief that the communicator … considers false" (p. 1487). This definition incorporates notions of a communicator's intentionality and prior beliefs. We will elaborate on this definition in several ways to make it more relevant and applicable to real world marketplace deception.

First, the inclusion of the concepts of "intentional" and "deliberate" deceptiveness in general social sciences definitions are there to provide an exception for cases where people do inadvertent deception, deception out of ignorance, and deception due to the understandable inability to know, remember, and communicate "the truth" competently. In general discussions much is made of distinguishing inadvertent or unintentional deception from real deception, which requires a consciously intended attempt to deceive. Usually, this distinction is meant to excuse individuals who did not know that what they were saying, showing, or implying was actually false. So, for example, a child or adolescent who misremembers or misreports on something she did or witnessed is not, in this view, really doing deception. The key issue here is that sometimes people will act deceptively without intending to even though they have done the best they can to be nondeceptive. It is our position that no such excuses should apply for marketplace deceptions.

In marketplace communication, all deceptiveness is intentional. All marketing communications are consciously planned, designed, and executed by communication professionals. In our view, a marketer is always responsible for any actions or inactions that have a reasonable likelihood of misleading and deceiving consumers. Marketers have access to the resources and expertise necessary to fully educate themselves about the deceptive implications of their marketing activities. So, for marketers to do "the best they can" to be nondeceptive requires that they educate themselves so they are in a position to understand when and how their actions or omissions may mislead. By taking this step marketers can control their actions so as to avoid deceiving consumers, unless of course they want to deceive consumers.

Our second adaptation of the Masip group's definition relates to the requirement that the belief being espoused is considered false by the communicator. We accept that in the realm of everyday deception by lay people, everyone cannot be expected to invest heavily in learning about the validity of their statements every time they utter something. However, in the marketplace, a better standard is that marketers should be held responsible if they even "suspect" that a belief they encourage consumers to hold is false, and that marketers should know if their representations are likely to create misunderstandings or inaccurate beliefs. The marketer, who has the resources, time, expertise, and responsibility to learn as much as possible about the validity of statements and about the way the overall presentation of those statements could mislead consumers, should be held accountable for deception that occurs through malevolence, negligence, recklessness, or carelessness.

Finally, in social science domains other than the marketplace, deception is typically defined so that it includes a wide range of inconsequential and benign communications which can be described as everyday, interpersonal "little lies" about one's beliefs, feelings, or autobiography (Depaulo, Lindsay, Malone, Muhlenbruck, Charlton, & Cooper, 2003). For example, in two studies where participants kept careful diaries of their conversations, college students reported lying in approximately one out of every three of their social interactions, and people drawn from the larger community said they lied in one out of every five social interactions (DePaulo, Kashy, Kirkendol, Wyer, & Epstein, 1996). These lies were mainly self-presentational statements about individuals' personal feelings, beliefs, achievements, past actions, future plans, and immediate whereabouts. In those studies, as in most of the research on lay people's deceptiveness in everyday conversations, the definition of deception included misrepresenting a private internal state, for example someone saying that they felt fine when they really felt a little stressed or sickly, or that they like someone when they actually do not. Also, in everyday social life, lay communicators may be deceptive because they have unreliable communication competencies that result in "unprepared" deceptions. They do not elaborately construct, redesign, rehearse, and pretest these little deceptions, so message recipients may often be misled and deceived because the speaker simply cannot craft and deliver a clear, nondeceptive, relevant message. Thus, for everyday interpersonal exchanges, the layperson's deceptions and communication incompetence may be confounded. However, it is our position that neither the claim that communicated misinformation is inconsequential nor that the communicator is incompetent applies to the marketplace where messages are professionally developed and delivered.

Legalistic Definitions

Deceptiveness in commercial speech, which includes all marketing communications, is defined and regulated more strictly than any other form of speech in America. Because of this, professional marketing organizations often have their own in-house or outside consulting legal staff and screening process to judge possible deceptions from a technical, legal standpoint. Beyond that, there are specialized legal consulting services that provide advice on how to interpret legal rules and precedents on deception. We suspect that many social scientists will be surprised at how broadly legal rules on deception are construed. Indeed, the legal viewpoint is more all encompassing and stricter in assignment of responsibility than the viewpoint on lying behavior that is found in most social science research. This is because marketplace deceptions are often serious and consequential to both consumers and to fair competition in general. The various definitions of marketplace deception that have been proposed within the American legal system reflect different purposes. One such purpose is regulation to protect consumers, making the legal definition by the Federal Trade Commission a good place to start. We examine legal definitions here because these provide us a distillation of societal thinking. These definitions reflect the thinking over time of legal scholars, educated lay people, and pragmatic attorneys and regulators.

The Federal Trade Commission (FTC) Act prohibits unfair or deceptive business practices defined as "a representation, omission, or practice that is likely to mislead the consumer acting reasonably in the circumstances, to the consumer's detriment" (FTC, 1984). The word *representation* suggests a wide variety of possible means by which deceptive practices can be conveyed, including different modalities (e.g., words, statistics, pictures, facial expressions) and different tactics. The definition explicitly notes that omissions can be deceptive. The phrase "likely to mislead the consumer" suggests that a practice can be deceptive even if no one has as yet actually been deceived, which is consistent with a focus on protecting the public from deception rather than punishing the seller after deception has been proven. By omitting any mention of seller motivation, the law does not require that deception be proven to be intentional. Proving intention would add a layer of difficulty to policing or prosecuting deception.

The Federal Trade Commission's policy on what specific acts will be considered as deceptive also provides an important perspective on current societal views (Richards & Preston, 1992). The FTC states that its staff members will presume any of the following to be potentially deceptive: (a) express claims by a marketer; (b) omitted information the seller knew, or should have known, ordinary consumers would need to evaluate the product or service; (c) claims the seller knew, or should have known, were false; (d) implied claims, where there is proof the seller intended to convey them; (e) misrepresentations or misleading information involving health, safety, or other areas with which the reasonable consumer would be concerned; and (f) misrepresentations or misleading information pertaining to the product's central characteristics, for example, anything involving the product's purpose, safety, efficacy, price, durability, performance, warranties, quality, or regarding findings by another agency (e.g., a research and testing firm; the Food and Drug Administration) about the product.

Further, marketing misrepresentations are deceptive in the FTC's view if they affect any important cognitive or overt behavior by a consumer that influences the person's prepurchase decision process, the actual purchase event, or postpurchase behaviors in using the product. So misleading acts that affect any of the following consumer activities, among others, can be defined as deceptive according to this perspective: (a) information search activities, such as a person's decision to stop searching for more information about the advertised product or another competing product; (b) consideration set formation—that is, a person's decision to exclude certain products from further consideration based on what he or she already believes about the advertised product or those other products; (c) important and useful evaluative criteria, that is, a person's judgments about which product attributes they want to learn about and how to weight different attributes; (d) usage beliefs, that is, beliefs about how to use a product effectively and safely under foreseeable usage conditions and given limited information-processing and physical skills; (e) purchase timing decisions, for example, a person's decision to not buy anything in a product category in the near future; a person's decision to buy the advertised product hurriedly and soon; or (f) the final choice of one specific product over another final contender.

The academic literature on marketplace deception, which usually has focused on deceptive advertising, has generated definitions that both mirror the legal definition and differ in some respects. Richards (2000) reviewed the differences between some consumer psychologists' definitions and the FTC's perspective. For example, Gardner (1975, p. 42) offered the following: "If an advertisement (or advertising campaign) leaves the consumer with an impression and or belief different from what would normally be expected if the consumer had reasonable knowledge, and that impression and/or belief is factually untrue or potentially misleading, then deception is said to exist." Gardner elaborated three categories of deception. The first was an "unconscionable lie" in which a claim is completely false; the second is a "claim-fact discrepancy" in which a claim would require a clarification for it to be properly understood and evaluated; and a "claim-belief interaction" which occurs because of an incorrect inference by consumers based on their prior beliefs. Gardner's focus on overt deceptive statements and claims thus excluded a large set of other deceptive tactics.

Jacoby and Hoyer (1987) expanded the boundaries of deception by describing a misleading or deceptive marketing communication as one that "causes … through its verbal content, design, structure, and/or visual artwork, or the context in which it appears, at least N% (some percentage to be decided) of a representative group of relevant consumers to have a common impression or belief regarding the advertised product, brand or service ... that is incorrect or unjustified." This definition reflects a concern with the operational measurement of deception to establish legal proof in court cases. By stipulating causality, this definition requires elaborate testing procedures in order to rule out other sources of incorrect belief. This definition also champions the idea that there should be some threshold quantitative standard (although unspecified) for the number of buyers who are misled, and that those who are misled should be "relevant" consumers. The stipulation that consumers have a common misimpression differentiates legal deception from consumers' own random-error mistakes in comprehension and seems to exclude cases where a marketing presentation creates a variety of misperceptions rather than one that all or most consumers share in common.

However, we believe that the most important thing to appreciate about legal definitions is that in actual legal proceedings the system relies heavily on human judgments about deceptiveness. While some researchers favor an empirically valid test procedure, the legal code defines a range of possibly deceptive acts and then lets judges, jury members, attorneys, expert witnesses, and FTC staff members determine whether or not specific actions by a marketer will be or have been deceptive and misleading. So, in many cases, it is the culturally learned lay theories or mental models of deception in the minds of these individuals that define given instances of illegal, sanctionable, or impermissible marketing communication. It is also worth noting that the FTC's broad perspective reflects the active participation by consumer behavior researchers in the agency's rule-making processes over the past three decades. That participation helps assure that deception is interpreted in this highly serious domain as realistically as makes sense, according to prevailing behavioral research on human judgment and social cognition.

Marketplace Deception Is Persuasion

All of marketplace persuasion need not involve deception, but all of marketplace deception is done to persuade. Marketplace deception is, in essence, persuasion (Miller & Stiff, 1988) and is always instrumental to a marketer's persuasion goals. It is not done purely to affect consumer beliefs as an end in itself, nor to simply entertain, amuse, or amaze. To be sure, marketplace deceptions seek to attract and hold attention and create a state-of-mind or state-of-mood, but the end goal is always persuasion. Deception is a major omnibus persuasion and social influence strategy. Any act or strategy of persuasion can entail deception. Any act or strategy of persuasion can be used as a "deception accomplice," so that it bolsters the success of a deception carried out somewhere in a given message or campaign. However, when we examined the prominent writings on social influence theory and research, we found scant mention of deception as a central defining characteristic of persuasion or as an essential class of persuasion strategies. In parallel, when we examined the abundant theorizing on deception in everyday social life, there is scant reference to or integration of the theoretical views offered by prominent persuasion theories. This latter void may be because deception research has initially focused so much on the everyday unprepared telling of little lies in conversations between individuals that conceiving of this as persuasion makes it seem overly formal and ominous.

We suspect however that this historic compartmentalization of deception research and persuasion research is due mainly to the pervasive specialization that occurs within fields in the social sciences, together with the way in which early influential research streams guided the topical progression in a field. For example, the pioneering deception researchers (e.g., Ekman & Friesen, 1969) did not approach deception from the perspective of the social psychology of persuasion, nor was it those researchers' forte or realm of expertise; they were initially concerned with facial and other signals of inner emotions. Similarly, attitude change theories did not develop in such a way that deceptiveness (vs. nondeceptiveness) was a theoretical concern. Indeed, the science of social persuasion is, to a large degree, a science of deceptive social persuasion. Lab experiments provide the lion's share of empirical evidence on the psychology of persuasion. And, in most of the lab studies that social psychologists and consumer researchers have done on persuasion, the message content and the contextual information vital to the persuasion tactics that were presented to the subjects were simply fabricated and staged (made up) by a researcher. The true goals of the actors and impostors playing their parts in the researcher's staged reality were hidden or misrepresented. The actual truth of the message statements in the stimulus messages was of little concern because these messages were made up to create content that operationalized a construct of interest to the researcher. DePaulo, Wetzel, Sternglanz, & Wilson (2003), leading deception scholars, discuss exploitative deception as follows: "We think that the skills of impostors and confidence artists are akin to those of the best experimental social psychologists. Working in a private lab, they need to stage a compelling reality, draw people into it, and then keep them so involved in the show that they have no time to question the authenticity of the performance" (p. 402). We are not criticizing these uses of deceptiveness for research purposes. However, it is important to recognize that what has actually been studied in lab experiments on persuasion is in essence successfully deceptive persuasion.

Deceptions Are Context Bound

An act's deceptiveness must be assessed within the overall communication context in which it is embedded. Some actions are deceptive across a wide range of contexts and audiences. However, an act which, by itself, is not inherently deceptive or misleading when taken out of its real-world communication context can nevertheless be misleading and deceptive within the specific communication context in which it is used by a marketer or encountered by a consumer. For example, a verbal statement that by itself might be clear and accurately interpretable in isolation from other message ingredients and external distractions, may well be deceptive and misleading when it is buried amidst unrelated information in a fast-paced, high-information-load telemarketing call or television commercial. So, examining an act out of context (e.g., having a consumer carefully read, reread, and consider, a written sentence shown to them in conspicuous typeface and asking them if they understand its meaning, when the statement was actually said aloud to consumers amidst a barrage of information in a telemarketing call or flashed on-screen in small print in a television ad) would be a meaningless way of judging the deceptiveness of the actual act by a marketer.

As another example of how overall context matters, an honestly executed persuasion tactic—for example, a valid statement that medical doctor so-and-so prescribes XYZ prescription drug for his own family—can be presented so that it bolsters the deceptiveness of a subsequent concealment, misrepresentation, or omission, in the same message. Buller and Burgoon (1994) noted that even in everyday deception, liars may not rely on a solitary lie, but rather they weave several lies together such that ancillary deceptions are used to bolster the apparent credibility of the false core deception, and to bolster the impression that the liar is a truthful person. The view that deception is more than a single act taken out of context is essential to understanding marketplace deception.

A Deception Agent's Definition: It Is Deception if Persuasion Targets Perceive It as Such

A compelling account of how a deception agent would think about practicing deception is contained in a remarkable document prepared for the U.S. Department of Defense. In this well-researched treatise, Fred Cohen and his colleagues (Cohen, Lambert, Preston, Berry, Stewart, & Thomas, 2001) explain how a deception strategist who is well versed in cognitive social psychology should plan and execute deceptions in the domain of covert military intelligence and national defense operations. Cohen et al. (2001) presented a definition of deception that is different in perspective from the social sciences and legalistic definitions. Their definition, which views deception strictly from the vantage point of a brutally realistic deception perpetrator, states that "Deception is the set of acts that seek to increase the chances that a set of targets will behave in a desired fashion when they would be less likely to behave in that fashion if they knew of those acts." The last half-dozen words are critical. This definition emphasizes the pivotal role of the target's perception of a deceiver's deceptive acts and intent. If a target believes or suspects, based on their own thought processes or through being told by a third party, that an act or a sequence of acts by the agent is "deceptive," then that belief itself ruins or seriously reduces the deception's intended effects, and thus dilutes or eliminates the impact of the agent's overall persuasion attempt. Thus, an action is deceptive if the target perceives it to be deceptive, and that interpretation by the target alters the whole of the person's responses to any other actions taken by the perpetrator.

Extending this highly pragmatic point of view from the world of secret agents to the world of consumer behavior leads us to a provocative representation of how a professional marketer bent on accomplishing persuasion could think. In this scenario, the marketer believes that they must not be suspected at all, certainly must not be caught, and must indeed pull off the entire deception (i.e., get total buy-in by the target consumers to the intended altered reality) in order to successfully achieve their marketing persuasion goals. If successful persuasion is the paramount and overriding goal, then acts that are perceived as deceptive by their targets must be defined as deceptions by the persuasion planner, because perceived deceptions act as "discovered" deceptions in a consumer's mind. It is the consumer's perception that gives the persuasion-related act a special meaning that then alters the psychology of the persuasion attempt (cf. Friestad & Wright 1994). That interpretation can undermine and ruin the marketing presentation's persuasive impact. The implication of this perspective is that for a persuasion planner, something that target consumers "could" reasonably interpret as a deception "must be" treated as a deception in judging what to include in a deceptive persuasion attempt.

This definition of deception highlights the target consumers' deception beliefs, and raises those beliefs to a position of great power because of their presumed impact on the effectiveness or ineffectiveness of a deception perpetrator's persuasion attempt. Thus, it does not matter if the communicator's act(s) do not adhere to a social scientist's, or a judge's, or a regulator's definition of a deception. What matters ultimately is that the intended effect of the act on a target consumer has been ruined by his or her belief that the communicator was attempting deception. This is a highly pragmatic, instrumental-effects definition of deception. Perceived deceptiveness is the significant issue in the case of marketplace deceptions. Consumers judge for themselves whether a perceived action by a marketer is to be treated as a deception attempt. The cognitive process by which that occurs is of central interest to researchers, as well as the process by which consumers issue their own penalties for perceived betrayals, without recourse to the lie-detection technologies, specialized definitions, or formal deception-detection security systems that get used in some other contexts (e.g., criminal investigations and national defense). Thus, even well intentioned marketers must be highly concerned, as Cohen et al. argue, with avoiding even the appearance of acting deceptively to individual consumers who are applying their own personal deception detection rules.

Ethics and Morality

One thing that makes marketplace deception complex to analyze is that in general, deceptiveness per se is not considered inherently unethical or immoral. In reading about deception, we sometimes found that deceptiveness gets confounded with ethicality. However, judging or believing that some act of communication is deceptive is not the same as judging or believing that that act is unethical. This is because people in and out of academia argue that deception can be used for benign purposes "in the target's best interest," that deceiving someone into doing something that turns out to be beneficial to them is indeed moral (or at least not immoral), and that deception enables gracious and cooperative human relationships, which would likely be destroyed by full disclosure of true opinions and beliefs. For example, in the authoritative *Handbook of Moral Development*

(Killen & Smetana, 2006), which reviews research on how children and others develop moral values and belief systems, there is scarcely a mention of how people learn to think about deception. When we asked one of the editors about this, she explained to us unhesitatingly that researchers on moral behavior believe that deception is not inherently immoral. It is relatively easy to think of situations where the ends appear to justify the deceptive means, at least according to some systems of ethics beliefs. For example, deceiving someone who is reluctant to try a new pharmaceutical drug into using it can seem justifiable and ethical when in fact using that drug alleviates their pain and cures their illness, while not using the drug leaves them in pain and debilitated. However, our point of view is that, in the marketplace, corporations rarely perpetrate deceptions on consumers "in the consumer's best interests," or with benign intent, and that actual deceptions harm consumers, harm fair competition, harm corporate assets, and destroy corporate cultures. Moreover, using or appearing to use intentional or negligent deception is a risky, desperate, and often ill-conceived management strategy. Relying on deceptive marketing is a failure of intelligent management, true innovation, and long-range vision.

Marketplace Deception Is a Special Domain of Societal Deception

To function competently in the clutter of the twenty-first century marketplace, people need to take into account the specific details of marketers' strategies and the real world task environment of marketplace decision-making. We believe that marketplace deception is itself a sufficiently complex domain of deception to warrant its study as a distinct research topic. Marketplace participants and observers are separated by the thought-worlds of their particular educational backgrounds, academic disciplines and professional training; by their personal value systems and the values they attribute to other groups; and by their chosen profession. People have difficulty communicating with each other about the problem or the realities of marketplace deception. Individuals and groups see only a part of the overall marketplace deception problem through the filter of their expertise (or areas of ignorance), personal values, and professional career agendas. However, the modern marketplace is a morass of specific contextual features, including its different types of communication media, marketing methods, product markets, and decision-making problems. And, with apologies to Mies van der Rohe (1969), the Devil rather than God is in the details. For example, what a twenty-year old adolescent has learned about how to cope with her friends' and suitors' persuasion and deception ploys will not, by itself, prepare her sufficiently to engage competently with sophisticated telemarketers, trained salespeople, or multimedia marketing campaigns. A major challenge for today's consumer is to become skilled at making successful cross-context adaptations when protecting against deceptive persuasion. Deception self-protection among high school friends or in everyday work environments is not the same as effective self protection against professional marketers' ploys. We highlight throughout this book the unique environment of marketplace deception. Doing so should help us better understand how research on deceptive persuasion in other specialized contexts (e.g., autobiographical lying between acquaintances; eyewitness reports; interrogations of suspected criminals; courtroom trials; auditing of corporate financial reports) applies, or does not apply, to the modern marketplace, and how future research on deception in the marketplace must proceed.

A Framework for Examining Marketplace Deception

In this section we present a basic general framework that we hope will give readers an organized overview of the phenomenon of marketplace deception. This framework is not a general theory or model of marketplace deception — that would be premature. Rather we describe what a complete theory of marketplace deception should ultimately be able to explain. Studying marketplace deception makes for an important, but manageable, domain of inquiry. It is sufficiently bounded to get researchers to initiate research projects. It gives us a specific, familiar, important, well defined, and richly detailed real world context to stimulate our thinking. And it yields insights of practical value to consumers, educators, managers, and regulators trying to make sense of and intervene in the marketplace. So, a conceptual framework of marketplace deception should include the following factors.

We must ultimately explain how marketing planners think about deception, that is, the belief systems, learning experiences, acquired skills, judgment processes, personal and professional values, organizational cultures, and situational conditions that influence marketing managers and their helpers in planning and executing attempts to mislead and deceive consumers, or in planning (or failing to plan) how to take reasonable preventive actions to protect consumers from being misled. A complete theory must explain how marketplace institutions and societal values shape the deception-related actions of marketers. In America societal values create a system aimed at promoting fair and vigorous competition, protecting free speech, encouraging consumer choice, and protecting consumer safety. The institutions that regulate marketplace deception in the U.S. were created by federal legislation, and reflect a societal attempt to accomplish the four goals cited above even when those goals may be in conflict with each other. Second, a complete theory would explain the specific belief systems, learning experiences, acquired skills, judgment processes, values, and situational conditions that influence how consumers try to self-protect themselves from marketers' deceptive persuasion attempts, and that influence their success at accomplishing this deception self-protection across their marketplace decisions. There is scant systematic research on how individuals can effectively detect, neutralize, and resist deceptive marketing. A third factor to explain is the role of regulatory bodies, communication technology and media, consumer education programs, popular culture, the economic system, and related cultural values in facilitating and hindering consumers' achieved level of protection from the effects of marketplace deception. And finally, a theory of marketplace deception should address the societal and economic consequences of all the above. At the societal level, pervasive marketplace deception probably contributes to the erosion of societal trust in all social domains. A marketplace where nothing can be believed makes it impossible to reward marketers for offering better products than competitors. Deception affects mistrust at the level of the individual consumer, and at another level, an organization's apparent reliance on, tolerance for, and rewarding of marketplace deceptions will affect the internal level of trust among its own employees and by extension its overall organizational culture.

The Scope of This Book

This book is not an encyclopedic research review. Rather, it is an attempt to selectively analyze and weave together some of the theoretical concepts and research from different fields that we believe help in understanding and researching marketplace deception in its many forms. The questions and issues that we discuss are the following:

What makes marketing communications misleading and deceptive?
What are the psychological processes that underlie deceptive persuasion tactics?

How do marketing managers decide to prevent or practice deception in planning their marketing campaigns?

What skills must consumers learn to recognize and effectively cope with marketers' deception tactics?

What does research tell us about how people detect, neutralize and resist misleading persuasion attempts?

What does research suggest about how to teach marketplace deception protection skills to adolescents and adults?

What should educators of adolescents, emerging adults, and mature adults understand to design teaching materials and learning environments that help consumers gain self-protection skills for detecting, neutralizing and resisting deceptive persuasion by marketers?

What roles can consumer behavior researchers and other social scientists play in helping others to understand the problem of misleading and deceptive marketing tactics?

And, especially, what are the exciting research opportunities?

More specifically, in Chapter 2, we examine behavioral scientists' theorizing about deceptive persuasion processes. In Chapters 3 and 4, we discuss the types of deception tactics that others have identified or that we have identified in writing this book. In Chapter 5, we examine how professional deception perpetrators think about strategic deception, as evidenced by their writings and by analyses of what they do in practice. We then shift our focus to deception from the consumer's perspective. In Chapter 6, we examine research conducted on how lay people cope psychologically with deception protection without the benefit of coaching and training programs. In Chapter 7, we discuss the types of deception-protection skills that consumers need to acquire. In Chapter 8, we discuss the learning and cognitive development processes that influence how children and adolescents develop deception protection skills, and the problems that make it difficult for people to master deception protection skills. In Chapter 9, we review studies in which researchers have designed and tested the effects of various formalized coaching procedures on consumers' deception protection behaviors. Finally, in Chapter 10, we discuss research needs and opportunities related to consumer deception protection programs, frontier issues that face regulatory agencies, and how marketplace deception practices affect trust in specific marketers, in marketing in general, and in the overall sociocultural environment.

2
Theoretical Perspectives on Deceptive Persuasion

To help understand marketplace deception, we first consider the perspectives offered by general theoretical conceptions of deception. These include Anolli, Balconi and Ciceri's (2002) miscommunication theory; Buller and Burgoon's (1996) interpersonal deception theory; Cohen et al.'s framework for deception (Cohen, Lambert, Preston, Berry, Stewart, & Thomas, 2001); Depaulo et al.'s (Depaulo, Lindsay, Malone, Muhlenbruck, Charlton, & Cooper, 2003) self presentation perspective on everyday deception; Ekman and Friesen's (1992) theory of deception cues; Johnson, Grazioli, and Jamal's information processing theory of adversarial deception (Johnson, Grazioli, & Jamal, 1993; Grazioli, 2006); McCornack's (1992) information manipulation theory; and economists' game theoretic models (Ettinger & Jehiel, 2007; Gneezy, 2005). These provide insights more or less applicable to the realm of marketplace deception. However, many of these accounts deal with everyday interpersonal deception in conversations between lay people, which limits their pertinence to the marketplace realm of organized professional deception campaigns affecting important consumer buying decisions.

Because deception is persuasion, we also consider what some contemporary theories of persuasion and social cognition imply about deceptive persuasion. These include dual-process theories of persuasion (Chaiken, 1987; Petty & Wegener, 1999), models of social influence principles and tactics (Cialdini, 2001; Pratkanis, 2008), and theorizing about lay people's persuasion knowledge (Friestad & Wright, 1994, 1995), metacognitive social judgments (Petty, Brinol, Tormala, & Wegener, 2007), self-protection motivation (Block & Keller, 1998; Higgins, 1987; Rogers, 1993), and aversion to being duped (Campbell, 1995; Vohs, Baumeister, & Chin, 2007).

Deception Theory

In pioneering theorizing on deception, the phenomenon examined was everyday lying in interpersonal conversations where the deceiver talks about their personal inner world and past behavior (Zuckerman, Depaulo, & Rosenthal, 1981; Ekman, 1992; Buller & Burgoon, 1996; DePaulo et al., 2003; McCornack, 1992). These deceptions concern the liar's purported personal feelings, attitudes, beliefs, and future plans, and their autobiography—what they claim they did, observed, said, thought about, where they were and when, on prior occasions in the past, and their past achievements. That research has focused on cues to lying in everyday interpersonal conversations, and lay theories of lie-detection—that is, what cues lay people use in deception detection and how accurate they are. In this domain of everyday lying, the lie telling is largely constructed and executed on the spot; these are unprepared, unpackaged, unrehearsed little lies. People deliver such lies for momentary personal convenience; to feel better about themselves; to appear more virtuous, sophisticated or desirable than they believe they are; or to protect themselves and others from disapproval, conflict, and hurt feelings. The liars and their target audiences regard these little lies as inconsequential; people feel little discomfort in telling them, and do not spend time planning them or worrying about being caught (Depaulo et al., 2003).

The rationale for spotlighting everyday lie telling was that these little interpersonal lies comprise the majority of deception experiences that fill up people's lives; everybody does this type of lying all the time and everybody has to cope with other people doing it. In their impressive review paper, DePaulo et al. (2003) express that viewpoint, saying that (they think that) only occasionally do people tell lies in pursuit of material gain or have to cope with other people's lies for material gain. However, a different view (our own) is that marketplace deception is a most important part of people's deception experiences over their lifespan because the deceivers transmit deceptions widely to large segments of the population, and those deceptions can influence people's health, safety, and financial choices.

In initial theorizing on everyday deception, Ekman and Friesen (1969) emphasized the "leakage cues" that liars emit but try to hide, cues which might convey inner emotions they are experiencing. They focused largely on facial expressions that might distinguish the experience of lying and concealing from honest conversation. Similarly, Zuckerman et al. (1981) focused on the thoughts, feelings and psychological processes that are likely to occur when telling lies versus not telling lies. In particular, they singled out arousal, guilt and anxiety, and the purported complexity of lying, relative to truth telling. Ekman (1992) focused more deeply on the role of emotions in lying. He examined, for example, leaked displays of emotion due to a liar's supposed detection apprehension, guilt, excitement from "duping delight", and the faking of emotions. Buller and Burgoon (1996) emphasized, in addition to inner emotions, the stresses and dynamics of ongoing social interactions that entail sequences of give-and-take actions and adjustments. Buller and Burgoon (1996) emphasized that the liar's early discomfort and awkwardness may dissipate as the interaction moves along, if the liar invests in monitoring the target's reactions, adapting the delivery, and thereby gaining more control, and experiencing less emotionality. They introduced a realistic but complicated view of everyday lying and lie detection, in which the deceiver's expectations, motivations and relationship to the target, and the target's general suspiciousness, interact.

Depaulo and her colleagues (Depaulo et al., 2003) have emphasized a self-presentational perspective on everyday lying. They focus on the large subset of instances when everyday lying about inner self and autobiographical details is done for self-presentational purposes. They noted that effective self-presentation requires effortful deception and equally effortful truth telling. This explains the now-abundant empirical evidence that cues to deception of the types studied so far are at best faint. They derive five theoretical propositions about better cues that might distinguish lie telling from not-lie-telling in everyday conversation. They predict that liars will be "less forthcoming" than truth tellers (slow to respond; express limited details); that their stories will be less compelling (less internally consistent, engaging, fluent, and active voiced); that liars will be less pleasant and more tense than truth tellers; and that liars will include in their stories fewer ordinary "imperfections" and less "unusual" content (e.g., meanderings in self reports of prior events from memory that stray off into unexpected associative "asides").

In our minds, the domain of marketplace deception is in many ways the polar opposite of the everyday lie-telling context. So, even though these pioneering ideas about everyday deception are rich and stimulating, they strike us as fairly irrelevant to understanding marketplace deception. In marketplace deceptions, there is lying per se, and there is also a huge array of other clever, deceptive acts and tactics beyond a blatant lie. The deception agents are professionally trained and professionally invested in the success of their deceptions. They collaboratively plan a deceptive strategy, consider alternate combinations of tactics to accomplish it, pretest it,

and revise it before using it on key targets, and then monitor and revise it
once it begins. They use professional communication craftspeople to construct every element of it. They rehearse and rehearse until the speakers
perfect their deliveries and the story presentation is as they intend it to
be. They carefully assess targets' vulnerabilities, distinguishing the easy
prey from the vigilant, skilled consumers. They usually do not display
emotional leakage cues, or reflect ongoing cognitive complexities from
suddenly overloading their cognitive processes during execution. They
choose the time and place for every transmission. They subjugate personal
self-presentational motives to strategic motives. They treat their professional deception activity as a distinct domain of deception, and try not to
confuse it with other interpersonal domains. They are savvy about what
psychologists and others believe will be "give-away" cues; they eliminate
such cues, pointedly do the opposite (display "truth-telling" cues), or
invalidate deception cues strategically by varying how they do a deception
attempt and how they do truth telling.

McCornack (1992,1997) presents the useful idea that deception can be
understood, generally, as doing the opposite of cooperative communication as described by the Gricean principles. The starting point here is the
well-accepted principle that in every communication between humans,
a listener must, to determine what a speaker means, go beyond his or
her understanding of the simple literal content of the message. To make
this interpretational process work fluently, there is a social "contract" in
which both parties apply shared pragmatic rules to allow the receiver to
accurately infer what the speaker intends to convey via the literal utterances. These Gricean maxims of cooperative communication (Grice,
1975) are:

1. Maxim of quantity: The speaker will hard try to make his or her message
   as informative as required, but not more so, for the current purposes of
   the exchange. Say just enough so the receiver can understand what you
   intend to convey, but no more than that.
2. Maxim of quality: The speaker will try hard to maximize the message's
   "quality" in terms of veracity and validity. Do not say anything that you
   believe to or suspect to be false or for which you lack adequate evidence
   about its validity, one way or the other.
3. Maxim of relevance: The speaker will try hard to say only what he or she
   believes will be directly relevant to the receiver for the purposes of the
   conversation or exchange.
4. Maxim of manner: The speaker will try hard to be brief, clear, and crisp,
   while avoiding ambiguity and obscurity of expression.

McCornack's robust insight is that a deception attempt invariably proceeds by violating one or more of these maxims or deviating from them significantly in some way. The deception agent willfully or recklessly provides too little or too much information, provides false or inaccurate information or information of unknown validity, includes information that is irrelevant and excludes information that is relevant, and presents in ambiguous language, arcane visual symbols and numerical forms. Turning this around, whenever we notice that someone deviates from or violates one or more of these maxims, that alone should alert us that deception (intentional and/ or reckless) is being attempted. Hence, a consumer's default interpretation in a social domain like the marketplace, where deception attempts are common and the communicators are skillful, should be that all apparent violations of cooperative communication norms are malevolent in intent, not just clumsy or discourteous communication.

Sperber and Wilson (1986) describe three pragmatic message interpretation strategies that message recipients can use which differ in sophistication. In using any of the three strategies, consumers realize that there are two basic ways in which the communication process can flounder: (a) the speaker may be incompetent, or (b) the speaker may want to deceive the consumer. Given that, the consumer can use an interpretive strategy of "naïve optimism." In doing this, a consumer assumes the marketer is both competent and benevolent (cooperative), so that the principle of relevance is operative, and the first interpretation available to the recipient consistent with that should be accepted. There is an intentional bias toward believing in the communicator's honesty, and confirming that interpretation. The second strategy is "cautious optimism." The consumer assumes the marketer is benevolent but quite possibly incompetent. The consumer believes the marketer is trying hard to be honest and relevant but is simply a poor communicator or did not understand fully what the consumer feels to be relevant, clear, and sufficient information. So potential deceptions are given the benefit of the doubt and attributed to poor communication skills. Sperber and Wilson (1986) call the third strategy "sophisticated understanding." In this case, the consumer does not necessarily believe the marketer is competent or benevolent, but assumes the marketer only wants *to seem* competent and benevolent. We can add to this a fourth interpretation strategy, which we call "sophisticated marketplace understanding." Here, a consumer assumes *the marketer is competent but is also malevolent.* The consumer thinks the marketer fully knows how to craft a clear relevant presentation tailored to the recipient's need and fully knows how to avoid being deceptive if he chooses to, but wants to be deceptive if it suits his or her purposes. So the sophisticated consumer stays vigilant because he or she expects a marketer to blend skillful honesty with skillful deception, and to shift from being competently relevant to competently deceptive within a message and across presentations.

Anolli, Balconi, and Ciceri (2002) describe deceptive miscommunication theory (DeMiT) as an attempt to move toward a viable general theory of deception. They echo McCornack's (1992) view that the early theories of everyday conversational lying embodied and promoted "hopeful myths" about the nature of deception and deception detection. These myths were (a) that the deception agent's act of constructing (encoding) deceptive messages necessarily entails on the spot active, strategic, and detailed cognitive processing; (b) that constructing and delivering deceptive messages therefore requires greater cognitive load than constructing and delivering clear, relevant, truthful messages; (c) that producing deceptive messages is significantly more physiologically arousing than producing truthful messages; (d) that there is an identifiable and consistent set of arousal-based behavioral cues, such as facial expressions, that accompany construction and delivery of a deception which deceivers "leak" when executing their messages; (e) that individuals are innately capable (without being tutored) of successful everyday deception detection; and (f) that deceptive messages have simple specifiable characteristics that render them distinct from truthful messages regardless of context.

Anolli et al. (2002) pursue what they see as the ultimate goal for a theory of deception: to explain how communicators and audiences distinguish benign fabrication of deceptive acts versus exploitative fabrication (Goffman, 1969). Anolli et al. make basic distinctions between acts of deception that help us locate marketplace deception relative to other deception contexts. First, they distinguish prepared deception from unprepared deception. A prepared deception is cognitively planned in advance and its main elements are carefully analyzed. Another distinction is between high-content deception and low-content deception. High-content deception concerns a serious topic, is carried out in an important context, and features notable consequences for the deceiver, the recipient, and other people. In contrast, low-content deceptions concern a fairly trivial topic, can occur in any kind of context, and have unimportant consequences for all concerned. In this framework, high-content deceivers risk losing face, being considered untrustworthy, losing self-esteem, and suffering strong negative emotions from being apprehended, such as guilt or shame. They also risk being openly accused of deceit by others who feel aggressive and prone to retaliate. And in the high-content case, the deception victim risks feeling duped, and suffering significant actual harm. High-content deception is done in complicated relational situations, where candid disclosure is a big issue. So the high-content deceiver's dilemma is, Is it better for me to be as nondeceptive as possible, as effectively as possible, and risk failing to persuade, or to do the deception, prepare some ways to avoid detection and accusation, and to fight an accusation or deflect it, and to live with having deceitfully harmed consumers physically, psychologically, or economically?

We urge that consumer researchers and other social scientists stay focused on the many highly consequential deceptions that consumers have to cope with, those that make marketplace deceptions so injurious to people's health and welfare. While marketers certainly attempt a lot of low-content deception concerning trivial products and illusory brand distinctions, we are more concerned in our book with marketers' well-prepared high-content deceptions. We believe that fretting about marketers' more trivial deceptions is a distraction. Of course, brand managers who advertise inexpensive, homogeneous, relatively harmless products may view their tactics to fabricate perceived distinctions between their brand and other brands as important to their career. And achieving a lot of these insignificant deceptions, each of which marginally influences brand choices by a lot of consumers, can add up to significant market share changes and cumulative profits. Still—eyes on the prize; research on high-consequence marketing trickery should be our priority.

Anolli et al. (2002) argue that a lay conversationalist's deceptive message generation usually does not result from a holistic top-down sort of planning system. That is, everyday lay deceivers rarely do prescriptive deception planning. They do not spend a lot of thought in constructing a deception plan. They do not carefully consider and choose among functionally indexed high-level strategies and forms of deception. Lay people adaptively construct deception attempts in the moment, in much the same way that they construct a process for making a decision (Bettman, Luce, & Payne, 1998). In Anolli et al.'s (2002) terms, lay conversationalists who try to deceive will quickly select concrete linguistic utterances, gestures, and facial expressions from functionally indexed, low-level forms of potential deceptors, using an interleaved planning system that goes back and forth from saying something, reading the response it generates, saying something else, and so forth. However, marketers do use top-down planning of holistic deception campaigns, selecting tactics to combine based on accumulated experiences in trying different tactics, and different ways of executing tactics. They use pretesting and revision in which strategies and executions in different forms are tried and refined. They formally build contingencies into their deception plan. Salespeople are given an "utterance library" to draw on to adjust what they say as the interaction with a customer gets cocreated. But "winging it" completely is rare in professional marketing, except in the case of a neophyte untrained salesperson or advertiser.

A different approach to analyzing deception is Johnson, Grazioli, and Jamal's (1993) examination of professional auditors' attempts to discern deception in corporate financial reports. In this work, now called the information processing theory of adversarial deception (Grazioli, 2006), these authors focused initially on financial frauds, commercial lending misrepresentations, and other contexts where corporate financial documents are constructed to mislead professional financial auditors and investment managers. This is the realm of corporate finance, cost accounting, and the financial investments marketplace. It is an environment that involves highly specialized expertise, high-stakes deceptions, modern accounting's arcane concepts, and formalized models. This marketplace is virtually unfathomable to laypeople and to most business managers, in the view of Bill Sharpe, winner of the 1990 Nobel Prize in economics (Sharpe, 2007). So, understanding how frauds are perpetrated and how to detect deceptions in corporate disclosures and capital markets must also be daunting and highly specialized. This work is especially helpful in understanding deception-protection skills (Grazioli, 2004; Johnson, Grazioli, Jamal, & Berryman, 2001). Therefore we will discuss it in more depth in Chapter 7 where we deal with deception protection skills.

Grazioli and Jarvenpaa (2000, 2003) argue that Internet deception is distinctive from other deception venues because it takes advantage of specific features of the Internet technology. They cite "page-jacking" as a particularly malicious deception tactic. In page-jacking one Internet marketer redirects an Internet user away from that user's intended destination site to another site that is controlled by the hijacker. This tactic is especially deceptive when the hijacker substitutes a site that looks very similar to the consumer's intended site. The hijacking is accomplished by engineering confusion via adjacency in a list, electronic redirection, and ad or site layout similarity. Further, the Internet can make it very easy to falsify the identity of information providers and marketing organizations, because it enables low-cost credible-looking "storefronts," and gives broad opportunity to reach potential victims privately (Grazioli and Jarvenpaa, 2000). Using the Internet also makes it easy for deceptive marketers to hide the proceeds from their deceptions and to escape consumer redress efforts and legal penalties. We add as another problematic factor the extremely transient nature of an Internet Web site content and display. The Web site design, icons, transfer routes, and page contents can be altered by a marketer significantly in a brief time, again and again, without leaving behind any lasting record of what information displays the site originally presented to a consumer when the consumer originally searched on it. This high transience is also the case with an oral interpersonal sales presentation, of course, which also leaves no record of its contents aside from what lingers in a consumer's memory and the salesperson's memory. However, the extreme transience of the Internet marketer's statements and deceptions may be more invisible to consumers because the site presents written and graphical information. Consumers are accustomed to written statements and visual images in other media that leave behind a lasting trail of evidence. Unless consumers create such a record of a Web site's contents by printing it out and storing the copy of a Web site whose content they think they will rely on or need to reinspect, the content that deceived them may not be there to demonstrate the deception later on. The Internet marketer can do posthoc sanitizing of their deceptions overnight.

Finally, completing our overview of deception theorizing, we found that economists' theories of market exchanges have embraced deception in only superficial ways. Game theoretic models have traditionally considered concepts of deception not related to belief manipulation (Ettinger & Jehiel, 2007; Gneezy, 2005). For example, these models deal with things such as playing mixed strategy and signaling games (Spence, 1973; Crawford, 2003) or repeated games (Kreps & Wilson, 1982; Kreps, Milgrom, Roberts, & Wilson, 1982) to avoid being detected. Ettinger and Jehiel (2007) recently argued that from the viewpoint of game theory, belief manipulation and deception are "delicate to capture" because traditional equilibrium approaches assume the players fully understand the strategy of their opponents.

Persuasion Theory

Dual-Process Models of Persuasion

Dual-process theories have been used widely by social and consumer psychologists to explain persuasion (Chaiken & Eagly, 1989; Petty & Wegener, 1999), social cognition (Petty, Brinol, Tormala, & Wegener, 2008), and consumer behavior (Schwartz, 2004), In these models, System

1 processes are quick, intuitive, and effortless, while System 2 processes are slow, analytical, and deliberate, and occasionally correct the output of System 1. System 2 processes are activated by cognitive experiences of threat, error, suspicion, difficulty, or disfluency during the processing of marketplace communications. Cognitive and metacognitive experiences like these serve as an alarm and a "disrupt" that activates analytic forms of thinking. The more analytic System 2 thought processes assess and sometimes correct the output of more intuitive forms of reasoning. In the context of deception, System 2 analytic thinking enables and facilitates deception detection, neutralizing, resistance, and penalizing activities. Further, the long-term result of a person's repeated System 2 thinking about deception protection can be to convert such thinking into System 1 marketplace deception protection heuristics. An important question for deception research is therefore, When will consumers notice that their System 1 processing of marketers' messages might be producing faulty (misled; invalid) beliefs and shift into System 2 thinking that makes good use of deception protection knowledge and skills?

Social Influence and Persuasion Tactics

Cialdini (2001) and Pratkanis (2008) describe types of persuasion strategies that research indicates can bolster persuasive impact. Each can be executed via deception, and each can become an accomplice to deception, whether it is executed honestly or via deception. Cialdini (2001) concludes that research indicates these persuasion tactics succeed mainly when they evoke only System 1 processing by consumers, that is, when they fly under the deception-protection radar. Cialdini identifies six factors that drive people to using automatized pattern matching responses to persuasive messages: being indifferent about the topic, being in a rush, feeling stressed in general, feeling uncertain, being distracted, and being fatigued. This is an important insight for our purposes. It implies that marketers will try to engineer situations characterized by several or all of those factors when executing a persuasion tactic deceptively or for deceptive purposes. While these conditions (e.g., indifference, distractedness, cognitive fatigue) may arise coincidentally in some situations, deception agents will tend to create those conditions. Indeed, if these persuasion tactics do depend on establishing conditions that weaken and suppress a person's deception protection capability, then these are inherently exploitative tactics. In a very real sense, therefore, the science of persuasion developed from lab experiments over the past 30 years may be a science of deceptive persuasion, that is, of persuasion as it occurs when one party skillfully creates a fictional psychological reality in another's mind via misdirection, lying, concealment, omissions and simulations of false reality. It is useful to appreciate, if readers already do not, that in many psychology experiments which are the backbone of the science of persuasion, intentional deceptions are common and rampant. Neither social psychologists nor marketers wait for favorable circumstances; they engineer them even if deception is required. Arguably, the level of and totality of deception in social psychologists' fabricated situations exceed that in marketplace analogs, because psychological researchers often just make up the content of the messages they present to subjects, without substantiating the validity or veracity of the statements made on a topic; routinely attribute the message's authorship to some person or source other than the true author (themselves); and routinely camouflage from target subjects the fact that some deception is likely to occur under the disarming easy-to-exploit mask of "this is research," a mask not available to marketers for the most part. We will not belabor this point, but readers should keep it in mind as they interpret (or reinterpret) the persuasion tactics that Pratkanis and Cialdini have catalogued as effective.

Resistance to Persuasion

Psychologists have not studied people's active resistance to persuasion nearly as much as compliance and persuasion acceptance (Knowles & Linn, 2004a). Research on resistance has increased recently and fresh perspectives on the mechanisms of resistance have been offered (e.g., Ahluwalia, 2000; Brinol, Rucker, Tormala, & Petty, 2004; Pfau, Comption, Parker, Wittenberg, An, Ferguson, Horton, & Malyshev, 2004; Sagarin, Cialdini, Rice, & Serna, 2002; Tormala & Petty, 2004; Wheeler, Brinol, & Hermann, 2007). In general, researchers believe that resistance to persuasion is motivated by a desire to hold valid attitudes and to gain control and consistency (Wegener, Petty, Smoak, & Fabrigar, 2004). Resistance is influenced by a variety of factors, for example, characteristics of the attitude under attack, the importance of the topic, and a message recipient's ability to resist (Brinol et al., 2004.)

However, none of this work directly identifies a person's skilled, learned deception-protective thinking as a particularly beneficial and effective mechanism of resistance to persuasion, and none explores the notion that persuasion resistance is a specialized type of acquired procedural expertise. Further, the prevailing view in the existing work is that resistance to persuasion is a bad thing, a problem for influence agents to overcome, rather than that self-protective resistance to deception and misleading persuasion is a very good thing. For example, in Knowles and Linn's (2004) recent volume on resistance to persuasion, only one of the 13 chapters deals with helping people learn to resist. The majority of these papers deal, more traditionally, with devising persuasion strategies for overcoming other people's self-protective resistance. Similarly, Wilson's (2002) book titled *Seeking and Resisting Compliance* exhaustively reviewed the research on compliance-gaining skills, but despite its title, the book's almost 400 pages include less than 30 pages on resisting compliance. In Chapters 7 and 8, we will present an opposing viewpoint (we resist traditional views on resistance) and discuss how deception-protective thinking, and indeed persuasion-resistance in general, is a basic survival skill to be refined and encouraged, rather than a barrier to be overcome to maximize persuasion.

The Persuasion Knowledge Model

Friestad and Wright (1994) take the view that people are "consumers of marketplace persuasion." The fundamental premise of the persuasion knowledge model (PKM; Friestad & Wright, 1994, 1995) is that people try to become skilled consumers of persuasive messages, and that skillful persuasion consumption is instrumental to successful product consumption. How skillful a person is at evaluating and judiciously using marketer's persuasion attempts determines in part the wisdom of their ultimate buying decisions and product consumption experiences. The persuasion knowledge model emphasizes a consumer's capacity to learn about persuasion and to eventually self-regulate in detecting, neutralizing, resisting, and penalizing unfair and deceptive persuasion. In first presenting the PKM, Friestad and Wright did not single out deceptive persuasion; their discussion of consumer self-protection dealt with persuasion in general. Here, we summarize some of the PKM's propositions with the emphasis on deception protection beliefs and skills.

   According to the PKM's principles, lay beliefs about deceptive persuasion and metabeliefs about our own deception protection knowledge are an especially important interpretive belief system because these tell people about situations where an intelligent purposeful outside agent is skillfully trying to mislead their inner self (their beliefs, emotions, attitudes, decisions, thought processes) and thereby alter the course of their lives. Individuals who allow unnoticed, uncontrolled invasions of their internal psychological world and consequent changes in their behavior do not survive and prosper. Consumers' deception protection beliefs help them to recognize, analyze, interpret, evaluate, and remember deception attempts, and to select and execute coping tactics they believe will be effective and appropriate. Lay people's deception protection beliefs and skills are developmentally contingent. They depend in part on an individual's development of basic capacities for social thinking, in part on continuous skill learning that is self driven over the lifespan, and in part on absorption of formal or semiformal coaching about marketplace deception protection. What consumers believe about marketplace deception is also historically contingent. The culturally supplied wisdom on marketplace deception changes over time, so that each new generation's thinking may differ somewhat from that of earlier generations. In general, deception-protection behavior encompasses cognitive and physical actions in anticipation of a foreseeable persuasion attempt, during a persuasion episode, after a persuasion attempt, or between episodes in an agent's extended campaign of persuasion attempts.

Friestad and Wright (1994) originally proposed that there are three critical belief systems that come into play when consumers process marketing messages. The most general belief system is marketplace persuasion knowledge (PK), beliefs about all marketers' goals and tactics, and about one's own persuasion-coping knowledge and skills. A second belief system is agent knowledge (AK), beliefs about the traits, competencies, and goals of the specific marketer who is presenting an immediate message. A third is message topic knowledge (TK), beliefs about whatever specific product, service, consumption problem, or transaction a marketer's immediate message deals with. We could now add, as a fourth belief system, the individual's system of marketplace deception beliefs or knowledge (MDK). However, we believe that MDK and PK are wedded belief systems, so we will refer in this book to marketplace deception knowledge as a third system of beliefs, not a fourth. Following Friestad and Wright (1994), an individual's allocation of mental resources to these different knowledge systems (deception protection knowledge, agent knowledge, topic knowledge) will vary across persuasion episodes. This will depend on how accessible and relevant each specialized belief system is at that time, on immediate message processing goals, and on message processing opportunities in the immediate environment. A person's use of deception beliefs and deception protection skills may ebb and flow over the course of a specific message-processing episode and over exposures to a multimedia campaign's different parts. Learning to fluently juggle the use of deception protection knowledge, agent knowledge, and topic knowledge is a challenge to consumers.

Friestad and Wright (1994, 1995) emphasized that beliefs about important psychological mediators of persuasion are a central element in everyday persuasion knowledge. A person's beliefs about deception tactics involve making a mental connection between an aspect of a persuasion attempt and a psychological event that the person believes (that the marketer believes) mediates persuasion. Realizing for the first time that a particular type of statement, pattern of statements, or mixture of audiovisual and verbal stimuli is a potential "deception tactic" is a critical persuasion event. Consumers may construe deception tactics as single message elements or configurations of elements. Metabeliefs are an important part of the deception protection process. These are one's beliefs about self-efficacy in executing important types of cognitive, emotional, and physical actions that accomplish marketplace deception protection. Marketplace deception protection skills include learning to schedule different types of thinking to best accomplish each that is needed without straining cognitive limits. In our work related to the persuasion knowledge model, we generated a number of ideas about the process of acquiring deception protection knowledge and skills over a lifespan (Boush, Friestad, & Rose, 1994; Friestad & Wright, 1994, 1995, 1999; Wright, Friestad, & Boush, 2005). We will discuss those and other ideas about how youngsters and adults learn deception protection skills in Chapters 8 and 9.

Metacognition and Deception Protection

Petty, Brinol, Tormala, and Wegener (2008) discuss how a consumer's metacognitive beliefs can affect their responses to a persuasive message. In general, metacognitive beliefs are "my thoughts about my own thoughts" in a specific message-processing episode or about my cognitive self-efficacy—my thinking skills, thinking strategies, and thinking effectiveness in a particular type of task environment. Here, we are most concerned with a consumer's meta-cognitive beliefs about their own thought processes when processing a potentially deceptive marketing message, as well as their perceived self-efficacy in doing effective deception protection thinking in the marketplace domain. Metacognition plays a prominent role in recent discussions of consumer psychology (e.g., Alba & Hutchinson, 2000; Wright, 2002).

Consumers will have various types of thoughts about their own reactions in response to deceptive marketing messages. For example, they may have beliefs about the "origin" of their specific thoughts, distinguishing between thoughts that "I myself generated" and thoughts that "the ad planted in my mind" (Greenwald, 1968; Wheeler, Demarree, & Petty, 2005; Wright, 1973). The thoughts they believe to be mainly self-generated are given more weight in their judgments about persuasion tactics and topics than are the thoughts they think occurred primarily because the ad momentarily supplied (made salient) such thoughts. Consumers should have beliefs that reflect "metacognitive confidence," for example, their sense of certainty or uncertainty about the validity or quality of their own thinking in response to a marketer's deception and persuasion attempt (Kruglanski, 1989). Doubt about the validity of "my thoughts" in response to a marketer's message ("I doubt I've accomplished much useful deception protection thinking yet") provokes a person to do more elaborated thinking about what was said and shown (Maheshwar & Chaiken, 1991; Petty, Tormala, Brinol, & Jarvis, 2006). Consumers' metacognitive confidence in the validity of their own deception protection thoughts in response to a marketing message increases when they perceive that the same thought has occurred to them often, that they have used that thought in analyzing and interpreting many other marketing messages, and that the thought is filled with rich details (Petty et al., 2008).

Petty et al. (2008) forecast that people's metacognition about their own persuasion-related thinking, skills, and experiences will turn out, after more research, to be a more important explanation of responses to persuasion than are the immediate thoughts and feelings evoked by a message. In a similar spirit, a consumer's metacognition about his or her own deception-related thoughts, deception protection skills, and deception protection performance may be a very important factor in future theories of deceptive persuasion.

Protection Motivation Theory and Regulatory Focus Theory

Several social psychological theories deal with what motivates people to try to protect themselves from harm and how this affects their processing of social communications. Two prominent examples are protection motivation theory (Rogers, 1983) and regulatory focus theory (Higgins,

1997, 2000). Protection motivation theory (PMT) identifies factors that increase or decrease a person's motivation or intention to learn how to self-protect from something harmful. PMT has been applied primarily in studying what makes people try to protect against health dangers, for example, what motivates someone to try hard, or not to try, to learn all they can about health care practices, products, and tools that can prevent or treat osteoporosis or herpes (Block & Keller, 1998). However, PMT also may help explain how people become more or less motivated to protect themselves from the harm that deceptive marketing can cause them if it seduces them into making poor-quality health care choices, for example, the harm caused by a deception-contaminated poor decision about buying and using a particular osteoporosis drug. Deception protection is thus a vehicle for health protection.

PMT proposes that people do a "threat appraisal" and a "coping appraisal" in judging how much effort to invest in any domain or form of self-protection. Accordingly, a consumer's motivation to invest seriously in marketplace deception protection is influenced by their beliefs about (a) the severity of the harm from being deceived and misled; (b) their own vulnerability to (likelihood of) being deceived and misled; and (c) the benefits to them and others who are important to them of doing successful deception protection. These considerations enter into a perceived-threat appraisal. Further, a consumer's motivation to do deception protection is also affected by her beliefs about (a) her already-attained self-efficacy in performing deception protection skills relevant to the immediate persuasion attempt; (b) the maximum level of protection that might be achieved in the immediate case from successfully performing one's known repertoire of deception protection activities (response efficacy); and (c) the cognitive costs of trying to do successful deception protection in the situation at hand. These considerations enter into what is called a perceived coping skills appraisal.

Block and Keller (1998) presented an integrative theory of health protection motivation and communication. They argue that the relative importance of people's beliefs about their vulnerability and self-efficacy, and about the severity of the threat, will change, depending on whether people are in a precontemplation stage of thinking about the health problem, in contemplation of it per se, or in an action-taking stage of thinking about health care self-protection. Now, regarding *deceptive health care messages*, we note that consumers must deal with both a deception threat and the disease/injury threat, and that one's success in coping with the deception threat mediates one's success in coping with the disease/injury threat. So, we see this as a two-part self-protection process: (a) protect from deception about health-related choices, in order to (b) make wise choices that best protect against the disease or injury. Therefore, someone's protection motivation in either step may be usefully explained via PMT in its original form (Rogers, 1983) or its extended form (Block & Keller, 1998).

Regulatory focus theory (Higgins, 1997) argues broadly for two distinct self-regulation strategies, one of which is preventing future harm. One strategy emphasizes the pursuit of gains (or the avoidance of nongains) and aspirations toward ideals. This is called a *promotion focus*. The other strategy emphasizes the avoidance of losses (or the pursuit of nonlosses), and the fulfillment of obligations. This is called a prevention focus. A promotion focus is characterized by strategic eagerness, and a prevention focus is characterized by strategic vigilance (Higgins, 2000). Some communications are more compatible than others with a particular self-regulatory strategy, resulting in a higher level of "fit" (Aaker & Lee, 2001; Higgins, 2000; Lee & Aaker, 2004). High processing fluency emerges from high fit, and is accompanied by greater enjoyment of the message-processing experience. Lee and Aaker (2004) argue that regulatory focus and loss–gain message framings (e.g., Block & Keller, 1995; Maheswaran & Meyers–Levy, 1990) are interrelated in complicated ways. Regulatory fit theory has most often been construed in terms of one's goal regarding the product domain or decision domain. That is, in choosing a car, am I eagerly oriented toward how it will change my life for the better or cautiously oriented toward assuring that the car I choose does not lessen the quality of my life? However, by adopting our two-step view of self-protection, we can shift self-protection goals back a step to examine a consumer's protective versus promotional goals regarding coping with possible deceptiveness by a marketer. As they open their mind to a marketer's message about a car, for example, is their main focus to prevent being misled and deceived, that is, being even worse off in their beliefs than before the message exposure? Presumably, a prevention focus in persuasive message consumption makes someone vigilant to deception and ready to access MDP skills.

Aversion to Feeling Duped

Vohs, Baumeister, and Chin (2007) argue that feeling duped by a marketer angers and frustrates many consumers. Therefore, this strong emotional aversion to being duped causes people to develop personality structures that are designed to prevent it from happening repeatedly.

Vohs, Baumeister, and Chin assert that some people have a chronic and possibly exaggerated fear of being duped, to which they give the charming label "sugrophobia," derived from the Latin *sugro*, which means "to suck". Sugrophobia is therefore "the fear of sucking," hence, the fear of being a sucker! Sugrophobia—a pronounced fear of being a sucker—is, Vohs et al. speculate, a chronic personality trait in some people. There are costs and benefits to being chronically sugrophobic, that is, repeatedly hypervigilant, cynical, and untrusting, just as there are costs and benefits to being chronically trusting and unsuspecting (Campbell, 1995; Cialdini, 2001; Friestad & Wright, 1994). Alternatively, we note that an individual's motivation to avoid feeling duped can also change adaptively from marketplace interaction to interaction.

Campbell (1995) explained a consumer's feeling of "having been had" by an advertiser (unfairly manipulated) in terms of an equity appraisal process. Similarly, Vohs, Baumeister and Chi (2007) propose that a person feels suckered when they (a) believed at the outset that shared standards of fairness operated; (b) realize now that they made some decisions along the way that in principle might have prevented the duping if they had made them differently; (c) believe that the agent intended to dupe them and thus dealt in bad faith; (d) believe that the perceived injustice was due to deliberate intentional acts by agent; and (e) feel that both the marketer and the buyer would now agree that the outcome violated a shared sense of what is fair. Sugrophobia's occurrence in exchange-based relations and its high degree of self-consciousness suggest that it evolved only recently in human history (Vohs et al., 2007). An aversive emotional state such as acute sugrophobia should be a powerful stimulant to counterfactual thinking (Roese, 1997). Thus, consumers who by nature or in a certain situation want to learn how not to be reduped the same way again may do after-the-interaction counterfactual analyses. They will replay what happened and ask, "How could I have prevented being deceived?" Sometimes, they might use downward comparison ("Imagine how much worse I could have been cheated"). However, upwards comparisons ("Imagine how I might have done things differently and thus avoided feeling suckered") are more likely if the situation will be repeated. Vohs, Baumeister & Chin (2007) argue that feeling duped evokes both anger at the marketer and self-conscious embarrassment or shame at oneself. Thus, they suggest that duped consumers will not readily admit to others that they were duped.

3
Marketplace Deception Tactics I

In this and the next chapter, we discuss the anatomy of deceptive persuasion tactics. In our framework, an act or configuration of acts by a marketer is misleading and deceptive if in our judgment it meets at least one of these criteria:

1. It meets the social sciences definition of deceptiveness discussed in Chapter 1.
2. It meets the Federal Trade Commission's broad definition of deception (Chapter 1).
3. It can be interpreted as an attempted deception by its targets, which exerts ruinous effects on the persuasion attempt's success, thereby meeting Cohen et al.'s (2001) instrumental-effects definition (Chapter 1).
4. Other social scientists have talked about it as a misleading and deceptive tactic.
5. We ourselves interpret it as misleading and deceptive because we understand how it can significantly aid in a marketer's overall attempt to misrepresent the product and/or to suppress a consumer's marketplace deception-protection skills.

There are other qualitative tests that can be applied to judge if some action is misleading and deceptive. One is to ask, Is this how a skilled communicator would communicate to consumers if he or she really wanted people to learn the truth, the whole truth, and nothing but the truth about a product or service? Another is to ask, after reading and reflecting on this book, would you describe that act as a potential deception tactic in teaching your own teenagers and family members marketplace deception protection skills?

We are not asserting that all these tactics are inherently unethical, only that they are deceptive. Different ethical belief systems will yield different views on the ethicality of these different tactics in specific situations.

As mentioned in Chapter 1, deception per se is not viewed as inherently unethical by social scientists and ethics scholars. We are not sufficiently versed in alternate ethical belief systems to analyze each tactic from alternative ethical perspectives, nor do we want to present broad personal judgments on this issue. Further, we are not asserting that these tactics are inherently illegal. We are not attorneys, and we have not adopted a legalistic perspective in judging these to be misleading and deceptive persuasion methods. In some cases, there is a family of tactics that have been discussed many times, and we will describe those en masse but not rereview each and every variation, for example, the exploiting of inferential tendencies. In some cases, we describe a tactic sparsely in this chapter, but go into more depth about it in Chapter 6 where we review research on consumer responses to that tactic (e.g., omissions). We dwell longer on some tactics to explain how and why these are misleading and deceptive, when that may not be readily apparent to all readers.

In Chapter 3, we first provide an overview of marketplace deception. We emphasize that deception as practiced by marketers is best conceived of as a theatrical performance rather than a single act, that marketers think in terms of integrated deception planning, and that deception involves both message content and message distribution strategies. Then we focus on methods of hiding damaging information from consumers, that is, concealment and omission strategies, and also on disarmament methods, that is, suppressing and discouraging the use of personal deception protection skills so concealments and omissions go undetected and unsuspected. In Chapter 4, we will deal with deception methods that directly involve the proactive presentation of deceptive information.

Overview of Marketplace Deception Strategy

Marketers' deceptions are all about controlling consumers' attention, suppressing their unfavorable thoughts and controlling the direction of their thinking. That is what the word *mislead* means: We lead you away from the truth; you follow where we lead. A deceit-minded marketer wants a target consumer to notice and process only the favorable message parts and to completely or substantially ignore all disclosures or suggestions of drawbacks, risks, and limitations. The word "drawback" perfectly captures the psychological braking and distancing reaction by a consumer that a deceitful marketer will do almost anything to prevent. The marketer wants to lead a consumer to rely on System 1 processing exactly when and how the marketer wants, and to only use System 2 processing when and how the marketer wants. When target consumers do System 2 thinking, the marketer risks losing control of their attention. To retain control, the marketer tries to direct System 2 thinking via proactive simulations that make it easy and tempting to think about favorable things and to suppress System 2 deception-protection thinking along with thoughts about a product's drawbacks and risks. Timing is critical in deception. Marketers therefore do well-timed distractions, concealments, and attention-control tricks that cognitive and social psychologists have learned will manipulate a consumer's attention and suppress self-protective thinking. Marketers distract when they need to, swamp the consumer's mind when they need to, delay disclosures, prime a consumer's mind to ignore deceptions, and so forth.

Large deceptions are built up from smaller deceptions. Real-world marketplace deception is an orchestrated process, not an isolated single act. It is best seen as a theatrical performance and production, a process of seduction. The single specific act, or different discrete acts, that execute the deception are embedded in an orchestrated and staged presentation. In contemporary marketing, managers think in terms of doing integrated marketing communication planning. So when deception is afoot, they will think in terms of doing *integrated deception planning*. Even within a single advertisement or sales presentation, there are "softening up" events, camouflage tactics that surround the deceptive act, and "close out" events that urge a consumer's mind away from the deceptive act to keep it unrecognized as such. So, we ultimately have to understand two things: (a) the specific acts that can deliver a deception, and (b) the strategic sequencing of the acts that precede, surround, and follow deceptive acts to make them work.

To get our minds around real-world deceptions, it helps to first think small. So we first examine the tactics that become the building blocks, and think in terms of a single marketing presentation or message, for example, a single television ad, a single sales presentation, a single brochure or Web site screen. But eventually we need to broaden our perspective to understand the big picture of real-world deception campaigns. In that world, a deception strategy often unfolds across and enlists multiple messages and/or repeated presentations that use varied formats, verbal statements, and visuals; that have different lengths and emphases; and that use different media and different communication modes (print, audio, verbal, still pictures, motion pictures, or any combination of these). The different messages are sequentially transmitted and are encountered by individual consumers across time in some sequence, either that the agent intended or some other sequence. Some of these messages may not be encountered and processed at all; for example, disclosures made only in materials made available late in a person's buying decision process may be missed. On the other hand, some of these materials may be reencountered and reinspected again and again by the same target consumer, especially someone who is vigilantly self-protecting against being misled and deceived.

Appearing to disclose something while really trying to conceal it is a major deception strategy. Marketplace deceivers must by law disclose in some way, at some point, damaging information about a product's substantive drawbacks, limitations, and risks. So companies devote special attention to deceptive "disclosure" tactics (DDT), that is, ornamental but ineffective disclosure. DDT is of course also the acronym for a pesticide (dichlorodiphenyltrichloroethane) used to kill insects in agriculture and insects that carry diseases such as malaria. DDT is poisonous, in either the pesticide context or the context of marketing. A DDT strategy's overall success or failure depends in large part on how long a marketer can delay a consumer's (a) learning about drawbacks, risks, and limitations, (b) suspicion that deception (concealment, omission, lying) is being attempted, and/or (c) realization that no meaningful disclosure of drawbacks will ever actually be made.

Therefore, the message distribution aspect of a marketing campaign is a determinant of its deceptiveness, as well as the contents of the specific messages. There are many possibilities. For example, marketers can attempt a one-shot, one-message, one-exposure deception. The whole deception is contained within that single message execution. Alternatively, a marketer can present such a message plus an ineffective instruction about "how to find out more" that weakly directs consumers to another message in another vaguely described location or medium, a message that itself may or may not really alleviate the deceptiveness (e.g., "See our ad in *Golf Digest*," "Consult the Terms of Purchase document"). Marketers can try to implement multiple-message transmissions so that every target person gets exposed in roughly the same sequence to the entire set of messages. In so doing, a deception-minded marketer can assure that revelations of unfavorable drawbacks are delayed to the end of the consumer's decision process, after the impact of the earlier deception tactics has created a solidified favorable inclination toward buying the product. Or, a marketer can intentionally practice a scattershot transmission that facilitates deception. Indeed, unless a marketer seriously plans the message distribution to prevent deception, any single consumer's exposure pattern to the full array of transmitted messages may be incomplete, such that many consumers never encounter the critical parts of the marketing communication array that could have prevented deception. For example, if there is one message (e.g., a direct mailing) in the overall message array that does contain a potentially revealing disclosure of a drawback, deceitful marketers will try to sabotage that message's arrival, for example, by mailing it in an envelope disguised to look like a piece of junk mail, to lure consumers into discarding or ignoring it. Deceitful marketers also mail rebate checks and other payments to people in junk-like envelopes, hoping these will be discarded unopened.

Types of Deception Tactics

Many deception theorists assert that all deceptions are comprised of dissimulations and simulations. Anolli et al. (2002) say that there are four basic types of deceptions: concealment, omission, simulation, and lying. Keep in mind that these are not mutually exclusive; real-world marketers use them in combination. For example, both concealment and omission are used to dissimulate (hide the true reality) and also to help in deceptive simulation (show the consumer false reality). In their work on adversarial deception, Johnson et al. (1993) adapted a deception typology from Bell and Whaley (1991). Johnson et al. defined dissimulation as tactics that hinder formation of a correct representation of the "deception core." They defined simulation as tactics that foster an incorrect representation of the deception core. The "deception core" concept is useful; it refers to the things the deception agent will try to misrepresent, or to induce the consumer to misrepresent in their own mind. In the marketplace context it needs to be defined broadly. Most obviously, deceptions can occur in misrepresentations of the product(s) and service(s) being marketed by the agent, including their attributes, usage consequences, and benefits, risks, and so forth.

The deception core can also include deceptive representations (statements, objects, pictures) about any element of any persuasion tactic(s) used in the message to bolster its persuasive impact. It includes misrepresentations of an alternative product or service to the one being marketed, for example, a competing brand or alternative type of product. It includes misrepresentations of bad things that might happen if the consumer does buy the marketed product, and of wondrous things that will happen from using the product. The deception core also includes misrepresentations about the terms of the transaction. It includes misrepresentations made about things that a social critic or a scientist has said or might say about the product's drawbacks and risks. It includes misrepresentations about how to search for and learn more about the product, and how users with different levels of knowledge and ability can use it safely and efficaciously under foreseeable usage conditions.

The forms of representation and misrepresentation that marketers use include visual and verbal devices of all kinds. Visual and verbal misrepresentation occurs via graphical designs; still photos; motion pictures; digitized image manipulation; numbers and numerical relations; arithmetic calculations; statistics; pictures (charts and graphs) of statistics and numbers; data presentations from research on humans, consumers, products; statistics (base rates, proportions, sample sizes) used to generate representations of relation; language choices; propositional logic; animation; digitized image invention; information overload, sparseness and imbalance; and storytelling. These forms of symbolic misrepresentation and the tools for executing them fluently have kept changing at a rapid pace throughout the last two centuries. Changes in the tools of misrepresentation probably outstrip successive generations' capacities to adapt and self-protect, or at least pressure people's learning capabilities to keep pace in both understanding a widening range of representational forms and grasping how they can be used to misrepresent.

Bell and Whaley (1991) identified three general dissimulation tactics for hiding the real. They call these (a) masking: hiding the real by making it invisible; (b) repackaging: hiding the real by disguising; (c) dazzling: hiding the real by confusion. Their three deceptive simulation tactics for "showing the false" are (a) mimicking: showing the false through imitation; (b) inventing: showing the false by displaying a different reality; and (c) decoying: showing the false by diverting attention from the real. We find those six compartments useful but somewhat confining for discussing the psychology of marketplace deception. In our own discussion of marketplace deception tactics, we aim for midrange tactic conceptions described by their psychological properties. These are not as specific as some practices prescribed by laws; for example, we do not talk in this chapter about specific stylized schemes such as a pyramid scheme, which have detailed legal descriptions, or specific scams, such as a pigeon drop. We do not discuss trademark confusion and counterfeiting because that specialized topic is dealt with in-depth elsewhere (Jacoby, 2001; Zaichkowsky, 2006). We also do not talk specifically about deceptive pricing tactics, although deceptive pricing can be usefully analyzed in terms of the tactics we do discuss.

Distraction and Camouflage

Malevolent distraction is one of the most prevalent deception strategies used by marketers. Distraction is well known to suppress protective cognitive response activities that require effort such as counterarguing or deception-protection thinking (Petty & Brock, 1981; Wright, 1981). In persuasion studies, researchers typically distract subjects for the entire duration of a persuasive message, authoritatively disconnect the distracter from the persuasive message per se, for example, by giving subjects an ancillary task to perform, or authoritatively impose a message-processing subtask such as counting the adjectives or studying the use of color in the message. However, deceitful marketers use distraction more artfully and tactically than that, by engineering distractions in an ad that are timed and located to disrupt processing of the specific disclosures in the ad about drawbacks, risks, and limitations. Marketers' distractions are cleverly constructed, pretested, and strategically timed to facilitate the deception of consumers. Modern communication media afford marketers with a wonderful arsenal of attention-getting technological capabilities; before marketers transmit ads, Web sites, and promotional materials on a widespread basis, they experiment with, tweak, pretest, and revise their uses of these technological capabilities to direct attention as skillfully as they can. Psychological research identifies many types of stimuli that are virtually irresistible as momentary attention-getters. These can be reliably used, alone or in combination, to distract consumers away from the damaging disclosure. Well known examples are visual size and prominence; visual brightness and vividness; loudness; surprise; novelty; pleasing or puzzling complexity; stimuli people habitually focus on in everyday life because these may be related to basic wants and needs, such as safety or sex; aesthetic beauty; processing fluency; and habits related to watching a particular medium, for example, center-screen fascination. So it is relatively easy to design and position effective distracters to aid in a deception.

To disrupt a consumer's consideration of a damaging disclosure enough to undercut its effectiveness and to also conceal the deceptiveness in how that disclosure is made, a marketer needs to distract a consumer without making the intent-to-distract obvious. In doing that, a marketer needs only to distract a consumer once or intermittently while the damaging disclosure is available to be, or likely to be, processed. A marketer can use a bevy of different attention-getting stimuli to accomplish a one-time or intermittent distraction away from a damaging disclosure. Even a scattershot distraction strategy works to achieve the deception. For example, in a television ad a marketer can do all the following things to distract while a damaging disclosure is being stated or printed on the screen: show something surprising at the top of the screen; have an actor voice a sudden exclamation and make sudden physical movements; show a foolproof "feel good" attention-getter (e.g., a baby, a beautiful face) in some region of the screen; show rapid scene changes; do a narrator talk-over about something unrelated to a damaging disclosure being shown in print at screen-bottom; and so forth. To the deceit-minded marketer, it doesn't matter which of these multiple distracters causes sufficient distraction; indeed, different consumers may be diverted from the disclosure by different distracters provided by the marketer. It is enough that any of them, or any combination of them, achieves the distraction. For example, in a TV ad for a pharmaceutical product, written on-screen disclosures about risks were shown via swirling ribbons of written text at the screen's bottom while a train roared through the top half of the screen and the celebrity spokesperson continued talking about a topic different than the risk disclosures.

To understand the uncorrupted honest design of information displays, Tufte (1997) examines what magicians say about how to produce misleading illusions. Tufte argues that a magician's goal is the antithesis of an honest educator's goal: "To create illusions is to engage in disinformation design, to corrupt optical information, to deceive the audience … The strategies of magic suggest *what not to do* if our goal is truth-telling rather than illusion making" (Tufte, 1997, p. 55). Magicians master the production of entertaining but inconsequential illusions. Marketers, however, try to master the production of highly consequential illusions. According to classic writings about magic, magicians aim to create astonishment and bafflement, an enjoyable perplexity and a mildly-frustrated confusion that is unpenetrable to the audience, caused by concealing important facts and factors or by making them overly intricate. They specialize in strategies of disguise and attention control. They do what skilled mystery writers do, contriving the show so that just as the possible clue is dropped a distracting incident occurs (Fitzkee, 1945). They do visual masking, which Breitmeyer (1984) describes as reducing the visibility of one stimulus by presenting a spatiotemporally overlapping or contiguous second stimulus (the mask).

Magicians know, as do marketers and most lay people, that movement attracts attention to a stimulus but also diminishes that stimulus's visibility. A large movement can be used to conceal a small one (Nelms, 1969). Tufte notes that professional designers of visual communication materials know, like magicians, that shrill and strident visual activities will tend to dominate the information space, thereby scrambling detailed but relevant content. For example, putting a thick-line frame around a cautionary warning statement that is written in "sans serif" capital letters will minimize the distinctions among letters and words, making it difficult for consumers to read the warning statement. Tufte (1997) believes that the intentional masking of substantive content pervades much contemporary graphic design in advertising, packaging, and other marketing materials. Rand (1993) calls this the triumph of decoration over information. He describes the graphic design in advertisements, packaging, and elsewhere as a kludge-like collage of chaos and confusion that arrogantly combines whiz-bang high-tech design toys and low art, aimless sprinklings, sleazy special effects, indecipherable and zany typography, and tiny-type cunning.

Early texts on magic advocate two primary principles for successful visual illusion-making: suppressing the target audience's awareness of context and preventing the audience from doing reflective analysis of what they are seeing or have seen. These principles apply well to the practice of deceptive marketing. These texts preach that the successful illusionist (magician, marketer) should never let the audience be acutely aware that deception is about to occur, never tell the audience beforehand what you are going to do, and try hard to prevent them from gaining advance insight on what you are going to do, because that gives their vigilance direction and increases the chances of detection. Magicians are advised to never perform the same trick twice on the same evening, because even a great trick loses much of its effect on repetition. Besides that, the audience knows precisely what is coming, and have all their deception detection skills directed to finding out how you "cheated their eyes" on the first occasion. Because a magician's audience often wants to maintain and enjoy their astonishment, they will often keep themselves "in the dark," not trying hard to learn too much and thereby spoil the fun. However, consumers seeking truth, not illusion, can try diligently to penetrate the marketer's trickery. Following the magician's principles, a skilled deceitful marketer will vary the deception tactics used in a stream of transmissions and materials, trying to avoid a situation where a consumer sees the same exact trickery in the marketer's

successive ads. Deception-minded corporations will also try to preserve
the vulnerability of their prey by implicitly pressuring, convincing, or
rewarding researchers and educators not to independently teach consumers helpful deception-protection skills, and will try to control the content
of consumer education materials used in classrooms by designing them
so they dilute teaching about detecting visual and verbal deception, and
by supplying such weak materials free.

Marketers use bookend distractions, not just concurrent distraction,
to create deception. Bookend distractions surround a damaging disclosure with a lead-in distracter and an immediate follow-on distracter. The
lead-in distraction occupies a consumer's mind right before the damaging disclosure appears, which makes it difficult for the consumer to
reorient efficiently toward the damaging disclosure once that becomes
available. The lead-in initially activates a particular belief system that
is different from what a consumer needs to use to understand and learn
from the damaging disclosure. The person easily continues thinking
within that initially activated belief system, but it takes nontrivial effort
to tear thoughts away from that topic to deal with the newly presented
damaging disclosure. Similarly, marketers place distractions right on
the heels of a damaging disclosure to immediately tear people's attention away from thinking about the disclosure if they have noticed it. In
some cases the lead-in and follow-on content of the ad each offers a vivid,
interesting, clear, conspicuous, and relevant presentation about favorable product attributes, sandwiched around a brief, boring, vague, tur-
gid, ambiguous, pallid presentation of a damaging disclosure. Marketers
also do overlapping distractions. The presentation begins an engaging
visual theme or story before the printed or spoken disclosure is made
and continues it while the disclosure appears, then shifts in the middle
of the disclosure to another visually engaging story or theme. The second
audiovisual distracter capitalizes on the easy pass-along of visual engage-
ment and keeps the consumer's attention on the visuals, away from the
audio or print disclosure, until that is well past. Concealment via distraction can involve a beguiling, dazzling display of enjoyable stimuli
that are either irrelevant to the substance of the marketer's case or that
represent an extravagant, showy, mind-occupying display of favorable
product information. This has been called the "razzle-dazzle." It is well
captured in a popular song that asks how can people see "with sequins
in their eyes?" and continues, "what if your engines all are rusting, what
if, in fact, you're just disgusting ... razzle-dazzle 'em, and they'll never
catch wise."

Camouflage is also used to hide damaging disclosures, as a complement to distraction. In an insidious version of this, the message's format buries the specific damaging disclosure right in the middle of a paragraph or section that appears to be about another topic, or in a section whose topic is vaguely headlined or titled so as to misrepresent that section's contents. This violates well-accepted norms of how to organize and "punctuate" a written or oral presentation. A consumer's default expectation will always be that the content in a single (titled, subheaded, or labeled) paragraph or section of a presentation will deal with the specific topic stated in the heading or topic label. This occurs in oral presentations where the speaker helps listeners by labeling what the next topic will be. People learn to rely on such labels and headings as a helpful orientation guide to the upcoming section's content, along with reading (listening to) the section's lead sentence(s). They do so because they trust that the well-intended communicator is carving up the presentation for them according to well-accepted norms for organizing written and oral communication. Burying an unrelated or a marginally related disclosure inconspicuously in the middle of such a section or paragraph, rather than separating it and highlighting it on its own, is a truly malevolent form of deception.

Corrupted and Subverted Persuasion Tactics

Well-known persuasion tactics that could be executed honestly and without deception are often corrupted when used in the marketplace. We call a potentially powerful persuasion tactic executed via deceptiveness a "corrupted persuasion tactic." A corrupted persuasion tactic is one that has been changed "from a state of uprightness, correctness and truth" to a state that is "depraved, debased, and error-filled." As noted in Chapter 2, Cialdini (2001) and Pratkanis (2008) have identified a number of persuasion tactics that are effective under some conditions. Cialdini identifies six social influence principles, based on engineering or exploiting: (a) reciprocation motives, (b) commitment and consistency motives, (c) longing for social proof, (d) liking for the persuasion agent, (e) deference to authority, and (f) belief in scarcity. Pratkanis (2008) identified over a hundred social influence tactics that psychologists have found to be effective sometimes. Pratkanis lumped these into four general categories of things a persuasion agent can do: (a) establish a favorable climate before the persuasion attempt begins ("landscaping"), (b) create credibility with the audience and thereby enhance the communicator–consumer relationship psychologically, (c) present the message about the product per se in a convincing manner, and (d) evoke emotions in consumers to persuade them.

Now, marketers could execute each of the broad or specific persuasion tactics Cialdini and Pratkanis discuss in a sincere, honest, nondeceptive way, so that the information conveyed to a consumer to execute the tactic is free from subterfuge and deceit. However, marketers often execute these persuasion tactics in a misleading way (Cialdini, 1997). In terms of deception tactics, the corrupted persuasion tactic's execution incorporates and depends on misrepresentation, omission, concealment, or lying. For example, to misleadingly execute the "authority tactic," the marketer incorporates fake cues that misleadingly imply "authority" to consumers. This deceptively created impression that this speaker is a true authority on the topic helps create a favorable state of mind that magnifies the impact made by whatever favorable claims about the product that the spokesperson or the ad as a whole make. Deceptiveness in a persuasion tactic's execution may also entail disguising the true goal behind some part of a presentation. For example, in executing reciprocity-based persuasion, the initial act of giving something to a persuasion target or doing a favor for the target may be done honestly and openly—for example, "I'm giving you this free gift because I hope you'll give me something in return … that you'll listen to what I have to say about …" Or "… because I hope to convince you that this product is a valuable thing for you to buy." But marketers often do it covertly and dishonestly, hiding for as long as possible that the action they took was not simply an act of benevolence but was really a key step in a sequentially-unfolding persuasion tactic.

To appreciate the consumer's deception detection problem regarding corrupted persuasion tactics, consider that a marketer's persuasion attempt may rely on just one of Cialdini's or Pratkanis's tactics, or any two of them in combination, or any three in combination, and so on. For example, a single persuasion attempt, or a group of messages comprising a campaign, could use a scarcity tactic, a scarcity tactic coupled with a social proof tactic, those two together with several credibility-enhancing tactics, and so on. A bit of math indicates that there are thousands of persuasion tactic combinations that marketers can use, any of which can be corrupted in various ways by deceit in the execution of the constituent persuasion tactics. For example, a persuasion attempt that incorporates five different persuasion-enhancing tactics might make each of the five into a corrupted tactic by using deception in its execution, or might only corrupt one of its persuasion tactics to better disguise its inherent deceptiveness amid honestly executed persuasion tactics.

As discussed in Chapter 2, these persuasion tactics appear to work mainly when a target is indifferent, preoccupied, distracted or heavily loaded with cognitive tasks (Cialdini, 2001). Hence, they rely on System 1 processing being the predominant mode of processing as these tactics are executed. But System 1 processing alone creates weak, transient state-of-mind effects, by and large (Petty & Wegener, 1999), which do not by themselves produce durable attitude effects. Instead, System 2 processing of message content and own thoughts is required for lasting, stable, effects that withstand competitive messages (Petty & Wegener, 1999). Thus, the persuasion tactics that Cialdini and Pratkanis discuss are effective (from a marketer's perspective) mainly because they create momentary states of mind that bolster the "favorability" of any System 2 processing that the marketer induces a consumer to do. The persuasion tactics also help by creating a momentary state-of-mind that is destructive to the specific types of System 2 processing that would be unfavorable to the agent's goals, e.g., deception protection.

We arrive at an important realization. These well known and well studied persuasion tactics often become "deception accomplices" in practice, because their inclusion in a message that also contains a substantive deception about a product's drawbacks, risks, and limitations bolsters the success of the substantive deception. Persuasion tactics operate as deception accomplices when they are used to help a deception agent accomplish the deception by weakening or eviscerating a consumer's deception protection capabilities and motivations while he or she processes the entirety of the deceptive message. Persuasion tactics function as deception accomplices in the way we just described whether or not the persuasion tactics are themselves executed honestly or dishonestly. For example, an *honestly executed* social consensus persuasion tactic can bolster a subsequent deception by a marketer by creating a state-of-mind favorably inclined toward accepting the marketer's deceptive message and disinclined to vigilantly examine that message for concealments, omissions, or misrepresentations of drawbacks and risks. Similarly, a *corrupted version* of a social consensus persuasion tactic—one that lies, omits, conceals, or misrepresents social consensus information—also bolsters a marketer's deceptions about the product or transaction, and undermines its deception protection capability (assuming the deception in the execution of the social consensus tactic is itself not suspected or detected). When persuasion tactics function as deception accomplices, as we have described, we can think of them as "softening up" tactics that disarm consumers' deception protection capabilities in the moment. They lull to sleep a person's deception vigilance, because deception protection readiness and skill require a protective mindset and a protection-focused effort to do System 2 thinking.

Suppressing Deception-Protection Motivation and Opportunity

Deceit-minded marketers try hard to suppress a consumer's motivation and opportunity to apply their personal deception protection skills when processing the marketer's messages. We treat effective deception protection thinking as a specialized form of System 2 thinking. By and large, for practical purposes deception protection requires effort. Consumers will need to do effortful, special purpose thinking to accomplish deception detection, deception neutralization, and deception resistance. Some consumers may reach a point in their lives where their deception protection skills are so well developed that doing effective deception protection is an automatic System 1 undertaking. But marketers try to suppress consumers' deception protection thinking because consumers' marketplace deception protection skills (MDP) are slow to develop, and their self-protective thinking is therefore vulnerable to disruption and resource depletion (Vohs, 2006).

Distractions can be timed to disrupt a consumer's mental deception protection activities before those reach fruition. For example, suppose that deception protective thinking has started to slowly accelerate. That train of thought can be derailed in mid-journey by an inserted distraction; the consumer is diverted before deception protection thinking becomes effective. A deception tactic called "disrupt-then-reframe" exemplifies this (Fennis, Das, & Pruyn, 2004; Kardes, Fennis, Hirt, Tormala, & Bullington, 2007; Knowles & Lin, 2004b). It is at its heart a deception strategy built on artful distraction and confusion. In it, a message is constructed to introduce a timely distraction and feeling of confusion at a key moment, so as to interrupt a consumer's deception protection thinking before it gains momentum and is productive.

Another method of suppressing the use of marketplace deception protection (MDP) skill is to swamp a consumer with assorted information processing tasks before staging a concealment or omission, attempting to disarm MDP capabilities via sheer cognitive fatigue. Cognitive swamping involves gradually inundating and overwhelming a consumer's mind with more information than can be dealt with or accommodated, especially with a goodly portion of irrelevant information. For example, having a consumer think about topic after topic after topic, or detail after detail after detail, before a key concealment occurs will tire out the mind. The more cognitive resources these various topic shifts and details absorb, the greater the depletion of cognitive resources available for continual vigilance (Wegener, Petty, Smoak, & Fabrigar, 2004). Flooding a presentation with details will not only disarm a consumer's self-protective weaponry but also create an impression that a lot of disclosure is being made, thereby suppressing suspicion that something relevant and damaging has been omitted. One form of this is "flash flooding." A flash flood of information is, like a flash flood of water, a sudden localized flood of great volume and short duration. For example, in a telemarketing spiel, a telemarketer will, after first swamping the consumer with assorted information, suddenly ratchet up the deluge by rapidly reciting a list of vague services that are part of a "free" offer, just before briefly and ineffectively disclosing that this is a "negative option" offer that is tricky for a consumer to understand fully. The general swamping of cognitive deception protection capabilities, bolstered by this sort of flash flooding, eviscerates self-protection armament.

Knowles and Linn (2004b) identify what they call "Omega" persuasion strategies for reducing a consumer's resistance to a marketer's messages. They note that these types of strategies are under-researched in the persuasion literature, and present them as viable parts of a persuasion agent's kit of persuasion tools. As it turns out, many Omega strategies are actually strategies that mislead and deceive consumers, and their impact is due in large part to the deceptions. Knowles and Linn did not advocate unbridled use of the more deceptive Omega strategies; they probably envisioned them mainly as methods to overcome resistance to messages that advocate "pro-social" causes, where in the perpetrator's mind some good ends justify the questionable means. One potentially deceptive Omega strategy (Knowles & Linn, 2004b) is to "redefine the interaction" so its true persuasive goals are masked from the consumer. This tactic is familiar to marketers. Knowles and Linn cite as examples the training of salespeople to define an interaction with a consumer to that consumer as a "consultation" to deflect the consumer from defining it mainly as a persuasion and marketing interaction. They listed the potential benefits of this method of deceptive persuasion, as they saw them, as follows: (a) it implies to the target that he or she is in control and therefore has little need to be wary, (b) it defines things so the goal seems to be creating a shared plan, which distracts a consumer's attention away from taking care of her own self interest, and (c) it focuses the consumer's mind beyond this immediate interaction to an inferred long-term interaction with the salesperson, which suggests that the consumer can defer deception protection—for instance, wait for future opportunities to deal with any deceptions or "misunderstandings" created by the marketer in this immediate interaction.

A second potentially deceptive Omega strategy is to use narrative storytelling as a means of hiding from consumers the persuasive intent or goals of a marketing presentation. Using narratives in marketing messages makes the presentation seem more like escapist, unimpeachable entertainment. The suspenseful story-unfolding structure of narratives enables marketers to hide for a while what the topic of their message is—that is, what specific type or brand of product or service is the true topic of the persuasion (Campbell, 1995; Dal, Cin, Zanna, & Fong, 2004; Escalas, 2007). The "this-is-entertainment" mindset prevents a consumer from getting mentally primed for self-protection early in processing the message, and also from exiting from the persuasion attempt early on. The narrative story sucks a person in, gets them engaged in nonsuspicious processing, and then springs the marketer's true topic on them when the marketer chooses to. Green and Brock (2002) argue that narrative forms create "plausible" mental simulations or scenarios—that is, these are not necessarily valid but still seem plausible to a consumer—and that consumers often treat a plausible storyline as a true storyline. Dal, Cin, Zanna, and Fong (2004) argue that narratives often rely on a receiver doing spontaneous inferencing about the story's details beyond what is explicitly stated. That is, the story implies things for the reader, viewer, or listener to mentally fill in, and indeed doing that filling-in work in one's imagination adds to the receiver's enjoyment of the experience. But, once a consumer gets caught up in this filling-in activity, which is essential to the fictional story, their mental momentum makes them keep on making inferences, often invalid, even when the topic switches to claims about the marketer's actual product. Green and Brock explain that a person becomes increasingly absorbed into a story via a convergent process wherein all of one's mental faculties get devoted to the narrative experience (Green & Brock, 2002; Green, Garst, & Brock, 2004). If so, then that constricts cognitive capacity available to "step away" from the story itself to do deception-protection and to carefully scrutinize the persuasion part of the message. Green and Brock call this a mental and emotional *transportation process*.

Thus, narratives stories served up by marketers are accomplices in disarming and disabling the vigilant scrutiny a consumer might otherwise apply to detect relevant deceptions. A mixed fictional–factual presentation, or mixed unreal (animated) and real (actual people and places) presentation, requires some special state of mind from consumers that lulls them away from serious deception vigilance. Dal Cin, Zanna, and Fong (2004) argue that narratives reduce a consumer's alertness to forewarnings, contextual cues, or message cues that would suggest that deceptive tactics are at work. Further, they believe that the content of narratives is difficult to discount, because plausibility is the yardstick by which consumers evaluate truth; the "implausible" must be untrue, regardless of whether it is fact or fiction, whereas the plausible, if not true, at least "could be." They argue further that the cognitive and emotional demands of absorption into a narrative leave readers or viewers with little capacity to think critically about substantive claims in a message containing big doses of narrative. Transportation is a convergent process where all mental systems and capacities become focused on the events in the narrative, thus unavailable for scrutinizing the validity of a marketer's product-related assertions.

The Run-Around

To facilitate a concealment strategy, marketers often give consumers inexplicit, hidden, or obtuse directions on how to find a clear disclosure—a definition, an explanation, a qualification—in another part of the ad or material, or in another marketer-supplied message in another medium. Further, if a definition, explanation, or qualification about drawbacks and risks is actually made at some other place, it is often not placed closely adjacent to the deceptive part of the original presentation. This forces consumers to disrupt their current message processing to hunt for clarification or enlightenment, or to remember to exert search effort later on to track it down. Further, even if such a disclosure is actually supplied once, marketers rarely repeat it again (voluntarily) even if the entire message or presentation is lengthy and tedious to process. When such a disclosure is made only once, without helpful redundancy and repetition, its chances of being neglected are greatly increased. So consumers have to seek out a repetition or explanation of something suspicious on their own.

When consumers do seek better information, marketers sometimes use a "run-around" strategy to deceive a consumer about the likelihood of obtaining useful information about drawbacks, risks, and limitations. One version of this is an outright discouragement strategy; the marketer tries to show a person that one or more of the necessary conditions for finding the elusive disclosure cannot be achieved (Rowe, 2007). Lying to accomplish this is tempting. Rowe (2007) argues that stalling is especially effective because it (a) is less suggestive of deliberate deception and (b) is also less discouraging to the consumer's determination to learn more. He reasons that by stalling the consumer's immediate efforts to learn more, but artfully leaving open the possibility in the consumer's mind that "if I just keep plugging" I will learn from this company what I need to, the deceit-minded marketer denies the consumer the sought-for information while also wasting that consumer's time and energy, thereby depleting the cognitive resources that could be used on other deception protection activities. Rowe illustrates how run-around tactics might be executed. A marketing representative communicating to a consumer via e-mail or telephone can, for example, (a) claim or imply that he or she cannot at this time find the information about a drawback, risk, or limitation needed by the consumer; (b) claim the consumer is not authorized to get the information or ask for passwords, codes, or other identification that the consumer does not have at that time; (c) issue an "error" or "cannot be opened" cryptic message in response, or simply not reply and not say anything; (d) say that the resource needed to obtain the sought-after information is not working, stop the resource from completing its search task in the middle, or put the consumer into a seemingly endless (discouraging) loop; and so forth. These are all deceptive excuses to string-along consumers who try to obtain information they need to judge possible product drawbacks. To a deceit-minded marketer, deception via a discouraging run-around may seem less obvious to consumers than risking a more detectable deception early in the communication campaign or actually disclosing a significant drawback early on. Further, the longer a marketer postpones the start of the run-around, and the longer the marketer stalls between successive consumer attempts to persist in detecting deceptions, the fewer such run-around iterations the marketer may need to do, and keep track of, to keep the overall deception story consistent (Rowe, 2007).

Omissions

Totally omitting information about a particular drawback, risk, or limitation, or several of these, is a commonplace marketplace deception strategy (Kardes, Posovac, & Cronley, 2004). Marketers both omit damaging disclosures and create their presentations to prevent consumers from reflecting on their decision-making criteria, to assure that an omission is neglected. Typically, marketer's presentations offer partial omissions or what are called "half-truths." For centuries, people have cited a half-truth, an omission blended among truthful revelations, as a particularly pernicious form of deception, often arguing that a half-truth is "the blackest of lies." To realize that something important is not being presented, a consumer needs to have a salient and accessible mental template of expectations about what all could be or should be revealed. Communication strategists hinder this by encouraging consumers into a sense of urgency and/or suggesting that "being decisive" and taking quick action is preferable to thinking and self- control, and by trying to isolate their own ads and materials from those of direct competitors whose ads and materials can provide alternate models of disclosure that make the marketer's omission noticeable. The problem consumers have in coping with omitted information has been discussed extensively (e.g., Gaeth & Heath, 1987; Kardes, Posovac, & Cronley, 2004; Shimp, 1979) so we will discuss that research in depth in Chapter 6.

4
Marketplace Deception Tactics II

In this chapter we focus on the sorts of deceptions that arise from what a marketer does explicitly say or show to consumers, not what a marketer conceals or omits. We will discuss simulations, framing tactics, impersonation, hedging language, and equivocation, exploiting consumers' tendencies to draw inferences beyond literal content, exploiting consumers' innumeracy and limited understanding of research methods, verbal and visual lying, verbal and visual rhetoric, and marketing bullshit.

Simulation

From a consumer's perspective, mental simulation is an internal process involving one's own imitative mental representation of an event or series of events (Taylor & Schneider, 1998). In deception theory, the word *simulation* is also used to reference the action by a persuasion agent to explicitly misrepresent to consumers an object, action, situation, event, or series of events, as an enticing lure for the individual consumer to embrace and "buy into" in doing their own mental simulations. Ultimately, consumers do the simulation mentally; to mislead that mental simulation process, the marketer proactively depicts or models for the consumer how their mental simulations should unfold. We clarify this because we have found that in discussions about simulation as a deception strategy, the term is sometimes used to describe the external agent's activity and sometimes the deception target's mental activity induced by the agent.

In conveying a representation of a reality, the simulation is what you explicitly say, not what you leave out. However, any simulation of a situation or event or process or object by a marketer will also be defined by its omissions and concealments. Any simulation of something by a marketer is a reduced-form conception of it; by definition, a simulation is not the all-inclusive entity. Simulating is sometimes a neutral good-faith activity, but in lay parlance and deception writings it refers to an insincere, inferior, fake, counterfeit, misleading representation. Marketers engage in deceptive simulation when they proactively misrepresent a basic element of the market offering. These include misrepresentations of the purported product per se; the physical service delivery site; the transaction site; the company's manufacturing or business operation sites; the service delivery "servicescape"; the procedural depiction of consumers doing the instrumental tasks, overt and cognitive, that apparently lead to depicted outcomes; the service delivery process that depicts a consumer's required or typical behavioral interactions with employees or other consumers within the site; the use of electronic, physical, or other tools as part of the service experience; the service delivery employees' statements, demeanor, and actions; the physical product's outer appearance from different perspectives—its size, its innards; the actions a consumer needs to perform effectively in operating it, using it, and learning its safety instructions and risks; and searching for vital usage information from the packaging, labels, other ads, etc., storing this and maintaining it. Research on mental simulation by consumers examines when and why particular forms of cognitive cause-and-effect simulations and process simulations guide a person's future actions and which forms of simulation exert positive effects on a consumer's life versus negative effects (Escalas & Luce, 2003; Gregory, Cialdini, & Carpenter, 1982; Keller & McGill, 1994; Taylor, Pham, Rivkin, & Armor, 1998).

Of particular importance here is the general finding that people are often dependent in their own mental simulations of future events on highly salient, easily accessible, concrete "simulation lures" that others present to them. People tend to imagine futures following the lead of an explicit, compelling scenario that someone explicitly shows them. Doing one's own hypothetical constructions of different future scenarios than the one a marketer explicitly presents is not an easy task, and people cannot imagine cause-and-effect scenarios or procedural sequences of future actions that they themselves have never or rarely observed happening in the real world.

Process simulations in a consumer's mind are of special concern because marketers often tell an if–then cause-and-effect story that misrepresents the bad things that will happen if a consumer keeps doing or starts doing something other than buying the marketer's product, and the wonderful things that will happen simply by acquiring and somehow using the marketer's product. This is a basic before-and-after story. It is the structure of what are loosely lumped together as problem-solving messages, before-and-after messages, anxiety-arousing or threatening messages, loss framing messages, and social-modeling messages. Deceptiveness occurs when that story's basic elements are misrepresented.

The concept of a decoy is useful here. A decoy is something used to lure someone into danger. A decoy is not just a momentary distraction used to conceal something. In decoying, the deception agent strongly wants to attract attention to something and hold it there, to induce a consumer to believe in it, because that lures the person's mind down the particularly deceptive if–then path the marketer needs them to simulate mentally. In the basic if–then story a marketer conveys, there are several fictional realities to be created. One is what can be called a "bogeyman decoy." A bogeyman decoy is a deceptive simulation of the consumer's supposedly horrible experiences if they do not choose the marketer's product. The decoy reality here is one a consumer will want to escape from, into the other invented reality (or actual reality) the marketer also conveys, the "candy-land decoy." The candy-land decoy is a fictional misrepresentation of a wondrous future. The third important part of this cause-and-effect story that marketers often misrepresent is the intervening sequence of actions that a consumer supposedly must take to avoid the bogeyman scenario and achieve the candy-land scenario. The marketer's proactive representation of these intervening actions is often woefully incomplete or explicitly misleading. It lays out an over-simplified, inaccurate, and often downright dangerous, set of actions to imagine, plan, and execute. It reduces this complicated action sequence to a "Madison Avenue two-step": buy the product, thereby avoiding the bogeyman and living in a candy land, pure and simple. This modeled action sequence is deceptive and misleading when it (a) inaccurately demonstrates, describes, or omits, any important action step or mental operation step vital to or beneficial to producing the depicted product usage outcomes; (b) explicitly misrepresents how difficult it is to do the specific acts in a required set of actions; or (c) misrepresents the conditions and consumer competencies that make executing specific steps especially difficult. Because consumers are usually unable to imagine themselves executing future action steps or cognitive operations that they have not previously executed under the pertinent conditions, they will be misled into danger by an impoverished or inaccurate simulation of the actions to be done. Note that when a new or unfamiliar product or service is being marketed, misleading representations of how to find out more, learn about drawbacks, and use the product safely and effectively are common when marketers do not take pains to help consumers mentally simulate the necessary conditional actions involved. For example, a company tried to introduce a new brand of infant formula for newborns via short TV ads, without educating medical professionals about the product's limitations. The brand manager responsible had previously worked on pet food marketing. The TV ads pictured mothers and babies but did not warn that this product was unsuitable for the sizable segment of babies who are lactose intolerant. Mothers who saw the ads bought the product, fed it to their intolerant babies, and some of those babies got really sick.

Deceptive Framings

This leads us into a broad, often deceptive, family of tactics called *framing tactics*. "Framing" amounts to presenting consumers with an incomplete and biased representation of a decision problem that misleads their perception and analysis of that problem, and thereby misleads their entire decision-making process. To frame a buying decision or preference judgment for a consumer, marketers present a narrow way of thinking that focuses on only one or a few aspects of a more complex decision problem, draws attention toward the marketer's favored framing, and says or implies that the frame presented by the marketer is objective and indeed the only reasonable framing to use. Incomplete framings involve discussing only one or a few of the relevant attributes or usage outcomes of a product, only comparing the marketer's product selectively against one or a few of the potentially viable alternatives, and representing the losses and risks associated with a product in a biased and incomplete way (Bettman, Luce, & Payne, 1998; Kahneman, Slovic, & Tversky, 1982; Kivetz & Simonson, 2000; Levin, Schneider, & Gaeth, 1998).

Framings of this sort are rarely discussed as intentional deception tactics by framing researchers. However, framing tactics inherently rely on omission and artful concealment of potentially relevant information, depend on these concealments and omissions escaping the consumer's scrutiny, and especially rely on concealing from consumers the possibility and benefit of adopting different framings of the decision problem from the one the marketer presents. Drawing a consumer into an incomplete, biased representation of the choice and judgment problem is what framing tactics are all about. Framing effects beneficial to marketers' persuasion goals exploit consumers' tendency to think only in terms of the explicitly-presented frame, and ignorance of how adopting the marketer's incomplete artful framing can bias their choices. To appreciate this, think about these two cases. In one case the marketer presents a classic one-perspective framing that gives consumers a partial incomplete perspective on the decision problem that is favorable to the advertised product. In the other case, a marketer presents that same identical biased one-perspective framing but in addition reveals to a consumer an alternate frame or two. ("In thinking about this, you may also want to consider these other unmentioned attributes, or these other unmentioned competing products" or "Here is an alternate way to frame your thinking that is just as good and accurate as the framing we just presented.") Or a consumer may be advised that "if you think about this from different perspective than the one we've foisted on you here, your preferences about these products may change somewhat; consumers should always reframe their decisions from several different points of view before they decide." Once we realize that persuasion agents can either keep their framing tactic covert, offer it as only one possible framing, or alert naïve consumers about the danger of this "frame it our way" perspective, the deceptiveness inherent in traditional covert framing tactics becomes apparent.

One type of framing is loss–gain framing. In representing the purported undesirable outcomes of not using the advocated product (e.g., the undesirable outcomes from not using a new drug or health care practice), there will always be multiple ways to depict bad outcomes which are each in themselves valid, but are more or less scary, graphic, brutal, anxiety arousing. In the abundant research on how to choose the best levels of anxiety arousal to create via persuasive messages, the prevailing but blinkered thinking has been to choose one, and only one, way out of the multiple valid ways to represent bad outcomes to consumers. However, even if the one representation a communicator chooses to employ is an accurate one, technically, if he or she presents only one depiction of the "negative outcome," that is deceptive to the consumer. This is a selective and biased framing of the negative outcome. It hides from the consumer other equally valid, but less or more scary representations, and thus deprives the consumer of a full disclosure in order to achieve the communicator's own persuasion goals. It is an artfully misleading simulation, and should be thought of as such.

In that situation, a nondeceptive way to represent the bad outcome of not using the advocated product or service would be to show it/describe it in a range of different ways, some true but graphic, some true but less graphic, some that show harsh cases, some that show milder cases, etc. These alternate depictions or framings of the negativity of the possible bad consequences together provide a realistic future scenario for the consumer to imagine, not a misleading future scenario biased to help the persuasion agents get their own way. The same applies to "loss framings" in so-called loss–gain framing strategies. If you present only one loss–gain frame, even if it is accurate and valid, that is deceptive unless you also present the other form of loss–gain framing of that same identical future scenario that you are representing. It is nondeceptive (or less deceptive) to present the framing explicitly from several different, equally valid, perspectives; it is exploitive and deceptive to present only one such framing intentionally to sell your product or idea, even if you believe it is a beneficial one. The deception inherent in choosing to present only one particular representation of a future negative event has rarely been mentioned, much less discussed openly in the huge literature. The overriding concern has been in understanding the effects that are set in motion by different ways of representing a threatening event, and in choosing strategically the "best" representation to use to maximize one's persuasive impact. This work is often done with laudable intentions in mind (e.g., to design effective ways of persuading reluctant sufferers of a medical condition to try a new treatment [e.g., Block & Keller, 1995]). We suggest that the deceptiveness in any one-frame-only persuasion strategy be better appreciated and accounted for in studying and using these tactics, even in health care persuasion.

Impersonation

Impersonation is pretending to be another person for the purposes of entertainment or fraud.

This includes impersonations in ads, scams (one person playing multiple roles on the telephone), and strategies where marketers deceptively obtain, then sell, identity-faking information and props to other marketers who use it to deceive consumers; by providing a target person with such information to establish authority; or by not disclosing to the consumer that you already know some key aspect of their private identity (e.g., their Visa card number), thus leaving them feeling they are safeguarded by the private part of their self when they are not. More obviously, it involves impersonating another consumer to make purchases in her or his name. Sometimes consumers knowingly and willingly buy "impersonating" gear and tools to use themselves in the misleading of others. Examples include a telemarketing services firm that sells deceptive scripts to clients to use as part of their own telescam impersonations, an Internet company that sells term papers for students to use to deceive their teachers, or a company that sells a neophyte real estate agent a counterfeit Gucci handbag for her to use to impersonate a successful experienced agent.

For the most part, any marketing agent—in person, as an unseen source of a message, or as a performer hired to be in an ad—is acting a part. Every consumer should interpret every act or utterance by a marketer as an acting job, unless they get strong, clear, proof that this specific marketer or marketer's helper is in fact putting their own selfish best interests aside and is operating as a true objective, honest, careful, friendly counselor. As with any covert acting performance, the people doing it try to lose themselves in the roles. They submerge their own personality, beliefs, and character for the moment. They learn to do the acting job well. Professional advertising strategists often describe their goal as establishing "verisimilitude." Verisimilitude is the *appearance* of being true or real, an *adequate* semblance of authenticity that is deliberately misleading but sufficient to pass light scrutiny. The staged setting, costumes, props, and even the actors' performances need not closely resemble the "real thing," as long as they match the targets' expectations about the real thing (Depaulo et al., 2003). For example, most adolescents and many adults probably have only vague notions about how an actual authority or specialized expert really looks and behaves, which makes them easy marks for impostors. Even if impostors seem a bit inept in their roles, lay people may readily overlook this because they think that most humans, regardless of role, authority, or expertise, communicate imperfectly. Professional actors who appear in ads posing as whoever their role calls for are in many cases good enough impostors to keep consumers from being jarred by their lack of authenticity. This charade is especially easy to pull off when audience members have rarely encountered and observed true examples of the particular type of person being portrayed in the ad.

Language That Misleads and Avoids Responsibility

A deception strategy includes plans and mechanisms to evade the negative consequences of being busted (detected, challenged, exposed, and penalized.) Guerin (2003) reviews research on how people use language to evade negative consequences from what they say. Linguistic strategies for evading the negative consequences of making misleading statements are called hedging, mitigation, equivocation, or disclaimers. Guerin argues that evading negative consequences means avoiding outright challenges. However, marketers also use hedging and equivocal language to try to evade the negative consequences in consumers' minds that accompany suspicion. A marketer can do this reactively, that is, wait for implicit suspicions about a presentation's integrity to occur in a consumer's mind or to be expressed (e.g., to a salesperson), and then try to respond via some evasion tactic. Most marketers, however, will try to do this proactively. Guerin (2003) reviews how research on hedges, mitigation, and equivocation has gone on in diverse social science disciplines under different names and with different categorization schemes (e.g., Caffi, 1999; Coates, 1988; Holmes, 1990). Hedges include giving preemptive "reasons" or "excuses" for one's perceived deception acts, distancing oneself from the presentation, and affirming one's social solidarity with the target. A common form of hedging is to use modal expressions such as "should," "could," "possibly," and "maybe," and quantifiers such as "a few" and "most likely." These expressions allow a definitive and clear phrase to be used and then qualify that definitive phrase by adding potential variation to it.

There are large lists of such hedges (Coates, 1988; Turnbull & Saxton, 1997). Abstract statements are "safer" to use than concrete statements and therefore mitigate or hedge the speaker's consequences. As academics well know, using abstract words heads off the consequences from overt peer challenges and rebuttals, while giving the appearance of being informative. Linguists believe that abstractions are hard to challenge formally, especially under demanding message processing conditions, because one must mentally review and challenge many examples of the abstraction to challenge its overall validity (Guerin, 2003). Of course, consumers need not do such scrupulous and exhausting cognitive analysis; they can simply learn to suspect deceptiveness whenever marketers use glib abstract generalizations and to discount such statements automatically.

Imprecision and ambiguity are also used as preemptive social defenses against being castigated for deception. To evade responsibility for any actions perceived to be deceptive, marketers will offer (and prepare salespeople to offer) vague and ambiguous reasons for their utterances and tactics (Adams, Towns, & Gavey, 1995; Miller, Joseph, & Apker, 2000). Bipolor categorizations used in marketing presentations are inherently vague while appearing to be precise. Using an obscure word can cause consumers to hesitate and question if they know what the term means, assume that the marketer may have used the term accurately, and believe that the failure to understand it accurately is their own responsibility; therefore, the consumer hesitates to challenge the usage as deceptive. However, here again, consumers can learn to assume automatically that when professional communicators use an obscure term, and do not try to helpfully elaborate it or define it for people, that is an intentional attempt to mislead in some way. Metaphors also have conversational properties that prevent or preempt challenges. Narrative story forms are accepted as incorporating and relying on a storytelling mode, in which some leeway is given to keep the story entertaining and fluent. Talking about one's mental or emotional world or "identity" is another strategy for avoiding deceit monitoring and negative consequences (Rose, 1999). For example, when ads portray a customer, spokesperson, expert, or employee stating what they "need," "want," "like," "feel," or "prefer," audience members can only weakly (suspiciously) contradict or challenge those disclosures. In everyday life, telling someone their report on their own mental world is a lie or a deception seems almost nonsensical; when you do it at all, you do it for humor. In marketing presentations, when someone talks about their supposed identity, values, or self, that is a possible strategy for resisting accountability and, importantly, for suppressing a consumer's motivation or tendency to do "truth monitoring," especially if the speaker in an ad or a salesperson talks confidently about a seemingly solid identity. This is the basic paradox of self-identities, corporate identities, and brand identities—that there is inherently nothing "real" there. These identities become "real" only when a person or a company learns to use them expressly for negotiating the "realities" of socioeconomic life (Goffman, 1959; Guerin, 2003).

Exploiting Automatized Inferencing Tendencies

Exploiting consumers' natural tendencies to draw inferences beyond the literal meaning of a marketing message is the most well discussed form of marketplace deception. Preston (1985) analyzed in depth how advertisers can exploit consumers automatized inferential tendencies, Harris (1990) discussed this from a legalistic perspective, and Kardes et al. (2006) provided an excellent review of recent research on the inferential tendencies that marketers exploit in order to mislead consumers. Consumers must draw inferences beyond a marketing message's literal content, in order to grasp the communicator's meaning. They might do this by applying

simple and uncontroversial symbolic logic or computational logic. They
are usually forced to apply their own pragmatic logic, however, a logic
that employs short-cut inferences and inferential heuristics. Among the
inferential tendencies that marketers may exploit to mislead are what
Preston (1985) called the following:

1. *Implied significance.* An ad states a fact, and simply stating it implies
   to consumers that it must be an important, significant piece of
   information.
2. *Implied contrast.* An ad states truly that there is a certain difference
   between the product and its alternatives, which implies to consumers
   that such a difference "makes a difference," that is, is an important distinction, when in fact it is not.
3. *Implication via ordinary meaning.* The advertiser uses several ordinary
   words that most people will predictably interpret as they do in ordinary
   usage, but which are used together to cause an unwarranted inference
   by the consumer.
4. *Implied proof.* An ad presents an explicit performance or benefit claim
   plus an explicit claim that some sort of testing or surveying of users has
   been done—for example, merely citing or referencing the test or study
   that was done, which is vaguely described, but which implies falsely to
   consumers that that test or study was done according to accepted scientific standards and is therefore meaningful proof.
5. *Implication via a reasonable basis for pragmatic inference.* Merely
   expressing a fact or claim about a product implies to consumers that
   the advertiser has indeed substantiated that fact, because the consumer
   applies pragmatic logic that governs normal social discourse and therefore believes the speaker would not state something without having a
   reasonable basis for believing it.

Verbal and Visual Misrepresentation

Both overt verbal lying and overt visual lying are especially troublesome
for consumers to deal with because manufacturing and video communication technologies have outstripped consumer self-protection capabilities.
Verbal lying is blatantly stating in words something about a real entity
in a way that misrepresents that entity's reality. *Visual lying* is blatantly
showing a visual image of something that is real in the world, in a visually
altered way that misrepresents its physical, observable reality. Marketers'
verbal lies are difficult for consumers to cope with because detecting the
lie as such depends on having some information in memory that indicates

the representation is inaccurate and false. Technological manufacturing innovations have placed consumers in a situation where they often do not have the requisite technical information for suspecting or believing something a marketer says about a product is a lie. Similarly, technological innovation for seamlessly altering visuals places consumers in a position of not being able to ascertain for themselves when something in a visual image has been altered unless they have verbatim visual images in mind of the reality of that entity. Consumers are increasingly dependent for their detection of verbal or visual lying based on the substance of the lie on the warnings of other people who are more informed about the reality, and can better detect lies. Marketers can now use as a deception tool the dramatically increased technological capability to do seamless alterations of authentic visual images. The creation of any visual image involves manipulation and interpretation (Wheeler, 2002). Historically, it has always involved a process in which a communicator selects, emphasizes, and sanitizes so that the presented image is more ideal appearing than the real referent. Paintings are compiled images completed over a number of sittings, blending together objects and people from different occasions or places. Paintings and photos have long depicted two people together who never met in person, in a place they never were.

In the past, faking photos required expertise and high motivation. A skilled photo faker tries to anticipate the types of cross checking a suspicious viewer will do, and then adjusts the visual evidence accordingly. But nowadays digitally stored photorealistic images can be produced and reproduced by virtually anyone, including lay consumers themselves. Whether generated via scanner, camera, or computer, these images are of the highest quality, and there is no trace of the alteration. Professionals and laypeople alike can alter details of a photo and video, combine multiple images, rearrange things, recolor, etc. Wheeler (2002) discusses how people create counterfeit photographic authenticity cues by technical tracing, matching edges, blending, gap filling, tone and color matching, and texture replications. Apparent originals can be generated from a computer itself. People can manipulate an image in the act of recording it. Professionals can make real-time video insertions of computer-generated ads into television broadcasts, creating seamless blending of moving images, seamless superimposing of single static image in to a scene in real time so it appears the image was originally part of the scene, and seamless superimposing or removing in real time of complex or moving objects from the scene. Virtualized ads intend to deceive at a very basic level, and there is the added complication that "participants" who are being filmed have no awareness of an advertisement being imposed into and invading their personal action displays, so they can become associated with a product without their knowledge (Wheeler, 2002).

How does all this affect the future of visual deception in the marketplace? That is unclear at this stage. The spread and assimilation within the general public and among amateurs of software that accomplishes these visual manipulations could end the myth of photographic objectivity. Consumers may soon simply distrust the validity of any and all visual images presented by marketers because easy manipulation has made it a standard commonsense practice that even consumers themselves grow up doing. Photography may already be discredited as a reliable witness. Digital technology usage by consumers may destroy the photograph's deceptive halo of truthfulness.

Exploiting Limited Numeracy, Research, and Statistical Understanding

Gigerenzer (2002) and Sowey (2003) explain how deceit-minded marketers can exploit lay people's "innumeracy," that is, their functional incompetence to understand and argue back to a statistic, and to draw accurate meaning from, and criticize, a statistical argument about the real world. Gigerenzer (2002) argues from experimental research that people are easily confused and misled when presented with information in the form of conditional probabilities. He argues that stating some event likelihood as a conditional probability impedes natural human inference, whereas stating the same information as a natural frequency demands less computation by the person in interpreting that statement, and has the advantage of using a form of expression analogous to how the individual human mind has experienced events over most of its evolution. We observe event frequencies in everyday life, not event conditional likelihoods which have to be calculated post hoc. He describes how consumers get confused and judgments get manipulated by the language that advocates use to express the risks and benefits from health care products or practices—for example, disclosing relative risk reduction versus absolute risk reduction; number of people who need to use a medical treatment to save one life; the proportion of users who are cured or saved; risks reported as absolute numbers and potential benefits as relative numbers, and so forth. Sowey (2003) further asserts that lay people's general innumeracy makes them more likely to accept a number or statistic that a marketer presents on trust than to argue back to it. Consumers confuse that number or statistic's apparent precision or exactness with its accuracy. They think it must be accurate if it is precise. Many people confronted by a marketer's numbers or statistics suspend otherwise natural skepticism in favor of regressive obedience to argument by authority. Sowey believes that most people, in school, learned what they know about math by rote, not by understanding. In that scenario, numerical results were meaningful because the teacher said they are meaningful. Later in life, they still believe a statistic is meaningful if the source of the statistic says or implies it is meaningful. Any marketer's "official" measurement of product or corporate performance gains credibility in an innumerate society of consumers simply by stating it. Statistical illiterates have learned as kids that stats are "true" under given assumptions, do not understand that statistical arguments are inductions, or that other logics are possible, and assume instead that a statistically expressed conclusion is necessarily a conclusion beyond question.

Best (2001) discusses the ways in which professional persuasion agents exploit the public's naivety about research methods and data interpretation. These include the inappropriate, incomplete, or inadequate reporting of survey or test results; reporting only the absolute number of survey respondents answering in a given way, and not the percentage or sample size, or vice versa; using but not reporting inappropriate sampling techniques in surveys; incomplete specification of the competition in a reported comparative tests; and only reporting the number of people who responded to a survey, not the number who refused to take part. One widespread deception strategy used by companies and industry groups is based on exploiting consumers' incompetency in evaluating research methods and data interpretations. Michaels (2008) describes in depth how industry executives use scientists, lobbyists, and captive congressmen to keep consumers confused and uncertain about the hazards of products, such as secondhand smoke, plastics, global warming, asbestos, and other toxins. The general deception strategy is to have a company's or industry group's consultants vilify as "junk science" any research done by outsiders, including renowned independent researchers, which might threaten corporate marketing goals. We call this a mud-slinging strategy—the spreading of murkiness, uncertainty and doubt. The companion deception strategy is a company's having its paid researchers and scientists sanctify the company's own bought-and-paid-for research as "sound science."

Michaels' book title (*Doubt Is Their Product: How Industry's Assault on Science Threatens Your Health*) draws from a notorious memo in which a tobacco industry executive said doubt is the company's real product since creating doubt about the health risks from smoking is the essential corporate marketing strategy. Michaels discusses how company-funded researchers design the company's studies to generate deceptive findings, and how companies then cherry-pick or frame their research results when presenting them as part of a marketing campaign. The pharmaceutical industry's shenanigans are an example. Pharmaceutical companies' commonly used methods for deception in designing studies of drug products include:

1. Testing the company's drug against a treatment that is well-known not to work or not to work very well.
2. Testing a company's drug against too low a dose of the comparison drug because that will make the company's product appear more effective.
3. Testing against too high a dose of the comparison drug because that will make the company's product appear less toxic.
4. Publishing and presenting the results of a single multicenter trial many times in many places because that will suggest that multiple studies reached the same conclusion.
5. Publishing or presenting only that part of a drug trial that favors the company's drug, and burying the rest of the results.
6. Funding many studies but publishing and presenting only those that make the company's product look desirable.
7. Data dredging, sometimes called Texas sharpshooting: fire a bullet at a blank wall, draw a circle around it, and then claim that you got a bull's eye. In this case, a company's researcher dredges through data long enough and creatively enough to discover something spinable, and the company's marketers showcase it (Michaels, 2008).

Michaels says that most consumers and many researchers are astonished to learn that the drug companies can get away with these sorts of deceptions. He states from experience that the FDA ignores research reports a company submits to scientific journals because the agency knows these can be badly incomplete or dominated by spin, not substance. This still leaves physicians who rely on the medical literature deceived and misled in making treatment choices, and consumers who rely on physicians and on their own understanding of misleading presentation of studies in ads and marketing materials doubly deceived.

Rhetorical Deception: Visual and
Verbal Figures of Speech

Semiotics involves the interpretation of symbolic behavior at its most fundamental level. Renowned semiotician Umberto Eco characterized semiotics as the discipline studying everything that can be used in order to tell a lie. Rich discussions of visual and verbal rhetoric by Stern (1992), Scott (Scott, 1994), McQuarrie and Mick (1996, 1999), and Philips (McQuarrie & Philips, 2005), among others, have focused on the figures of speech or expression that add meaning in consumer's minds to literal statements by advertisers. Some forms of figurative expression in marketing communications may be inherently misleading to consumers. Indirect claims can elicit inferences for which no explicit statement was made; they "invite" consumers to construct multilayered meanings that are not actually given in the ad's text. Metaphors represent a type of indirect claim because they make claims in a figurative away. They are artful deviations that require resolution and point the way to resolution (McQuarrie & Mick, 1999; McQuarrie & Philips, 2005).

Advertising sometimes resembles literature in the way it seeks to get audiences to experience things in new ways. And like literature, advertising sometimes takes poetic license with words and images to convey meanings that go beyond literal truth. In so doing, deception can occur through the use of tropes, or figures of speech, that change the literal meaning. Tropes can be represented by images as well as words, and both can have a positive impact on the way advertising is evaluated and remembered (McQuarrie & Mick 1996, 2003). Stern (1992) described several of these as potentially deceptive. A metonym is a trope that relies on association through contiguity rather than similarity. For example *the crown* is a metonym for royalty and *the press* is a metonym for the news media. In both cases the concepts are represented by something that happens to be associated with it rather than something that is similar to it in any way. Irony relies on creating a discrepancy between what the words in a statement appear to say and what they really mean. An ironic advertisement therefore carries a real meaning below a surface meaning. The effect is often humorous. Absurdism describes a type of drama in which causal sequences of events are illogical, characters behave irrationally, and strange juxtapositions of people and things occur. Absurdism challenges the assumption that the world is rational and that objective meaning exists at all. This kind of dramatic treatment essentially dissociates language from meaning and therefore encourages perceivers to fill in whatever meaning they like. Stern (1992) describes absurdism as an especially subtle form of deceptiveness, because it disrupts conventional notions about meaning by questioning its very existence. She argues that, in advertising, characters like "Smooth Joe" Camel qualify as absurdist heroes who allow advertisers to convey messages about the desirability of smoking through juxtaposition of images. "Smooth Joe" is a humanized Camel shown smoking Camel cigarettes in various scenes that feature sex and status symbols. It is interesting to consider the potential effect of similar imagery using a real person rather than an animated character to convey the message. Distancing the product spokesperson from a real human seems to make the imagery less literal and therefore more palatable.

Pictures that associate unrelated things via visuals, such as healthy young adults and cigarettes, cause viewers to do multiple inferential interpretations. McQuarry and Philips (2005) point out that many have argued that advertisers use metaphorical pictures when they do not want to take responsibility for the covert content of their ads or dare not make such claims flat out for legal reasons. Pictorial metaphors may suppress counterarguing and deception-protection thinking by spreading consumers' attention along multiple inferential pathways, and because people simply cannot counterargue pictures, thus causing inferences favorable to brand that could not be legally stated without substantiation (McQuarrie and Philips, 2005).

Marketing Bullshit

It is timely to examine a form of marketplace deception that we all call "marketing bullshit." Renowned philosopher Frankfurt (2005) and eminent sociologists Mears (2002) and Goffman (1959) have discussed the meaning and ubiquity of "bullshit" in contemporary popular culture, including the realm of marketing. Frankfurt (2005) lamented that we have no clear understanding of what bullshit is, why there is so much of it, or what functions it serves. The *Oxford English Dictionary* suggests that to engage in bullshitting is "to bluff one's way through something by talking nonsense." Bullshit ("BS") is in many cases "talk for talk's sake," because an opportunity or perceived need to talk presents itself, but it is also a form of misrepresentation that differs from lying or concealing the truth. The bullshitter's distinctive characteristic is hiding from the audience that the intention is neither to report the truth nor (as with the liar) to conceal it; that the speaker just does not care about the truth one way or another in saying what he or she says (Frankfurt, 2005). Mears (2002) conceives of BS as a person's attempt to question, change, or control another person's impressions of the speaker's "true self" by deliberately and playfully creating misleading yet possible, though improbable, accounts or impressions of that self for instrumental or expressive reasons. He proposes that this only becomes "bullshitting" when it is so recognized and labeled as "that's BS!" by the audience members.

Participants in any interaction must interpret it by some frame of reference. A marketplace interaction can be defined by two or more frames of references, a bit of education, some persuasion, some entertainment, some deception, some nonsense, which makes interpreting advertising tricky for consumers, and one of these perspectives can be bullshitting if the consumer and/or other observers define it as such. Mears and Frankfurt assert that a bullshitter's goal can be much broader than denying or obscuring a specific truth. It can include fabrication of entire events and contexts, and has a "panoramic" rather than a particular focus. Further, faking just who you are and what you have done can be an authentic creative activity (Goffman, 1959). Individuals experiment with other "possible selves" that could become more and more one's "true self" if these individuals find that this originated-in-bullshit self "works" in the minds of others. It is a way for adolescents, young adults, and others (including corporations) who have no well-formed identity to manage identity problems. Thus, brand image creation often entails bullshitting in the sense that a company tries to "become" whatever persona it finds handy to become, to take on a "personality" that it fabricates out of whole cloth. The brand image is something the company makes up and "tries on," like an outfit or costume or a role, simply by associating the company or product line with a set of characteristics without concern for whether or how deeply these are rooted in reality. The brand creates its own "self" and presents it to others to see if anyone will believe in it. In this view, branding amounts to a company's tentative, temporary identity tryout for an audience on whom it might work.

It may be that BS is especially pronounced in marketing contexts. The propensity to deceive varies widely within and across communities and domains of social life. Frankfurt (2005) sees BS as ubiquitous because communication technologies and corporate worlds put so many people so frequently in a position of having to say stuff when they have no clue about what is valid to say and when the pressure to talk outweighs concern for whether what they say is valid or relevant.

Marketing managers, salespeople, and advertising copywriters feel such pressures repeatedly. Brand managers and advertising creative types may be so accustomed to bullshitting in their personal lives, in searching for a personal identity or for instrumental courting purposes, that simply transferring that behavior to their work lives comes naturally; when in doubt, bullshit. In many contexts other than the marketplace, BS performs useful functions. Goffman (1959), for example, says that the practice of "playful deceit" exists in all societies, so that individuals contain and create different selves to perform for the purpose of having fun themselves and creating fun for others. In this view, BS has a socialization value for children and adolescents. It enables them to experiment with self-reality negotiations and to learn how to survive in social environments where some types of deceit may be functional. By creating fantasies, lying, deceiving, teasing, and being playful, a child or adolescent learns there are diverse ways of framing and playing with reality, that there are limits on how far you can go, and that how far the BS is allowed to go depends on how far the recipient is willing to play along before eventually signaling "That's BS!"

Marketing BS can also entail cool-minded instrumental deception. It includes the act of achieving specific goals via strategic manipulation of reality, for example, expressing empty values or taking credit for policies, social trends, and environmental events for which in reality the marketer or the products had little or no responsibility. It also involves dramatic BS. In 1983, British movie director Ridley Scott created a TV ad to introduce the Apple McIntosh computer to the world for the first time. It was a 60-second ad titled "1984," which was shown only one time on national television, and went on to become the most renowned TV ad ever made; it was later chosen as the best ad of the 20th century. Scott had previously created the movie *Blade Runner*, with its stunning visual depiction of a Los Angeles of the future populated by humanoids who can't feel emotion. Modern audiences know him best as the director of the movie *Gladiator*. In the Apple McIntosh ad, an audience of grey-cloaked drones sits in a dreary auditorium watching a huge video screen on which a Big Brother figure is preaching a future of total control by big corporations. Then, a young woman in vivid red shorts sprints down the center aisle swinging a sledgehammer over her head, which she launches into the screen, shattering it, and a wind-of-change blows across the stunned drones. Later on, Ridley Scott explained that he had taken the trouble to mount giant

Boeing 747 jet engines on the auditorium walls, and to cast the hundreds of skinheads recruited from the streets to play the drones, because the ad needed some "good old marketing bullshit." The only validity test applicable to this display of "good old marketing bullshit" is whether it has verisimilitude. Does it resonate in a viewer's mind as an immediately understood, plausible and dead-on representation of a *possible* reality? Do we get it? Or does it fall flat, from some inherent falseness we recognize or from ineptitude in its staging and enactment? In any case, how marketing BS fits into the menu of other deception tactics we have identified, and how consumers cope with it, are interesting research issues. Is it harmless-tongue-in-cheek experimentation, or clever deception that can sometimes confuse and mislead consumers about serious buying decisions?

5

How Deception-Minded Marketers Think

In this chapter we consider the deception-related thinking of a professional marketplace deception agent. We gain insights on this from several sources. One stimulating discussion is Cohen et al.'s (2001) Framework for Deception, originally developed to explain deception planning in the context of covert intelligence operations. A second useful source of insights is Mitnick and Simon's (2002) candid revelations about how so-called "social engineers" use low-tech interpersonal deception techniques to penetrate organizational security systems. A third source of insights is the unique study by Pratkanis and Shadell (2005) of recordings of hundreds of actual telemarketing calls made by professional telescammers. Further, we present our own analysis of the factors that can influence a marketing manager's decisions about practicing misleading marketing.

A Mental Model of a Professional Deception Planner

We return to Cohen et al.'s (2001) discussion of how a professional deception strategist who is well versed in cognitive social psychology should plan and execute deceptions. Recall that in Chapter 1 we discussed these authors' provocative notion about how to operationally define deception when one's overriding goal is accomplishing successful persuasion. Cohen et al.'s (2001) discussion does not depend heavily on specific or exotic details of national intelligence operations. Therefore, we feel that the "mental model" of a deception agent's mind illustrated in the Cohen et al. "Framework for Deception" provides an approximation to how sophisticated marketers think as they consider how to deceive consumers while minimizing their risks of being caught. Cohen et al. (2001) did not claim to be presenting a model of how real-world marketing strategists actually think; they prescribed how a deception strategist who is as smart, psychologically literate and pragmatic-minded as they are should think. So as we examine their ideas, we should keep in mind that the deception "agent" represented in Cohen et al.'s discussions is state-of-the-art insightful. Cohen et al.'s discussions show us how a marketer might think if that person understands the cognitive psychology literature, or understands in lay terms the basic notions of cognitive functioning that arise from that research, and has carefully thought through what to do to from a practical perspective to apply this knowledge intelligently to important real-world deceptions that are complicated to execute. On the other hand, the level of analysis about deception illustrated in Cohen et al.'s document probably does not reflect the thinking of inexperienced marketing managers or others who clumsily try to apply psychological research to complex situations without really appreciating the practical problems in doing that.

To synthesize Cohen et al.'s (2001) lengthy prescription for successful deception and show how it would apply to the marketplace realm, we interpret it and reexpress it as a first-person narrative spoken by a prototypical deceptive marketer, briefing his or her team of deception planners. Our hypothetical corporate deception maestro speaks:

We, the deception team at Profits, Inc., seek to control the set of data available to target consumers and control the focus of attention of target consumers. Our deceptions are designed to emphasize things we want target consumers to observe over the things we do not want them to observe. Ideally, we could control all the observables that are available to consumers but, failing that, we want to so tightly control their focus of attention that we only really need to control a small part of what they might observe. Consumers have limited memory and must use some standardized ways of thinking. That makes their thinking predictable to some degree. Even though we cannot totally know each consumer's memory state and belief system, there will often be enough predictability in all consumers' attentional focus and judgment processes to plan deceptions that will work, although with uncertainty about our results. However, consumers have the capability to learn from previous deceptions they've witnessed. So, to be effective our deceptions must be novel or varied across time in cases where a target consumer's memory about prior deceptions can affect the viability of our current deception. We can continue to effectively reuse the same deceptions, however, on successive cohorts of younger, less experienced consumers who continually replenish our supply of fresh, naive targets, as long as more experienced adults in society do not efficiently and effectively pass along what they have learned about our tactics to each newer cohort of younger consumers.

[The Profits, Inc., deception team leader continues.] While we might construct simple deceptions quickly, we are best served by preplanning all deceptions that are somewhat complex and are important to our marketing goals. Doing that takes time. Therefore, our marketing deceptions will almost always be a result of organized planning on our part, not just a serendipitous occurrence. When we have to execute a deception that encompasses multiple marketing media and messages, and if we must prevent leakage and detection, then we must anticipate that our deception-related planning, research, and refinements will take months. Additionally, our salespeople and marketing communication copywriters must be prepared to implement each part of a sequential and contingent deception process very rapidly and spontaneously, so they must be scripted, well rehearsed, and adept at conditional adaptations.

In most cases we must sustain the deception long enough for some key desirable psychological event or action to occur in the target consumer's mind or behavior. For one-shot deceptions that we use to gain a momentary compliance or a brief psychological effect, we need only sustain control over their attention for a few seconds. However, the realities of marketplace time lags and inefficient communication imply that we often must sustain our deceptions for long periods (days, weeks, months) before those deceptions pay off. Because our deception campaigns usually require us to execute complex sequences of acts, and often entail branching "if–then" decisions about communication tactics based on some feedback we receive from or about a target consumer, we must set up critical criteria to control our sequencing of deceptive acts. We cannot hope to prepare and train for a lot of different multiply sequenced deception plans and contingencies; our marketplace environment moves too rapidly, and our control over what is said by our communication agents and our competitors is limited. Further, consumers have allies: individual friends and family members, marketplace observers in the media, or consumer protection institutions. We have to take into account differences in the vantage points of a target consumer's available allies.

[The deception team leader further explains.] Our deception will be negated when a target realizes that we are doing something to hide information from them. So we must try very hard not to be caught or, especially, not to be penalized if we are caught. So, we must maintain operational security. We do not want to inform too many of our colleagues or "marketing helpers" about our ongoing consumer deception program to prevent leakage from careless or outraged field personnel, or from coworkers who quit or change jobs in the midst of our deception campaign. However, we do not want our own marketing people to be so uninformed that they do not play their parts appropriately. So, deciding who is in and who is out of our internal deception-planning loop is important. We should screen deception methods according to how well known they become among the general population. If knowledge gets widely diffused about a deception strategy in general and about how marketers execute it specifically, its usefulness to us gets reduced. However, if the strategy's various execution details remain "secret" or at least hard to recognize, that method of deception remains viable for our purposes. Of course, we and other marketers partly control this spread of deception execution knowledge; the more people we train in how to execute a deception strategy, the more widely the "how it gets executed" knowledge gets dispersed and the less viable the deception strategy becomes. So, from our manipulative perspective, there is an "optimal" level of nonsecret "how to do it" deception knowledge in the world at large.

[The Profits, Inc., deception team leader continues.] Our marketing interactions with target consumers are recursive and reflective. We can only judge the effects of our attempted deception from observable signs that the consumers present to us. We can use pretesting to prompt such signals in advance, or can try to monitor consumer reactions as we execute our strategy. Of course, our own marketing personnel are limited in how efficiently they interpret that feedback; for example, their own expectations about the effects of our deceptions will color their interpretation of consumer reactions. Further, some, maybe many, consumers will mask their responses to attempted deception from us or even misrepresent their reactions to mislead us. Because of this noise in our feedback, we really cannot plan too much beyond a single layer of recursion. So, practically speaking, executing a number of small, controllable deceptions of a consumer is usually preferable to trying to envision and orchestrate one grand deception that requires a lot of specific things to happen precisely, concurrently, and interdependently, as we originally envisioned them. Similarly, if we need to deceive multiple consumers, for example, all members of a household or organizational-buying decision-making unit, it is preferable if we can focus on effectively deceiving one or two key people. This limited initial deception of these key opinion leaders will get magnified as they themselves spread its poisonous effects to their less informed (not yet deceived) followers.

Large deceptions are built up from smaller ones. For example, consider the "big con." The big con is built up from small steps, as follows: (a) find a likely victim, (b) gain that victim's confidence, (c) show the victim "the money," (d) tell the victim "the story," (e) deliver a sample return on investment, (f) calculate the total benefits for the victim, (g) send the victim for more money to invest, (h) take them for all they have, (i) kiss the victim, and (j) keep the victim quiet. This seems complex, yet it works reliably again and again if each small step in it is carefully planned. In particular, experienced con artists have ways out at every stage—escape plans—so they can limit damage if needed, and keep the victim ignorant and quiet about what was going on. Further, they train the con actors in a number of ways to keep the victim engaged at each step along the way. In our deception efforts, we should follow that "big con" model. Accordingly, we will emphasize escape routes to limit the damages from being detected and busted, prepare a kitbag of variations in how to execute each step of the overall deception, and persevere with each step (while concealing the steps to come) until we accomplish it or until detection seems imminent (and we call off the deception effort). We will also rely on our deception-apprehension damage control experts—that is, our legal staff and public relations spinners—to minimize and excuse away penalties we incur if we are caught. However, we always prefer not to get those folks involved because that indicates we screwed up in our deception maneuvers.

Our deceptions entail concealment, simulation, or both. To effectively do deception via concealment or simulation, we need to know about target consumers' response thresholds, response capacities, and response predictability. Some of this we know from prior psychological research. Some we can learn about if we do our own experiments on marketing communication stimuli. Much of it we can only know with uncertainty because research-based knowledge about some psychological activities exists only at a general level, and these activities are difficult for us to study in our own experiments under realistic marketplace conditions.

To effectively conceal damaging information from consumers, we must know the details of stimulus detection thresholds and action thresholds for various elements of our marketing messages and materials. To conceal, we need only to suppress attention and comprehension.

Effective simulation of favorable product-related scenarios requires knowledge of thresholds of detection, capacity for response generation, and predictability of responses. To present believable, simulated realities and get consumers to encode and internalize those (misleading) simulations, we must get them to detect (notice) our (misrepresented) reality and to devote adequate resources to encoding it and to elaborating it predictably (favorably, from our perspective). We have to engage and convince their imagination. Knowledge of attention thresholds and selective attention getting is required. Response capacity knowledge is even more complex.

To execute deceptive simulation, we must try predicting the quantity of available cognitive resources that target consumers will have and their ability to use those resources effectively to engage with our misleading simulation. We must try predicting these things in general (with uncertainty) or via our own experiments. Finally, advance knowledge of consumers' response predictability (e.g., exactly how they will interpret and respond to the simulated reality we suggest; the types and nature of the thoughts and associations elicited by our presented simulation) is difficult to acquire.

[The deception team leader goes on.] We should think in terms of three levels of deception, related to three levels of cognitive processing. Lowest-level deceptions operate on perceptual processes. For example, concealing some element of a presentation may be accomplished by making it invisible to a target consumer's sensors. Or, if we can technologically create a perfect sensory simulation of a false situation we want target consumers to believe in, that would be ideal. To do that, we must not evoke any perceived anomalies or dissonance or even uncertainty about how to categorize or interpret an element of the "altered reality." Low-level deceptions work by keeping the consumer functioning fluently at the (desired) perceptual level, without bumping her up into "mid-level" cognitive processing. Mid-level processing deceptions work by affecting pattern-matching and slightly thoughtful consumer responses to our marketing communications. The deception capitalizes on automatized pattern-matching responses to conceal damaging information or to generate inferences helpful to our intended misleading simulation. Our lowest-level marketing deceptions are designed to make the target consumer physically unable to observe something (a damaging piece of information) or to get her to selectively attend to certain elements of our presentation to the exclusion of others. We can engineer low-level deceptions predictably based on what is known about human physiology and psychomotor reflexes. We can run experiments that give us precise quantified results on what stimuli in an ad, a store display, a Web site, or a package consumers will detect and attend to, and which they will not detect or attend to. We need only achieve these low-level effects for a few seconds at most to facilitate our deceptive goals. If we choose to, we can reliably reproduce the same sorts of low-level effects repeatedly in a marketing presentation, for example, draw a consumer's attention away from or to a particular element via the same distractive or focusing manipulations at different moments in an ad or sales presentation. Our mid-level deceptions will have one of two goals. We will sometimes design them to *encourage* the consumer to invoke practiced pattern matching responses that are favorable to our concealment or simulation. Our intent here is to get the person to rely only on these predictable pattern match interpretations, or on simple-to-execute inference or judgment heuristics evoked by the patterns they observe, if we know these simple ways of thinking will help our deception goals. Expressed differently, we use a deception to get them to avoid deep thought. Alternately, we will sometimes design mid-level deceptions to *prevent* the target consumer from relying only on fast pattern matching responses and simple interpretation heuristics. We do this to get them to ratchet up their thinking and become thoughtful and deliberative.

[The deception team leader concludes.] Our risk analysis deception algorithm is illustrated in this example. Assume you (deceiver) have two possible deceptions you might use, A (low risk) and B (high risk). Then, if the situation is such that the success of either A or B means the mission is accomplished, then the use of both simply raises the *quality* of the success (e.g., it costs less), but not the *chances* of success, but the discovery of either by the target will increase the risk that the other will fail; in that scenario then we should do A first to assure success. If A succeeds then we do B to improve the already successful result. If A fails, we either do something else or do B out of desperation. On the other hand, if the situation is such that the success of both A and B are required to accomplish the mission, and if the discovery of either by the target early in the execution will lead to substantially less harm than discovery later in execution, then we should do B first so that losses can be reduced if, as is more likely, B is detected. If B succeeds, we then do A.

Our sequencing rule is as follows: We will sequence deceptions so that the deception story succeeds for as long as possible. The clearest giveaways of our deception—the tactics consumers are most likely to perceive as a "deception" should be held until the last possible moment. Riskier elements of a deception, in terms of potential harm if the deception is discovered, should be done later rather than earlier so that they may be called off if the deception is found to be a failure. We must create backup plans to use when a deception is detected and one of our in-field deception pawns is caught. These backup plans should be convincing enough to keep the alerted target or watchdog third party from using high-level cognition to interpret the deceptive act—we need a plausible excuse or explanation that fits into other people's routine patterns of thinking. For example, can we claim that the salesperson was a newbie who just did not understand our training or principles? That we couldn't have known that the consumer would be distracted?

Social Engineering

Kevin Mitnick's book *The Art of Deception* (Mitnick & Simon, 2002) provides us with another valuable perspective on how skillful deception agents practice their craft. Mitnick was a notorious cyber-desperado whose invasions of corporate security systems made him a fugitive from the FBI and led to a prison term. His book is in the best tradition of "set a thief to catch a thief." He explains in detail how con artists like himself, who euphemistically call themselves "social engineers," deceive the people who control access to private confidential information by using "low tech" methods of deceptive persuasion. While computer hacking has an exotic high-tech element to it, Mitnick emphasizes in this book the interpersonal communication tactics that someone can use to get people to unknowingly help an outsider to breach their employer's internal security systems. For our purposes here, Mitnick's thinking is applicable to any marketplace context where a marketer's goal is to deceive a consumer into revealing private confidential information about self, household members, or anyone else to a stranger. We conceive of social engineering as an attempt to breach the individual consumer's "psy-curity" system. An individual's or a household's psy-curity system is the mental protective apparatus that consumers construct to perform personal security functions for themselves, akin to a corporation's formal and informal information security systems. In our analogy, a consumer's mind per se represents the information system that social engineers seek to invade. We do not mean that people's minds necessarily operate like computers, but that the consumer's mind contains the private confidential information that marketers treasure and try to steal. Mitnick and Simon (2002) note that the popular saying that a secure computer is one that is turned off is clever but wrong; the social engineer simply talks someone into going into the office and turning that computer on. In our analogy, the marketer seeking to breach a person's psy-curity system is not deterred because the targeted part of a person's mind is not at the moment accessible; the marketer merely deceives the consumer into opening up that dormant part of their belief system and letting the marketer raid it.

Mitnick emphasizes trust-building impersonation tactics, that is, how to get someone to feel enough trust in a total stranger to give them access to private personal information. For example, a marketer who thinks like Mitnick will try to pose as an authority who has "automatic rights" to ask for and be given the key information. To do this, the imposter will first gain knowledge of the lingo used by a company the consumer does business with or knows about (or create a fictitious organization) that will sound plausibly authoritative to the consumer. The impostor will also learn about that company's organizational structure, or invent a plausible fictional structure containing specific department names and job titles. The impostor can gain this impersonation information via chats with the company's employees, blending key inquiries with other unimportant innocuous questions. The impostor will then refer to other people by name who the mark knows, to give the mark the impression that the impostor is "one of us" and to lead the target to infer that helping the impostor by supplying some information will gain the target favor and recognition within the company.

Here is a hypothetical example modeled on a scam the authors learned about. It illustrates how this authority impersonation unfolds by capitalizing on a lot of "inside" information about the consumer already acquired via preceding deceptions. The scam works like this. Caller: "This is (name), and I'm calling from the Security and Fraud Department at VISA. My badge number is 12460. Your card has been flagged for an unusual purchase pattern, and I'm calling to verify. This would be on your VISA card, which was issued by (name of bank). Did you purchase an Anti-Theft Device for $497.99 from a marketing company based in Arizona?" When you say "No," the caller continues with, "Then we will be issuing a credit to your account. This is a company we have been watching and the charges range from $297 to $497, just under the $500 purchase pattern that flags most cards. Before your next statement, the credit will be sent to (gives you your address). Is that correct?" You say yes. The caller continues: "I will be starting a fraud investigation. If you have any questions, you should call the 1-800 number listed on the back of your card (1-800-VISA) and ask for Security. You will need to refer to this control number. The caller then gives you a six-digit number. Here is the key part of the scam. The caller then says, "I need to verify that you are in possession of your card." He asks you to "turn your card over and look for some numbers." He says, "There are seven numbers; the first four are part of your card number, the next three are the security numbers that verify you are the possessor of the card. These are the numbers you sometimes use to make Internet purchases to prove you have the card." The caller will ask you to read the last three numbers to him. After you tell the caller the three numbers, which is the key nugget of private information he was seeking from you, he'll say, "That is correct, I just needed to verify that the card has not been lost or stolen, and that you still have your card. Do you have any other questions?" After you say no, the caller then thanks you and states, "Don't hesitate to call back if you do," and hangs up.

Mitnick (Mitnick & Simon 2002) discusses a variety of common social engineering tricks, as follows:

1. Posing as a fellow employee, as a friend of a friend, or as a member of the same activity group as the target
2. Posing as a vendor, work partner or law enforcer—someone in authority
3. Posing as a new employee (neighbor) seeking help
4. Offering help if a problem occurs, then making that problem occur, to manipulate the target into calling the impostor for help
5. Using insider lingo and terminology to gain trust
6. Planting a Trojan horse document or file in a target's work or home vicinity to be picked up and used by the target
7. Asking a target to transfer a file to an apparently "internal" location (e.g., to a friend's e-address)

Mitnick emphasizes that social engineers should focus on the weakest links—inexperienced, naïve, and untrained targets who are unaware of the value of the information being sought and unpracticed in fending off strangers' inquiries. In an organizational context, these would be front-line employees, receptionists, telephone operators, administrative assistants and, ironically, security guards. In a household context, these would be inexperienced adolescents or socially starved stay-at-home adults. Mitnick identifies vulnerability factors as follows: (a) large number of employees (big family; extended family), (b) multiple facilities (household members dispersed and isolated from each other at different locations throughout the day and night), (c) household members who leave information about their whereabouts and contact info on voice mail messages, (d) households without any member who is professionally trained in security methods at work (no one to coach or alert other household members), (e) households without any reporting or response plan in place to cope with attempted breaches of family members' privacy and confidentiality.

The Mind of a Telescammer

Anthony Pratkanis and Doug Shadel's fascinating book *Weapons of Fraud* (2005) provides a unique window into the mind of a fraudulent telemarketer. Pratkanis and Shadel studied 645 undercover audiotapes of telescammers who thought they were pitching potential victims. The "victims" were in fact undercover investigators posing as elderly consumers. The tapes they analyzed were obtained from 1995 to 2003 by investigators in 12 states who set up hundreds of unsuspecting telescammers by identifying individual consumers who had been the victims of multiple scams and who therefore received a lot of telemarketing calls, and then transferring these people's incoming phone calls into the investigator's office, where the calls were taped. Pratkanis, a social psychologist, is a leading researcher in persuasion and social influence. Shadel is a former fraud investigator and assistant district attorney, who co-led a three-year study by the U.S. Department of Justice and the AARP Foundation to identify scam prevention strategies. They transcribed about half the 645 tapes. Then they carefully analyzed the tactics repeatedly reused to execute telemarketing frauds. Their research team located dozens of examples of each main tactic in the thousands of transcript pages. In their book, Pratkanis and Shadel (2005) supply readers with the verbatim excerpts from the taped calls to vividly illustrate how telescammers implement each tactic. The main tactics Pratkanis and Shadel identified in the telescammers' taped calls were as follows. They found that the cornerstone to each scam was a phantom dream. The phantom dream is something that a person desperately wants but which is normally completely unavailable. The phantom dream is something the consumer has never seen or experienced but hopes will become real for her. Over half the scam tapes involved holding out the hope that the consumer wins a lottery or some prize. The scammer holds out hope to the victim to the extent that the victim becomes disconnected from reality and logical reasoning. Scammers create a variety of phantom dreams to float to victims: winning a foreign lottery, winning a sweepstakes, creating a "better world" by contributing to a phony charity, providing for loved ones setting up a phony trust, huge payoffs from investing in phony rare coins, secret stock offerings, get rich work-at-home schemes, phony health plans and cures, and psychic communication with dead loved ones.

Pratkanis and Shadel (2005) also found numerous cases where a scammer created fictional characters and false relationships. The scammers played various roles, sometimes taking on multiple roles in talking with the same consumer. Each persona the scammer takes on puts the victim in a particular role relationship with the scammer's fictional persona. This could be a dominating authority character to be obeyed, a new friend who supposedly shares the victim's interests, or an anxious young salesperson who seems dependent on the victim to save his job. Some telescammers play multiple roles in a fictional company to create the illusion that it is a large (hence, successful) organization. The scammers often try to appear to be doing the consumer a favor, such as pretending to help get the consumer's money back from a prior bad decision or bending the rules to help the victim win an even bigger prize. They will present themselves as having nothing to gain personally from the consumer's choices ("I get paid whatever you do") or as an ally of the victim. They will pretend to share a secret with the victim—"inside information". They will convert whatever they learn about the victim into an invented "point of similarity" between themselves and the victim. They will falsely tell the consumer how much they like and admire her. They will reciprocate a victim's self-disclosures with their own (false) self-disclosures.

Pratkanis and Shadel's analysis of the tapes identified three major "landscaping" methods. One is agenda setting, in which the scammer explicitly lists the issues or topics to be considered and the sequence of actions the consumer must take to pursue the phantom dream successfully. A second is limiting the choices presented to the victim. A third is controlling the victim's opportunities to learn information from anyone other than the scammer by stressing that the victim should not tell anyone else about what is happening. Pratkanis and Shadel also found instances in the tapes where scammers were making use of other well-known influence strategies such as presenting false social-consensus information, false scarcity information, false fear-building information, and so forth. More than anything, these tapes of actual calls showed how savvy telescammers have become about how to use the full range of influence tactics discussed over the last 25 years in popular books on social influence research findings.

Marketing Managers' Deception Decisions

In this section we identify factors that impinge on a marketing manager's mind as he or she judges whether and how to attempt a marketing deception. To start with, the individual marketer often draws on their own personal marketplace knowledge and skills when making judgments about practicing or preventing marketing deceptions. For many marketers, these personal skills and knowledge may be the primary cognitive resource used to make their professional deception-related decisions. In essence, they rely on simple projection to all consumers of their own beliefs and tendencies. The manager's knowledge and skill for practicing *nondeceptive marketing* comes into play as a constraint. This refers to a marketer's beliefs about how to effectively communicate with and persuade consumers without misleading them, including beliefs about the persuasion process, the possible persuasion tactics to use, and the effectiveness of those tactics. It also includes the marketer's beliefs about the deception process, for example, understanding of deception tactics and communication practices that mislead, and beliefs about what consumers in general, or in a specific target market, know about deception tactics, about their skills in detecting such tactics, and about what practices consumers and others will subjectively judge to be misleading and deceptive. Many managers may not really understand how to go about implementing a truly nondeceptive marketing program. Managers may have poor or good understanding of consumers' cognitive limitations and the importance of task-load effects in determining what consumers can do to protect themselves from being misled. Finally, managers will have varied beliefs about consumers' reading skills, numerical skills, attention control skills, memory storage and retrieval skills, and so forth.

A marketer's beliefs about his or her firm's, brands, or product's competitiveness in the relevant marketplace environment should strongly influence the decision to rely on deception. These include beliefs about the capacity to compete successfully by differentiating current products based on actual product quality, value, and performance distinctions; by innovation and new product introductions; by creating supply-chain and distribution system advantages; by sales force training and relationship building; and by devoting dollar resources to nondeceptive marketing communication programs. If a marketer is pessimistic about the chance of competing successfully on substantive undeceptive grounds, then resorting to deceptiveness becomes attractive in the short run, even if risks are incurred. Or, if a marketer does not really care about establishing enduring competitive success on substantive grounds, deception may seem like the only available or necessary means for a short-term short-lived success. For example, fly-by-night business operations may be established only to enter a market, deceive an initial wave of buyers, get some immediate profits, then disappear, in which case its managers will perceive deception as the cornerstone of their business strategy. A manager's beliefs about the deceptive tactics of the firm's major competitors come into play, as well as beliefs about how to respond to deceit by a competitor about one's own company and products or about that competitor's product. These beliefs include the marketer's personal beliefs about whether or not deceptiveness is a normal and/or required part of a marketing manager's professional business role in the company, and hence whether or not "clever" deceptiveness is a valuable part of this marketer's skill set.

Marketing managers plan marketing programs in a dynamic decision-making environment. They often operate in an environment where they need to make multiple decisions about different elements of a marketing strategy, participate in departmental short-term and long-term planning meetings, and interact with people from other functional areas such as manufacturing and finance. That busy environment may limit the marketer's actual or perceived opportunity to monitor and eliminate deceptiveness during the critical period when planning and construction of marketing communication materials is done. Given that environment, a company's provision, or lack of provision, of deception-prevention resources, and establishment (or lack thereof) of managerial processes aimed at deception prevention, loom large. At one extreme, a company may ignore deception-prevention processes entirely, leaving every marketing manager on their own to deal with it as they see fit. Alternately, a company may enable and encourage its marketers to make full and systematic use of marketing research and expert reviews to learn about probable deceptions, and set up formal requirements that deception be considered in the planning of all marketing communication materials and campaigns. We are not aware of companies that do deception protection this stringently, but some may exist.

Many different individuals take part in planning, creating, testing, and producing the final ads, sales brochures, and so forth that get used. Last-minute revisions and final decisions may get delegated to individuals in outside ad agencies or lower-level materials production people. Further, internal conflicts and disagreements among managers about deceptiveness issues and ambiguities can produce stalling, paralysis, and avoidance regarding deception-prevention judgments.

Finally, an individual marketer may believe that his or her personal responsibility to try to prevent deception is low. The corporate culture may undercut a manager's sense of deception-prevention responsibility if internal or external deceptiveness is practiced, prevalent, celebrated and/or rewarded in employee promotions and career advancement. Or, the manager may believe that deception-prevention is a matter for the legal department, which provides the manager a shield against personal accountability ("not my job").

To be effective in preventing corporate deception, a marketer needs to acquire skills for proactively coping with deception prevention, analogous to the same sort of self-regulatory skills consumers need. A marketer by profession knows she or he will repeatedly encounter communication-planning problems where deception-prevention issues and opportunities loom. These strategy meetings, creative decisions, and testing decisions are complex, and deception-prevention is only one aspect of what must be considered. A marketer therefore needs to build proactive coping skills in resource accumulation, problem recognition, and so forth, so that she or he is well prepared to deal efficiently with deceptiveness judgments and decisions when these must be made. Similarly, a marketer needs to build skill in judiciously conserving and allocating cognitive resources for use across communication planning episodes. This meta-skill allows a manager to pick and choose which communication planning situations present big risks of deceptiveness and which are not worth fretting much about, and to avoid depleting her or his cognitive deception-prevention skills unnecessarily.

Of course, some individual marketers may derive inherent satisfaction from playing and winning "the game." This duping delight is more than just "I like deceiving people." What makes it enjoyable is winning against a favored opponent, outwitting people who are ostensibly smarter than you are, or more successful, or more privileged, or who believe that you cannot outwit them. There may be an underlying sense of social justice—stealing from the rich. There may be a sense of life's necessities—that the only tool you have to even things up and compensate for your other disadvantages and limits is trickery and deceit. There may be an underlying feeling that the target consumers got what they have by deceit and cheating, so this is just getting even. Finally, there may be implicit victim denigration, for example, "If you cannot protect yourself, you deserve to get duped ... I'm just fooling fools."

6

How People Cope With Deceptiveness
Prior Research

In this chapter we examine the existing empirical research pertinent to understanding how consumers process potentially deceptive marketing messages. The studies discussed here were done by researchers in different fields and have not necessarily shared a common conceptual foundation. Some of this work reflects the findings from many related studies. For example, there have been over 200 laboratory studies of people's lie detection accuracy in everyday conversations about mundane personal topics. In other cases, the empirical evidence for some interesting propositions is still sparse. The studies we discuss in this chapter focused on people coping with deceptive persuasion on their own without having been tutored formally about either deception and persuasion tactics or specific self-protection methods. Further, these studies focus largely on how individuals in late adolescence or emerging adulthood (ages 18 to 23) cope with deceptive persuasion. The research covered in this chapter deals with issues such as (a) the effects of uncertainty and suspicion about a message's validity, the effort invested in scrutinizing that message, and how suspicion affects responses to subsequent ads; (b) inference made about information that is omitted from marketing messages, how consumers draw inferences from implied claims in marketing messages, and how consumers infer manipulative intent; (c) the "truth bias" in processing misleading claims; (d) how consumers activate and use personal persuasion knowledge in processing ads and how metabeliefs influence resistance to misleading persuasion; and finally, (e) everyday lie detection in lab studies or on the Internet, and how deception-base rates affect lie detection accuracy.

Uncertainty and Suspicion

When consumers feel uncertain about an element of a persuasive message, they will try to identify the element of the message they are uncertain about, the reasons why that particular element evokes uncertainty, and whether or not the message is trying to mislead them. Schul (2007) offers a superb review of work on how people cope with feelings of uncertainty and suspicion aroused by a seemingly misleading element of a persuasive message. One of his conclusions was that when people feel uncertain about a message's validity or suspect deception, they appear to increase the complexity of their thinking (Fein et al., 1990, 1997; Hilton et al., 1993; Schul, Mayo, and Burnstein, 2004; Schul, Mayo, Burnstein, and Yahalom, 2007). For example, Schul, Bernstein, and Bardi (1996) found that when people were presented with several messages about another person and they suspected that one or more of those messages might be invalid, they took more time to read and integrate the entire set of messages compared to people who were not suspicious of deception. These researchers proposed that suspicion of deceit causes people to increase the complexity of their message encoding, by considering alternate scenarios that might apply. In particular, people who are suspicious may consider both what the presented information means to them, if it is indeed valid, as the marketer wants them to believe, and what it means to them if it is biased and invalid. Schul et al. (2007) also noted that suspected deception evoked more elaborative thinking whenever the overall message response environment was hospitable to thoughtfulness. However, when a significant distraction is present, that distraction prevents people from accomplishing the elaborative thinking about deception they want to do. Finally, Chiappe et al. (2004) found that in basic social exchange situations, people who are perceived to be acting deceptively and unfairly (i.e., cheaters) tend to be looked at longer and remembered better than cooperative people. Some evolutionary psychologists explain the remarkable human capacity to remember and recall strangers' faces as a vital part of a basic cheater detection system that we have developed to enable keeping track of who has tried to deceive us, to help us protect against and punish the cheaters. In any case, doing increased elaboration about the message's meaning may give consumers a heightened sense of personal control when they are faced with the threat of a marketer's perceived attempt at deception. Deception represents danger, and danger elicits thoughtful consideration. By slowing down and shifting into an elaborative mode of thought, consumers may increase their opportunities to notice details of the deception tactic, look for other clues that a deception strategy was being executed, and thereby better judge the magnitude of the attempted deception and what psychological process is being targeted (Friestad and Wright, 1994).

It is also the case that when a deception attempt creates suspicion, some sort of a coping and correction strategy is called for. One such coping strategy would be to discount some or all of the information in the suspicious message. Schul (2007) proposed that a person's success in doing this type of elaborative discounting depends on the density of the associative links between the deceptive part of the message, which needs to be ignored or corrected for, and the rest of the message, which is valid and may be useful. He goes on to say that during the initial encoding of a message, the meanings a person gave to the valid parts of the message may have been altered by the deceptive content. This process may then make it more difficult for people to consider the valid part of the message by itself. Separating the wheat from the chaff is very difficult if not impossible once they have bonded, so that even if you use a correction strategy, you will not rid your mind of the deception's effects. Thus, discounting should be better when the valid parts of a message and the deceptive parts refer to unrelated issues, than when the tainted and untainted message portions were readily relatable, and therefore bonded in memory, when first processed.

Schul (2007) goes on to explain that ideally a person will reencode the valid part of the message starting from scratch, as if the deceptive contents had not been encountered. He speculates that a total reencoding like this is unlikely because of the complexity of the correction process, which also includes beliefs about the direction and magnitude of the biasing effects on one's thoughts, and cognitive resources and motivations sufficient to do an effortful correction (Martin, Seta, & Crelia, 1990; Schwartz & Blass, 1992; Strack & Hanover, 1996). Schul (2007) also suggests that people may discount a deceptive message more strenuously and successfully when a third-party external source urges discounting on substantive grounds (e.g., a consumer is told that the prior message is deceptive and unreliable) than on procedural grounds (e.g., a consumer is told that the misleading message is not allowable under the rules of law). Finally, there is also research to show that deceptive messages are discounted more strongly when the consumer believes they have had a high impact on his thoughts and judgments than when they are viewed as having only a weak impact. There is support for this idea in studies of people's corrections for perceived context effects (Petty & Wegener, 1998) and source attractiveness (Petty, Wegener, & Fabrigar, 1997).

Beliefs about the powerfulness of a marketer's deception tactic will also affect the relative ease or difficulty of making a correction. Schul and Goren (1997) suggest that it will be easier to correct for a type of deception you believe probably exerted strong influences on your previous message processing than to correct for a deception you believe was not very effective. They also propose that people are more aware of their beliefs about the more threatening types of persuasion and deception tactics. For example, they point out that in a courtroom setting, respondents were told, after hearing testimony, to ignore it. People did better at discounting (ignoring) prior testimony when that testimony had features that people believe are strong persuasion and credibility-enhancing tactics, than when the prior testimony had no such features. Schul (2007) also asserts that precisely accurate corrections by consumers will be difficult. Technically, an accurate correction requires a consumer to both block the influence of the deceptive parts of a message and to still use the full legitimate parts of the message to their own benefit. Doing this disentanglement and accurate gauging of how much to keep and how much to shed will be difficult for most consumers. Finally, researchers have proposed that consumers will be better at discounting a message they realize was deceptive if they were prevented from doing integrative elaboration, or were unmotivated to bother, while originally encoding the valid and the deceitful parts of a message (Schul & Mazursky, 1990). It is our position that successfully executing a correction or discounting tactic is a skill to be learned via focused practice; that doing it is more vulnerable to opportunity and motivation effects when it is not well practiced than when it has been well learned; and that if it becomes well learned and hence automatized, then a skilled consumer can do discounting without much effort (even if it is a crude, simple, super-cautious discounting).

So, although we believe consumers can learn to use discounting and correction processes, one can ask why they would need or want to achieve this level of normative accuracy. If the marketer's partly deceptive message was in fact the only source of information, or the best source of information despite its flaws, then maybe it would be desirable to precisely extract its discounted value. However, there is usually no major loss from overcorrecting on the side of caution where a particular marketing message is at issue. Furthermore, corrections can be carried out by getting accustomed to doing after-the-fact strategies that do not require getting the correction done precisely in the heat of the moment. For example, in mock courtroom situations, mock jurors who are told to disregard prior testimony because it is misleading are apparently successful at that; their judgments turn out to be the same as other mock jurors who did not even hear the tainted testimony (Elliott et al., 1988). Thus, in the courtroom context where jurors are likely to be aware that witnesses may lie, people will activate a vigilant self-protective mindset, which makes corrections, once deception is revealed, easier to execute. We note that the courtroom context is similar in many ways to a marketing context in which a wary consumer is aware from the start that marketers may well try deceptions of many sorts.

Hence, it may be that invalid beliefs go uncorrected primarily in sterile unfamiliar contexts that maximize trust and reduce deception vigilance. In fact, we would characterize the vast majority of the laboratory studies of attitude change and social influence as only mildly threatening to a subject's attitudes and beliefs, and thus only weakly arousing of a deception protection state of mind. This is because most of the time the subjects know that the messages the experimenter presents to them were not actually created by a real marketer, the subjects' motivations are to fulfill a class requirement or receive a modest reward rather than make an actual decision, and if subjects do become suspicious of some parts of the messages they are eliminated from the study.

We note that when people are alert and aware that to stymie being deceived they must not do immediate integrative encoding, they can strategically reduce their elaborative processing of all message content during an initial exposure to the message. Thus, one can withhold integrative work until one has a chance to see what cues there are to deceptive content at the middle and ends of the message. Doing this allows the message recipients to minimize the amount of belated disentangling needed, and to postpone dealing with the tainted part separately and differently than with the seemingly untainted part until the message is processed a second or a third time (e.g., rereading a print advertisement, product brochure, or terms of agreement document). In these reexposures integrative thought can be directed to the seemingly valid portions and strongly negative elaborative thought can be directed to any hidden, negative disclosures that came at the middle or end of a message. Alternatively, a person who is well-prepared and skillful may attack a message vigilantly from the start by increasing the complexity of message processing, taking care to delay any freezing of a belief (Kruglanski, 1989) and looking for alternate interpretations if some message claims or tactics are misleading. This type of counterfactual thinking is what Fein, Hilton, and Miller (1990) and Fein, McCloskey, and Tomlinson (1997) found. When people come to suspect a hidden motive behind a presentation, they may process the content as if

(a) there is no hidden motive, and also as if (b) there is a hidden deception motivation. One line of thinking involves considering what the conclusion would be if the message was entirely valid, complete, and undeceptive. A second path involves considering what the conclusion would be if one or more parts of the message are untrue. In essence, the consumer does sensitivity testing of deceptive versus nondeceptive scenarios.

A consumer may also adopt the perspective that it is not really functional for me to do elaborative encoding of this incoming message until I can assess whether it contains a disturbingly high amount of suspicious, potentially misleading tactics and claims. If it turns out that my first inspection of this message suggests its content is a misleading quagmire, I will then have no need to elaborate on it for later use, and I will treat it as garbage content. If my first pass through it indicates it may be relatively untainted, then and only then will I bother doing elaborative encoding (Friestad & Wright, 1994).

Significant cognitive load is widely acknowledged to undermine and stifle someone's mental self-regulation and deception resistance even when vague suspicion is aroused. Mazursky & Schul (2000) put people in a situation where they first learned about six attributes of a car or a computer, then learned that the information on one attribute was actually invalid. Subjects then processed another message from the same car maker (computer maker) who had provided the tainted information before, or from a different source. They found that people who realized they had been misled the first time they processed a message changed their mode of processing the second time they encountered a message from a now-suspicious source. Subjects who first had done elaborative processing of that initial message now became more oriented toward the message source, and less focused on the attribute information, in this "once burned, twice shy" second chance. And, interestingly, people who had first been more shallow and source-focused also changed upon learning they'd been misled; they now focused more intensely on the attribute details and less on the source the second time.

Suspicion Effects on Processing of Subsequent Persuasion Attempts

Darke and Ritchie (2007) and Main, Dahl and Darke (2007) analyzed how a consumer's suspicion of deceptive intent in an ad, once aroused, can affect processing of the both the initial ad and subsequent ads. They argue that suspicion can be aroused by many factors. One would be that a person recently had a strong "I was duped" experience, the effects of which remain prominent in the person's mind when they encounter subsequent messages. The person may not in retrospect know exactly how they were misled, they just feel that they were somehow taken advantage of. The emotional impact of feeling duped is sometimes strong enough to cause lingering distrust and carryover effects. A second scenario is that a person has had over time a number of closely bunched exposures to ads that used noticeable deception tactics, such that the person has developed a highly accessible, enduring suspicion that ads from the same advertiser, ads for similar products, or all ads should be treated suspiciously. A third scenario is that something in the immediate ad processing situation primes and heightens a person's suspiciousness, and that this leads the person into a suspicion-biased processing of the immediate ad, which gets the person's mind highly focused on detecting deceptions. This intense bout of deception-sensitized thinking may enable the person to do more effective deception-protection activities than might otherwise occur. They may become better at deception detection, neutralizing, resistance, and punishment in this situation because these skills are now activated. Further, that intense deception protection experience will make the deception-protection state of mind and accompanying skills more accessible to reapply later on to other persuasion attempts. Sometimes, acute suspicion may also cause some people to become overly suspicious, so they see sinister deception tactics at work everywhere. This sort of overattribution of hostile intentions to advertisers has been called "making the sinister attribution error" (Kramer, 1994; Main, Dahl, & Darke, 2007).

Darke and Ritchie (2007) proposed that when a persuasive message seems dangerously threatening, people shift into elaborative protection-focused ad processing, When the situation seems only mildly threatening, people remain somewhat protective but try to rely on simple cues to help detect, neutralize, and resist deceptions. For example, they might easily call to mind negative stereotypes of the message source, which provides some level of protection, perhaps. Darke and Ritchie (2007) proposed that when someone initially performs elaborative deception-protection activities on one ad, they also apply the same systematic suspicion-focused elaborative thinking to a subsequent ad from the same advertiser. This can flood their mind with both specific memories related to the prior deception attempt by this same advertiser and perhaps evoke any negative stereotypes they have in memory. However, when confronted soon afterwards with an ad from a different advertiser, the person retains some suspicion but switches into more automatized reliance on only a prior negative stereotyping for self protection purposes. They demonstrated this sort of carryover effect when there was a 24-hour lag from the initial deceptive ad to a subsequent ad exposure. Further, this effect may depend on a person having engaged in the deception-protection activities of their own initiative during the exposure to the first ad, rather than, for example, being told afterwards that the ad was probably deceptive.

Omissions, Misleading Inferences, and Message Tactics

Kardes, Posavac, and Cronley (2004) provided a superb review of research on consumer inference formation. They examined research on how consumers mentally convert information provided to them by marketers into judgments or conclusions that the consumers generate themselves. This review was not explicitly framed in terms of deception. However, the focus was on consumer judgments that are based on limited, incomplete and missing information, and because intentionally omitting unfavorable information is a major deception strategy, the Kardes, Posavac, and Cronley work is germane to understanding consumer inferences when marketers have acted deceptively to intentionally hide unfavorable information. Unfortunately, at this time, most of this research does not examine inferences made when people are in a suspicious and deception-vigilant state of mind. Rather, the studies typically present people with displays of incomplete information in nonpersuasion contexts. That is, the missing information just happens to be missing, typically without any explanation.

As discussed earlier, information may be missing from a marketing presentation for several reasons, one of which is that the marketer omitted it as a deceptive act to keep consumers from learning about it. Consumers are frequently insensitive to what is missing from a marketer's presentation (e.g., unmentioned attributes, options, warnings), and they rely heavily on whatever information is clearly and explicitly presented to them. In doing so, they are willing to form evaluations based on information that may be intentionally incomplete, selective, and thereby biased. Consumers may overlook the issue of what information or how much information was intentionally left out of a marketing presentation, and treat whatever is presented, even if it is meager, as sufficient for generating judgments about the product. However, when individuals are highly knowledgeable about a product, and when the judgment context provides cues or reference points that suggest that some information that is potentially relevant and available was left out, the salience of the missing information is increased. In that case, people may adjust their immediate judgments about a product toward more "normatively appropriate" evaluations (Muthukrishnan & Ramaswami, 1999; Sanbonmatsu, Kardes, & Sansone, 1991; Sanbonmatsu, Kardes, & Herr, 1992; Sanbonmatsu, Kardes, Houghton, Ho, & Posovac, 2003).

Conversely, a marketing communication context that facilitates comparisons of brands described by different amounts and types of attribute information will increase a consumer's sensitivity to missing information (Broniarczyk & Alba, 1994; Simmons & Leonard, 1990; Simmons & Lynch, 1991; Sanbonmatsu et al., 2003). Notably, even without strong cues of deceptive intent by a communicator, products are evaluated less favorably when information is missing than when people are explicitly told that a missing attribute value is "average" for the product category (Huber & McCann, 1982; Jaccard & Wood, 1988; Johnson, 1987, 1989; Meyer, 1981). One explanation for this tendency is that consumers display a general discounting for any missing information, so that missing information is a negative cue in itself, which is separately integrated with the presented information about product attributes. A variant is that a consumer's overall product evaluations from presented information are generally adjusted toward the middle to correct for uncertainty. In general, people use their implicit theories of bias to correct their tentative judgments (Gilbert, 2002; Wegener & Petty, 1995; Wilson, Centerbar, & Brekke, 2002).

Consumers' sensitivity to omitted information grows when they are forewarned that information will be missing, when they have high product-category knowledge and well-articulated mental standards of comparison (Sanbonmatsu et al., 1992) and when a cursory examination of the information display makes it blatantly obvious that some products are described by relatively large amounts of information and others by small amounts (Kardes & Sanbonmatsu, 1993; Muthukrishnan & Ramaswami, 1999; Sanbonmatsu et al., 2003). Consumers also recognize and deal with omissions more readily when an ad makes explicit product versus product comparisons on specific attributes, rather than simply presenting selected information about one product and when a consumer encounters an ad that presents abundant attribute information soon after processing an ad that sparsely described the product (Kardes & Sanbonmatsu, 1993). And finally, the saliency of omitted information can increase when adjacent ads describe rival products on different and incomparable attributes. In any case, increased salience of omitted information alerts people that their immediate judgments will be based on weak, limited evidence, and the increased awareness of omitted information may cause them to try to correct toward a moderate and tentative view, which may be more accurate, can be updated, and seems justifiable to themselves and others. As the perceived importance of the information that is explicitly provided increases, its perceived sufficiency in a consumer's mind also increases; this, in turn, may reduce any negative discounting effect for deceptive nondisclosure in a consumer's mind. In essence, consumers may take into account whether the omission seems justifiable, or at least whether they are provided enough important information. This sufficiency effect suggests that by providing enough one-sided, favorable, important information, a marketer may mask from a consumer that other important, possibly damaging, information was omitted.

Identifying deceptive or persuasive intent is a fundamental skill applicable broadly in daily life. It is a topic that arises in societal debates about youngsters' vulnerability to marketplace and Internet persuasion and in legal proceedings because statutes dealing with acts of solicitation or fraud specify the "intent to persuade" as a part of criminal behavior. Once someone infers that a communicator has some degree of persuasive intent, further higher-order inferences may then occur. The capacity to infer human intentionality is a cornerstone of human social thought (Baldwin, 2005; Gibbs, 2001; Malle, Moses, & Baldwin, 2001; Zelazo, Astington, & Olson, 1999). The most fundamental intentionality inference people learn to make is whether or not a specific act by someone is an intentional one. If it is deemed intentional, then further intentionality inferences may occur. For speech acts, theories of basic message comprehension processes in linguistics and psychology describe how people infer the intended literal (semantic) meaning and/or the intended pragmatic meaning of a social message (Sperber & Wilson, 1995; Wyer & Radvansky, 1999; Wyer & Adaval, 2003). Pragmatic meaning is the meaning that the communicator intends the message to convey beyond its literal meaning. These models of message comprehension describe psychological activities that precede detection of persuasive intent. Wyer and Radvansky (1999) proposed a two-stage model that depicts the process of message comprehension with four steps: First, a person infers the literal meaning of the words and statements. Second, the person assesses whether the literal meaning meets expected normative principles (e.g., informativeness, relevance, politeness, truthfulness, modesty). Third, if there is some suspicion that there is added intended pragmatic meaning, the individual infers that intended meaning. And, fourth, the individual generates further responses to the message.

Other researchers have studied the higher order inferences about things such as the hidden motives behind the communicator's intent to persuade, the fairness of the methods used to persuade, or the communicator's personal traits (Campbell, 1995; Campbell & Kirmani, 2000; Decarlo, 2005; Fein, 1996). Campbell (1995) conducted pioneering research on factors that affect judgments about a communicator's manipulative intent. She defined inferences of manipulative intent as inferences that the advertiser is attempting to persuade by inappropriate, unfair, or manipulative means. Hence, manipulative intent is not quite identical to deceptive intent, but it is close. We believe that implicit in her conceptualization is a three-step model: (a) Infer persuasive intent: yes or no. (b) If yes, consider the methods being used to produce persuasion. (c) Assess the fairness or appropriateness of those methods in this situation. Presumably, deception is considered unfair or inappropriate. Although in this conception, only the initial step involves the detection of persuasive intent, Campbell's theorizing about the process of inferring manipulative intent depicted a potentially complex inferential process involving people's judgments of their own benefits from, and effort investments in processing, an ad, and of the persuasion agent's perceived benefits and effort investments. To test her theorizing, Campbell (1995) analyzed how different advertising tactics (e.g., borrowed interest) alter inferences of manipulative intent as measured by responses to items such as "I was annoyed by this ad because the advertiser seemed to be trying to inappropriately manage or control the consumer audience." The basic inference of persuasive intent is distinct from this more complex inference about manipulative intent. Successful inferences of persuasive intent can and do occur even though higher order inferences of manipulative intent do not follow. In four experiments, Campbell and Kirmani (2000) studied people's inferences about a communicator's hidden or ulterior motives in situations where a salesperson makes flattering comments to a customer. Campbell and Kirmani argued that inferring disguised motives and making attributions about a salesperson's sincerity was a higher-order and more effortful inference than some other types of social inferences. Their results indicated that these higher-order inferences may be affected by cognitive load and the accessibility of "hidden motives" information in memory. For our purposes, we note only that in Campbell and Kirmani's studies the primary dependent variable was a higher-order inference about a salesperson's motives, fairness, and traits (sincerity), not the possibly more basic inference about deceptive or persuasive intent per se. Similarly, DeCarlo (2005) examined how someone's suspicion about ulterior motives behind a salesperson's behavior affects their attitude toward the salesperson, but did not examine the process of inferring intent-to-persuade. We believe that identifying deceptive intent seems a less effortful inference than manipulative intent or ulterior motives because the latter evokes fairness and other types of appraisals, which may be highly context specific. Deceptive intent could be inferred simply by noting a known deception tactic, or could be evoked automatically in tandem with an inference of persuasive intent in all marketplace contexts.

Kricorian, Wright, and Friestad (2007) examined people's inferences about persuasive intent based only on the message content. No information about the communication agent or about the circumstances motivating the message's construction or delivery was provided to subjects. One experiment tested the effect of priming persuasion-related versus education-related concepts on inferences about the persuasive intent and educational intent behind messages that had different amounts of persuasive content and educational content. A sentence-construction priming task was used to activate persuasion-related concepts, education-related concepts, or no particular concept prior to a subject's exposure to a message. Subjects in the persuasion-primed condition and the education-primed condition unscrambled different proportions of persuasion-related and education-related sentences. Then, they read a single-minded persuasion message, a single-minded educational message, or a dual-intent message about a pharmaceutical product. The single-minded persuasion message contained five statements that a pilot study had indicated were perceived as intended mainly to persuade. Conversely, the single-minded educational message contained five statements perceived as intended mainly to educate. The dual-intent message contained a mixture of the two types of statements. The priming treatments affected the inferences about persuasive intent and the inferences about educative intent. In another study, KWF examined differences in perceived intentionality based on more fine-grained variations in the structure and content of dual-intent messages. A dual intent message could display any pattern of persuasive and educative statements. Messages varied in the proportion of these types of statements or the clustering of the two types of statements. Presenting items perceived to belong to the same category in immediate succession might activate that category knowledge structure more strongly than just presenting the same items in a less organized manner. But this requires that the immediate encoding of each such statement in a multistatement message as a persuasion statement vs. an educative statement, from its style and wording, be quite automatic, and that the proportions and density of these types of encoded statements be noted fairly automatically, too. The studies suggested that when consumers of at least late adolescence process a multistatement message about a product, they naturally encode information about the apparent persuasive versus educational intentionality of the respective sentences, and use that to form an ongoing impression of the overall message's level of persuasive intent or educative intent.

Kirmani and Zhu (2007) examined how a consumer's preexposure mindset affects their suspicions about an ad's manipulative intent. The salience of a marketer's manipulative intent may be increased by the presence of tactics such as delayed sponsor identification, borrowed interest, negative or incomplete comparisons, or even disclosures of drawbacks. These message cues will have an effect as long as a consumer recognizes those as potential deception tactics (Campbell, 1995; Johar & Simmons, 2000; Barone, 1999). Other message cues may make a marketer's manipulative intent less salient, and there are ambiguous cues that have multiple interpretations. For example, a consumer may interpret a marketer's incomplete comparison as a good-faith attempt to show actual superiority or as a manipulative deception because the marketer did not compare their product to the leading brand. Kirmani and Zhu (2007) proposed that a person's regulatory focus as they process an ad may affect how they interpret ambiguous cues about manipulative intent in an ad. Prevention-focused consumers are more likely than promotion-focused consumers to interpret ambiguous cues as strong signs of manipulative intent. Higgins (1987) proposed that promotion-focused people pursue message processing with hopeful eagerness, while prevention-focused people approach it with defensive vigilance. For example, Pham and Higgins (2005) found that during information searches, promotion-focused people focused on positive signals about available purchase options, while prevention-focused people focused on negative signals. Kirmani and Zhu (2007) reasoned that chronically promotion-focused individuals activate persuasion-protection beliefs, such as suspicion of deception, only when blatant cues push their thinking in that direction. In contrast, chronically prevention-focused people activate persuasion-protection beliefs even when message cues are ambiguous, rather than blatant. They found in one study that the prevention-focused mindset made ad readers more skeptical and more deception-sensitive when these cues were either moderately salient or highly salient, but promotion-focused people became deception-sensitized only when the cues made the agent's manipulative intent highly salient. In another study Kirmani and Zhu (2007) externally primed a person's level of suspicion, so that even chronically promotion-focused individuals might feel prevention-focused. They found that priming via a magazine article about fraud increased subsequent ad suspicion among typically promotion-focused people, but had no effect on the suspiciousness of people who are typically prevention-focused, and already suspicious. In a third study, these same researchers found that the combination of a chronic prevention-focus and high suspicion evoked strong perceptions of manipulative (deceptive) intent even for ambiguous cues. Kirmani and Zhu speculated that prevention-focused consumers may use "sentry" ad processing strategies more so than promotion-focused individuals. Sentry strategies, as described by Kirmani and Campbell (2004) include forestalling, reverse deception, assertive resistance, overt confrontation, covert punishment, withdrawal from the interaction, preparation for the interaction, and enlisting a companion to act as a super-sentry.

Another widely researched tactic (Rucker, Petty, & Brinol, 2008) that takes advantage of consumers' inference processes is the use of so-called "two-sided appeals." The marketer presents, in addition to much favorable content, a smidgen of information about one or two possible drawbacks, but then explicitly explains why those are actually only trivial or highly unlikely drawbacks. That is, the marketer chooses only to discuss specific possible drawbacks that are easy for the marketer to convincingly dismiss. Thus, the marketer hopes that by presenting some negative information about a product, this small step toward full disclosure will increase consumers' trust and thereby work to the marketers' benefit (Kamins and Marks, 1987; Pechmann, 1992) Thus, the partial disclosure by the marketer or persuasion agent of some negative information is not motivated by a desire to avoid being deceptive, rather the partial disclosure of some possible drawbacks is itself part of a broader deception strategy to reduce a consumer's unease upon realizing that information is missing. In an even more subtle variation on the two-sided tactic, Rucker et al. (2008) describe how an alternate form of this type of partial disclosure about negative product attributes is executed. In this strategy, the marketer only discloses and discusses the product's positive attributes, but claims to have considered both positive and negative information about the product before recommending it. Rucker et al. (2008) referred to this as "framing" (describing) the message as two-sided without actually presenting a two-sided message. In five studies Rucker et al. (2008) examined ads that featured recommendations by potentially credible prior users of the product, who explicitly say in the ad that they "had considered all the attributes" or "considered both the negatives and the positives" before arriving at their recommendation. These testimonials did not actually reveal just what the negative information was that was supposedly considered; they only made the claims that it was considered. In these studies, having someone in an ad merely claim to have considered the negatives as well as the positives increased adolescents' postexposure certainty that they had gotten the whole story and bolstered their confidence in their favorable product attitudes. This effect was moderated by how much knowledge a person had about the product category and their chronic propensity to think (need for cognition). Framing a message as two-sided, which we prefer to call "claiming that drawbacks were considered," is deceptive in two ways. First, and most obviously, it creates the illusion in consumers' minds of having been fully informed when they have not really been fully informed. It seduces them into believing that any negative product attributes had already been duly considered and judged to be unimportant by a potentially credible prior user of the product. Hence, they themselves need not fret or feel uncertain about what was not revealed in the ad. It is important to note that unless the ad's content explicitly told these subjects that both sides had been considered, these subjects did not make an inference that the person in the ad who recommended the product had actually considered all the unmentioned negative attributes. So, the default assumption consumers make, unless told otherwise, may be that people in ads doing product endorsements have at best only considered the product's favorable attributes, or at least have not seriously considered the product's drawbacks. The second reason is that executions of this strategy cannot be authenticated. Marketers can easily lie when they claim that their spokespeople or even their experts had seriously considered all the relevant drawbacks. What a prior user considered or did not consider in making their favorable judgments about the product is inherently hidden from others. Indeed, people do this all the time in everyday interactions by saying things such as "Oh, I already considered that" when we know they are fibbing to appear convincing and thoughtful. The prevalence of this tactic in everyday life may alert consumers to it as a deception tactic when marketers do it. Most likely, it tends to deceive people who know little about a product category, and hence cannot imagine on their own what potential drawbacks were omitted from the ad, or it deceives people who rarely bother thinking about what might be missing. Finally, Rucker et al. (2008) argue that "Do I have all the information?" is a key metacognitive consideration in whether or not a consumer feels either highly certain or not-so-certain about their postmessage attitude toward the recommended product.

Finally, as mentioned in Chapter 3, a deception tactic called "disrupt-then-reframe" (Knowles & Lin, 1999) is built on artful distraction and confusion. In the disrupt-then-reframe (DTR) tactic, a message is transmitted so that it interjects a timely disruption and confusion at a key moment, which interrupts a consumer's line of persuasion protection and deception protection thinking before it produces rejection or neutralization of the message. Then, the communicator offers a simple way of framing the judgment in hopes that the now-confused consumer will seek quick closure and seize on to that simple framing as the basis for a judgment or decision (Fennis, Das, & Pruyn, 2004; Kardes, Fennis, Hirt, Tormala, & Bullington, 2007; Knowles and Lin, 1999). Kardes et al. (2007) studied the intervening psychological processes, especially the role of need for cognitive closure (NFCC) in moderating the DTR tactic's effectiveness. As their NFCC increases, consumers seize on information that helps them attain quick closure, so they can make a hurried decision and start acting on what the message suggested to them. They therefore seize on a message's earliest unambiguous, easy-to-process information that has obvious direct implication for making a judgment or decision. Because marketers usually front-load their persuasion attempts with content favorable to the product or service, delaying any mention of drawbacks to the end, consumers high in NFCC are seemingly a deceptive marketer's easiest prey. Once they attain quick cognitive closure while processing a marketer's presentation, consumers high in NFCC freeze these early judgments (Kruglanski & Webster, 1996; Kruglanski, 1989). As NFCC increases, consumers tend more and more to neglect later information, ambiguous information or difficult-to-process information (Kardes et al., 2007). So, to execute a deception, a marketer will try to front load the presentation with favorable stuff, capitalize on and encourage a heightened NFCC, stall on disclosures of drawbacks, risks and limitations, express belated drawback disclosures in ambiguous, vague language, and make those disclosures as difficult to process as possible. Kardes et al. theorize and demonstrate that the DTR confusion technique frustrates someone acutely in need of closure. Then, the rest of the DTR tactic, the reframing, becomes an easy way out for the impatient, confused consumer. This can be understood as thwarting a consumer's System 2 self-protective thinking, then shifting her to System 1's quick, superficial thinking, and eliciting a thoughtless compliancy. It may be especially frustrating to, and thereby effective on, consumers who feel themselves on the verge of *resistive* closure due to the persuasion-protection and counterarguing they have done before the disruptive confusion occurs. Kardes et al. (2007) further reasoned and showed that people with lower chronic NFCC are not as likely to be thrown off or frustrated by the marketer's confusion tactic.

Kardes et al. (2007) followed Kruglanski in treating NFCC as a trait-type individual difference variable, which is measured, not manipulated. We note that while high NFCC can be a chronic trait, it can also be an acute situation-induced state of mind, thus something that deceptive marketers can try to engineer. Emphasizing the need for urgency and quick closure is one method for that. For example, in a brochure touting a well known health care program, the first part of the brochure tells consumers to read the brochure's lengthy info but then urges them dramatically to hurry and sign up (commit to) the program "today"! To heighten someone's acute need for cognitive closure, marketers will make it as frustrating as they can for consumers to find and wade through the delayed, concealed, ambiguous disclosures of drawbacks, risks, and limitations. If even the chronically low NFCC types become sufficiently frustrated by the marketer's concealment and obfuscation tactics, their tendency to let the final confusion tactic affect them could increase. Kardes et al. (2007) suggest, to our surprise, that marketers and consumer researchers should initiate research on different ways to accomplish the confusion, for example, technical jargon, overwhelming product assortments, and behavioral disruptions.

The Heard-It-Before "Truth Effect"

There is evidence of an increasing "truth effect" over repeated exposures to the same ambiguous statement. In essence, people seem to infer "if I've heard/read that statement before, it seems 'truer' than if I had not heard/read it before." (Arkes, Boehm, & Xu, 1991; Hasher, Goldstein, & Topino, 1977). In some studies, the same statement was judged more truthful once it was repeated than it had been on first exposure to it (Haserf, Goldstein, & Topino, 1977), including claims about products (Hawkins & Hoch, 1992). This truth-effect boost in perceived validity may be more pronounced when one's first exposure did not yield deep encoding and consideration of the statement's truth or falseness, as when you were slightly distracted that first time (Hawkins & Hoch, 1992). This is because elaborative processing on the first exposure may well yield a pronounced truth, suspicion, or false judgment, which is not swayed much later by the subtle, vague sense that something has been heard before. Roggeven and Johar (2002) examined how the truth-effect boost is influenced by whether or not the statement is repeated by the same source or by several different sources on different occasions. They found that when a claim about a product is not very plausible, feelings of subjective familiarity aroused by hearing the claim repeated can lead to boosted truthfulness ratings, but that repetitions by different sources can enhance this effect even more. Skurnik, Yoon, Park, and Schwarz (2005) noted that reexposing people to a statement increased the perceived truth of the claim even when it had been identified as false in the initial presentation. They argued that memory of a prior exposure to a claim about a product can exist without a memory of the original context in which you encountered that claim or its original source. They reasoned, therefore, that the truth-effect might even occur when one's later reexposure to the same claim occurs as part of a warning stating that the previously-heard product claim was (is) actually not true. Thus, if a truth-effect operated in this manner, then the reexposure from the warning message would not yield disbelief in the prior claim but instead it could neutralize the warning disclosure or perhaps even reverse it by making the previously heard claim seem more valid. Skurnik et al. tested this hypothesis by comparing the responses to repeated warnings about a statement's falsity of people in late adolescence/early adulthood (ages 18 to 25) to elderly adults (ages 71 to 86). In this case, when younger people were repeatedly told that a previously heard statement was false, they did not show a truth effect. The repeated warnings increased doubt about the statement immediately afterwards and after a three-day interim. The elderly subjects likewise did not show a truth effect immediately after being told repeatedly that a product claim was invalid. However, after three days, the elderly people who had been told once that the claim was false misremembered 28% of the false claims as being true. Those who had been told three times that the claim was false misremembered 40% of the claims as true after three days. So the added restatements of the claim in the course of repeated warnings that it was false decreased the effectiveness of the warning. This provided evidence of a limited truth-effect in this specific elderly subpopulation but, interestingly, not in the younger segment which was exactly the segment where truth effects had previously been found. What is also noteworthy here is that after three days the elderly subjects accurately recalled 72% of the false claims as false, after receiving just a one-time warning. After three such earlier warnings, inaccurate recall of false statements as true was higher, but these elderly people still recalled false statements as false almost two-thirds of the time. In another study by Skurnik et al. (2005), younger and elderly subjects were presented three exposures to a product claim followed immediately each time by a disclosure that the statement was false, or with the falsity warning made only once after the third exposure to the product claim. For both younger subjects and elderly subjects, delaying the single falsity disclosure until after three claim repetitions led to poorer recall that the claim was actually false. However, in this study, the falsity disclosures were made by simply flashing the single word "false" or "true" on the screen briefly after each of thirty-six different product claims. This provided a brief, sparse, unelaborated warning within a high-information-load, low-stakes setting. Skurnik, Moskowitz, and Johnson (2005) have also shown that the truth effect can change into an "illusion of falsity" effect when people judge retrospectively that the past claims were probably misleading and false. Other studies have also found that a lie bias can be activated when suspicion of a forthcoming deception is created prior to message exposure (Buller et al., 1996; Buller, Strzyewski, & Hunsaker, 1991; McCornac & Levine, 1990) and sometimes after message exposure (Buller, Strzyewski, & Hunsaker, 1991; Levine & McCornac, 1991). Finally, there are circumstances under which increased involvement in the outcome of a decision based on the message has caused a decrease in the truth bias, and sometimes the opposite (e.g., Hubbel, Mitchel, & Gee, 2001).

Johar and Roggeven (2007) analyzed the effectiveness of direct refutations of prior false product claims when the original claim had been an implied false claim versus when the original was a direct, explicit false claim. In their complex analysis, they called a refutation of a claim that directly contradicts an original direct claim an "aligned refutation" and reasoned that refutations that are closely aligned with prior information have stronger impact than nonaligned refutations. For example, a company's direct statement in an ad that "The Safeguard Car Rental Company offers collision damage insurance" is directly refuted by an aligned contradictory statement that "Safeguard Car Rental does not in fact offer collision damage insurance." In contrast, consider the case where the prior advertisement had used an implied claim that successfully enticed the consumer to infer something beyond what was actually stated. For example, suppose the ad stated, "All responsible car rental companies offer collision damage insurance." And also stated "Safeguard is a responsible car rental company." The inference made by some consumers would have been "Safeguard must offer collision damage insurance." Suppose that belief is incorrect and Safeguard does not offer collision damage insurance. In this case, that false belief stemmed from the person's own self-generated inferences. So, a subsequent refutation statement that says "Safeguard does not offer collision damage insurance" is not aligned with what was previously stated because it contradicts a claim that was never stated by the advertiser. In essence, this subsequent refutation contradicts the consumer's own self-generated belief. So consumers may engage in meta-cognitive processing such as "This newer claim challenges my own self-originated thinking. Therefore, I will be more suspicious of the validity this new statement and will defend my own prior belief." When a self-generated inference is originally evoked by an implied ad claim, that inference may be embedded within other self-generated elaborative thinking that occurred at the same time. This would make it easier for the consumer to access support arguments that bolster the prior false belief and counter-argue against the current, valid refutation. Clearly the aftereffects of having fallen prey to an implied false advertising claim and the processes that would be required to correct that mistaken inference are complex.

The Use of Marketplace Persuasion Knowledge

Friestad and Wright (1994) in the persuasion knowledge model (PKM) discussed the persuasion-related beliefs that individuals develop to help themselves cope with persuasion attempts. They challenged researchers to study real-world persuasion from a persuasion target's point of view, focusing on consumers' development (or lack of development) and use (or nonuse) of marketplace persuasion knowledge. The PKM was framed around persuasion attempts, not deception attempts, and we reiterate the point that persuasion need not involve deception by a marketer. However, in a marketplace, context deception is a prominent, pervasive, and threat-ening persuasion suprastrategy. The most basic judgments consumers must make as they interpret a marketer's actions are whether or not this is a persuasion attempt as opposed to an educational or entertainment pre-sentation. If it is identified as a persuasion attempt, then the next judgment is about whether these actions represent cooperative persuasion, in which there is little or no meaningful deception attempted, or hostile persuasion that is likely to contain deception on meaningful relevant issues. We can-not assume that activating persuasion knowledge invariably coactivates deception knowledge. However, we suspect that coactivation is common, and that consumers reach a point where they think automatically about the possibility of deception whenever they recognize that a marketer is try-ing to persuade them. Further, a person's marketplace persuasion knowl-edge may significantly exceed their deception knowledge as their overall marketplace sophistication grows throughout their lifetime. We propose that the development of marketplace deception knowledge typically lags somewhat behind marketplace persuasion knowledge. Nevertheless, research to date on how people apply persuasion knowledge should be able to help us understand how consumers use their deception knowledge to cope with marketers' deception attempts.

Inferences about agent's motives have been a central research topic, because these underlie a person's beliefs about what constitutes a persuasion tactic and about how persuasion works. For a marketer's specific actions to become interpreted as a persuasion tactic in a consumer's mind, there must be at some point in that person's life what Friestad and Wright (1994) called the "change-of-meaning" process. We will relabel that concept here as a "critical persuasion insight." Before having a critical persuasion insight, the naïve person simply does not apply any particular interpretation to specific types of statements and actions that marketers use for persuasion purposes. However, after having a particular critical persuasion insight, the person now interprets the specific type of statements and actions as an important persuasion weapon in a marketer's arsenal. There are two key parts to this insight. It requires that the consumer comes to believe that "marketers think that tactic X causes psychological effects in people that are instrumental to the marketer's persuasion goals," and that "it is plausible to me that tactic X does cause psychological effects instrumental to successful persuasion." Given that consumers form those two beliefs, then the consumer is prepared to infer that when they notice a communication that exhibits that tactic, the marketer's primary goal is to persuade.

Meg Campbell and Amna Kirmani, two leading researchers on marketplace persuasion knowledge, have recently reviewed and critiqued this emerging body of work (Campbell & Kirmani, 2008). Although most of the work they reviewed has not focused precisely on deception-protection knowledge, they concluded that how people make inferences about a marketing agent's persuasion-motivated tactics has been studied widely. Campbell and Kirmani (2000) initiated this work and subsequent studies indicate that suspicion about a firm's or agent's persuasion motives can be evoked by many types of marketing actions—that is, flattery (Campbell & Kirmani, 2000), rhetorical questions (Ahluwahlia & Burnkrant, 2004), incongruent placement of brand names in television programs (Russell, 2002), prosocial advocacy advertisements (Menon & Kahn, 2003; Szykman, Bloom, & Blazing, 2004), negative comparisons between brands (Jain & Posavoc, 2004), partial or incomplete comparative pricing (Barone, Manning, & Miniard, 2004), biased sources (Williams, Fitzsimons, & Block, 2004), and expensive default options (Brown & Krishna, 2004). Researchers have also found that consumers consider a diverse range of marketer's actions as persuasion tactics. Examples of this include delaying the identification of an ad's sponsor or using attention-getting stimuli (Campbell, 1995), a marketer's perceived investment of money and effort in launching a product (Kirmani & Wright, 1989; Kirmani, 1990, 1997), the number of ad repetitions (Campbell & Keller, 2003; Kirmani, 1997), an agent's choice of which alternatives to discuss (Hamilton, 2003), asking questions about intentions (Williams et al., 2004), using rhetorical questions (Ahluwalia & Burnkrant, 2004), or using guilt appeals (Cotte, Counter, & Moore, 2005). In some of the earliest work in this area, Boush, Friestad, and Rose (1994) examined adolescents' potential knowledge about advertiser goals and tactics. They identified eight possible psychological effects that children and adults may believe advertisers intend to produce via advertising (e.g., grab attention, learn about product, like the ad, like the product better, remember the ad, trust what ad says). They also identified eight types of advertising tactics that people may think advertisers use to produce those psychological effects (e.g., show a popular TV or movie star; use humor; show people similar to you; compare one product to another). Then they asked youngsters in early and late adolescence what they believed about the specific psychological effects that advertisers intended to achieve through the use of each of those tactics. Their cross age-group comparisons and longitudinal tracking of these persuasion beliefs indicated youngsters gradually develop increasingly adult-like mental representations of how tactics in ads generate psychological persuasion effects.

Friestad and Wright (1995) also examined the content and structure of lay adults' belief systems about television advertising tactics, and compared those lay beliefs about the psychology of persuasion to those of social psychologists and consumer psychologists who study persuasion. First, in exploratory depth interviews, twenty adults watched videotapes of television ads and expressed their beliefs about "things that the advertiser did in the ad to make it more effective." This initial qualitative study provided two hundred samples of lay adults' everyday thinking about persuasion tactics. Subsequent questions about why the advertisers included those tactics yielded thirteen types of psychological activities that people viewed as instrumental mediators of persuasion. These included attending to an ad, categorizing a product, associating the product to other things in one's life, feeling strong emotion, framing a product evaluation in a particular way, imagining future sensations or events, comprehending the ad's content, remembering the ad's assertions, inferring a conclusion, feeling overall positive affect toward the product, trusting in the ad's credibility, and wanting the product strongly. The insights from the qualitative research were used to create structured questions probing cause-and-effect beliefs about how TV advertising evokes these different psychological activities and how these activities in turn affect successful persuasion. These questions were administered to several hundred lay people, ages 20 to 54 and to a sample of 149 consumer behavior researchers and social psychologists. Both groups were asked to express their beliefs about how difficult it is for advertisers to elicit each type of psychological effect; how noticeable to consumers is each psychological event; how strongly each psychological event influences overall persuasion success; the causal sequence in which different effects occur; and the degree to which each psychological activity that occurs is more under the control of the consumer versus the control of the advertiser. Finally, extensive comparisons of the responses from these two groups were made. Friestad and Wright (1995) interpreted the overall results as indicating several important possibilities. First, there was enough sharing of common beliefs among lay people to suggest that people in the American culture develop and pass along to each other a folk model of the psychology of advertising. Second, there was enough commonality between the persuasion beliefs of the lay adults and those of the researchers to suggest that the culturally supplied folk model, together with gradual diffusion of researchers' theories into the public mind, gives consumers, marketing professionals, and other marketplace observers a basis for understanding how each other thinks about persuasive advertising.

Detecting Deceptions

As we noted in Chapter 2, there have been numerous studies on people's accuracy in detecting lies from nonverbal cues in everyday conversation situations. Because these studies have been widely publicized, we will explain just how and why these data are not very relevant to the marketplace deception context. These studies create a situation unlike marketplace persuasion in the following ways.

The message recipient in these studies must rely largely on nonverbal cues to deceptiveness emitted by the lie teller. The person who is the speaker intentionally tells an outright lie, or not, in talking about some aspect of their life. The speakers are assigned to either be a lie teller or a truth teller, and they do not have a choice about whether to lie or not. Often they are not assigned to discuss any one particular event or aspect of their own mental world, so the person who is trying to be the lie detector observes different speakers talking about different things, and lie tellers who lie about different things. Speakers may lie about some aspect of an everyday happening in their prior life, distant or recent, or about some private aspect of themselves (e.g., their emotions). The event or situation they talk about is often mundane; it is not necessarily something of consequence in their life and definitely not to the other person who they talk to. The general type of situation or internal event the speaker talks about may or may be a familiar one to the listener. The speaker can lie about exactly what they did or did not do (a specific action; a sequence of actions) or said; when this took place; where it took place; who else was there; what some other person did in response to what they themselves did; and so forth. The speaker can also lie about some part of their private internal experiences or state-of-mind such as something they like or do not like, what they believe or do not believe, their emotions, personality traits, political beliefs, or even their brand preferences. The person receiving this message indicates whether the speaker did or did not tell an intentional lie. The receiver does not know the speaker, nor anticipate or want any further interactions or relationship with the speaker. The receiver is not trying to learn something useful from the speaker that is relevant to making a future decision. So the receiver has no motivation to try to remember what the speaker says, or revise beliefs or attitudes based on what the speaker says. The receiver is not seeking to be entertained. The conversation holds no interest to the receiver beyond the immediate single-minded task of judging if the speaker's statements are valid or contained an intentional lie. The only type of deception to be detected here is an intentional lie of commission. The receiver is not asked to try to detect an important omission from what is said. The receiver is not trying to judge if the speaker is trying to mislead without telling an outright lie, for example by distracting the receiver from hearing or comprehending some part of the delivery or engineering the delivery so as to mask certain parts of it. The receiver typically observes the speaker on videotape, with just one chance to listen and watch. The receiver is often told in advance what proportion of the speakers they watch and hear will be telling a lie (usually this is set at 50%), so the receiver accurately expects half the speakers to be lying. There is no access to other witnesses or participants describing their reactions, and the receiver operates in isolation.

What people expect about other people's deception tendencies may affect their judgments about specific persuasion attempts. This is true in the everyday lie detection context as well as in the marketplace context. Levine et al. (1999) took the perspective that people's accuracy in everyday lie detection often depends not on an individual's true skills at that task but on the actual proportion of lie-telling versus truth-telling attempts the person historically encounters, together with the person's general expectation (bias) about the prevalence of truth-telling compared to lie-telling. This perspective is useful to consider as research on marketplace deception protection success goes forward. In essence, if someone expects a lot of truths and few lies, and simply guesses that most statements are truths, they will achieve coincidental accuracy when the people they interact with are indeed being truthful. However, if they expect that truths will be prevalent, and therefore guess that most of the statements they encounter are truths, when in fact many of the statements are lies, they will not be especially accurate—and vice versa. In fact, the lie-detection accuracy rates across several hundred studies that used the classic lie-detection paradigm described above was 54% (Bond & Depaulo, 2006). Across these same studies there was evidence for a truth bias, in that about 56% statements made in conversation and general social discourse were judged to be truthful. Explanations for the truth bias include the supposedly lower cognitive effort needed to represent incoming information as true versus the higher effort in immediately representing it as false or invalid (Gilbert, 1991), and fundamental principles in how language understanding occurs (Grice, 1999; McCornack, 1992). In some cases, this truth bias has been more pronounced in face-to-face communication contexts than mediated-communication contexts (Buller et al., 1991), and when people feel that they know the speaker fairly well (McCornack & Parks, 1986).

In a related, and timely context, Grazioli and Wang (2001) hypothesized that many instances of failures to detect Internet deception tactics arise from consumers' poorly formed expectations and understanding of the Internet, coupled with low effort invested in trying to detect deceptions. They studied college students' reactions to a "clean site" (defined as one without deceptive tactics) versus a "forged site," which was an exact copy of the clean site, except that it used seven different types of deceptive tactics. Grazioli and Wang had designed the stimulus deception tactics so they could be readily detected by a skilled, alert consumer. That is, they built the forged site so it provided deception detection cues and opportunities, rather than a site where the deceptions were so well executed that detection by typical college-aged adolescents was unlikely. The seven deceptive elements were a fictitious "assurance seal" from the Better Business Bureau; a warranty statement that was unrealistic according to industry norms; fictitious news clips from trade publications; a phony photo of the company's store front; store sales figures that were grossly unrealistic; fictitious testimonials; and grossly overstated claims about the store's reputation. Detecting these deceptive elements required that a site searcher do one or more of these things: (a) follow the link to the Better Business Bureau's searchable Web site, where the fraud could be discovered; (b) be sufficiently curious or informed to suspect that the warranty was much too good to be true; (c) follow the links to the fictitious articles, which revealed they were nonexistent; (d) realize that the photo of the store was merely a generic building photo without any store name; (e) realize that a wrong area code was given; (f) follow the links to the quoted testimonial givers, which proved to be nonexistent or unusable; and (g) search a bit on popular Internet search engines that would reveal that this store is not well known or regarded. The college students displayed little skill or motivation for detecting any or more than one of these deceptive elements of the forged site.

Finally, another aspect of lie detection is related to the presence of linguistic cues in spoken or written messages. Zhou, Burgoon, Twitchell, Qin, and Nunamaker (2004) proposed that a deception agent's choice of language might reveal the attempted deception. They cited a large number of linguistic indicators that might distinguish a message that contains deception tactics from one that does not. They speculated that deceptive messages may display less formal language and grammar; be less complex (e.g., have lower lexical diversity, lower lexical complexity, fewer long sentences, shorter words, fewer pauses or punctuation); demonstrate distancing from the audience (fewer self references, more passive voice, and/ or less spatiotemporal language); and may contain more misspellings and uncertain language. Their analysis related to contexts in which the deceiver is telling spontaneous, unprepared lies, or minimally prepared lies. Whether these linguistic cues have some validity as deception cues in such situations remains to tested, but it seems unlikely that they would be valid as cues to deceptions in marketing contexts where the messages are constructed by skillful communication experts, written and rewritten, tested and revised, and where people delivering the message have trained and rehearsed their deliveries.

Overall, we suspect that the marketplace context is one where there should be either a prevailing lie bias or a high variability in lie biases and truth biases across people and immediate situations. This variability would depend on the consumers' states of mind and deception protection skills, and on the success of a specific marketer in suppressing a lie-bias state of mind and encouraging a truth-bias state of mind. The main point of this perspective is that when people's beliefs about the deception rate in any particular social domain approximate the actual deception rate, that happy alignment enhances apparent lie detection accuracy. For example, if a person expects deception in 30% of marketing messages, and there is in fact deception in about 30% of the marketing messages that person encounters, he will be more accurate in apparent deception detection just by guessing than he would have been if he expected, say, deception in 70% of marketing messages. The skill here, if there is one, is in becoming good enough at preassessing communication situations and predicting the motives and methods of particular types of communicators so that one can fairly accurately adjust one's expectation about how likely it is that deception tactics will be attempted in the context at hand. Underestimating the likely base rate of deception will reduce one's accuracy even if you have specific lie-detection skills available to you. This is because your tendency is not to deplete those skills in situations perceived as mainly helpful and not dangerous. However, your default tendency is not protecting you well because it is out of touch with the level of deception you face. You can let your deception protection skills rest on "pause" without too much risk if you've accurately aligned your general expectations about deceptiveness accurately with what unfolds. All this raises the question of what might be said about the actual base rate of deception attempts in marketplace contexts and about people's general assumptions about the deception base rates in important marketing contexts. As far as we know, there is no research on that issue.

7

Marketplace Deception Protection Skills

In this chapter we discuss the marketplace deception protection (MDP) skills that a consumer can develop to be well prepared for marketplace encounters. The point of skill development is that individuals eventually come to do a specific task reliably again and again, and that some people become more skillful than others at doing those tasks. A well skilled young adult, for example, would successfully reapply their MDP skills whenever they face a telemarketing call, an Internet Web site, a salesperson, or a mass media advertisement. The research reviewed in Chapter 6 establishes that when a consumer does note something suspicious or potentially misleading in a message, he or she may slow down processing and shift into a System 2 thinking of some sort. However, that is a sometime thing. The effects observed indicate that some people sometimes do that adjustment, not that it is a dominant uniform move that all people have mastered. Conditions can make it more difficult to do this self-protective adjustment, so learning to do successful deception protection even when situational conditions inhibit that is important. Finally, it is still unclear from prior research just what type of self protective thinking people do once they make the shift into System 2, especially whether it is skillful, fluent, effective deception protective work or just a general but unproductive slowdown and shift.

A person who is skilled in deception protection will have well-learned mental procedures designed to detect, neutralize, resist, correct for, and penalize deception attempts; to prepare the mind for such attempts and tasks in advance; to self-prime acute vigilance when needed; to conserve and wisely allocate the self regulatory resources that are needed for MDP; to do fluent, assured shifts from System 1 to System 2 processing when suspicious of deception; to strategically use postmessage opportunities efficiently to do MDP thinking; to do counterfactual thinking about alternate ways a marketer could have presented the message, and alternate ways he or she could have processed it; and to do prospective alternate framings of future events. Beyond these personal self-regulatory skills, a consumer could learn counter-deception skills to disrupt and befuddle the deception provocateur. More broadly, consumers adept at deception self-protection will learn to warn and protect friends, kin, and loved ones, to shine bright sunlight on a specific marketer's deception activities, and to thereby help to deter deception. Most broadly, consumers must learn to adopt a deception protection goal as their default, starting-point goal for confronting all marketplace communications about important products and services. They must expect deceptions and therefore focus on scanning for these deceptions as a primary selective processing goal. Searching first for deceptions becomes the main objective, rather than first trying to credulously absorb the marketer's story-as-delivered or trying to cognitively multitask and thereby achieve only partial and ineffective deception protection.

Deception protection skills have not been studied in research on communication and social interaction skills. Communication skills are predominantly defined in our society as the communicator's skills rather than the skills developed by persuasion targets. For example, in Greene and Burleson's (2003) milestone book that surveys research on human communication and social interaction skills, there is hardly any discussion of a persuasion target's skills in detecting, controlling, and resisting real-world persuasion and deception attempts. The discussions in that volume deal almost entirely with a communicator's performance skills in getting other people to understand and go along with what the communicator seeks from them.

Deception Protection Skills: Detection, Neutralization, Resistance

A consumer's conceptual understanding about deceptive marketing tactics underlies her or his development of deception protection skills. However, declarative knowledge like that is insufficient to enable consumers to cope with actual deceptions. The individual must convert that conceptual knowledge into functional deception protection task-performance skills. Persuasion detection skills enable a consumer to recognize in a specific situation that persuasion is being attempted and how it is being attempted. Deception detection skills provide a personal forewarning or early-warning system that orients individuals to potential deceptiveness in a social communication. Deception-neutralizing skills enable a consumer to modulate, slow down, and suspend the deception process that a marketer seeks to engineer in the consumer's mind. Neutralizing activities are stepping-on-the-brakes activities that impose a freeze on the deception process, delay it, disrupt it, suspend it, or hold it in check. Consumers do this by learning to manage their message-processing environment and alter the flow-of-events associated with the persuasion attempt, rather than accepting a message-processing environment and flow-of-events engineered by the persuasion agent. Neutralizing achieves a grace period, an opportunity for a consumer to consider, plan and do cognitive activities of his or her own construction before either actively (a) internalizing a marketer's positive conclusion, implication or recommendation about the product, or (b) discounting severely, counter-arguing, or rejecting the marketer's advocated conclusion or recommendation about the marketer's product. Neutralizing a misleading persuasion attempt for deception protection purposes does not inevitably lead a person into actively resisting and rejecting it. Successful neutralizing may lead ultimately into self-regulated acceptance. Often, neutralizing will suspend in mental limbo any meaningful cognitive resolutions that favor or challenge the marketer's point-of-view, so that the possibility of deception simply vanishes the persuasion attempt as if it never began.

Active, skill-based deception resistance requires, in addition to deception detection and neutralizing, learning to judge when it is, and is not, in one's best interest to try doing intense focused deception-protective scrutiny of a suspicious message, and how much effort to invest in that, and learning specific ways to discount, dismiss and penalize specific deceptive practices. We distinguish skill-based resistance to deceptive persuasion from other mechanisms that result in a no-persuasion outcome but that do not directly entail deception protection skills. For example, one type of non-skill-based "resistance" is a simple automatic motivationally driven reactance against any form of pressure (external or internal) on or threat to one's freedom to choose anything, to prefer anything or to do anything.

Recognizing deceptive intent is a fundamental skill that has widespread practical application. Many marketplace messages are mixtures of entertainment, education, assistance and persuasion.

Developing skill in identifying the specific persuasion tactic(s) being used in a specific marketing message is difficult, because any persuasion tactic can be executed in a myriad of ways, using varied language and message forms. Beyond that, developing skill in recognizing deception tactics of the types discussed in Chapters 3 and 4 is a challenging task. For example, there are many specific ways to execute a distraction tactic or an impersonation-of-an-authority tactic in everyday discourse or marketing. Knowing such a tactic exists in concept is only a first step toward readily noticing specific instances of it being executing within a specific communication context, via specific language and/or visuals. So, one key learning task for every adolescent and adult is to create for themselves a mental deception-tactic library that contains a concise typology of the ways in which authority impersonations get implemented, the ways that distractions to conceal disclosures of product drawbacks get executed, and so forth. The deception detection process may proceed roughly as follows (Johnson et al., 2001). A consumer discovers an anomaly in the presentation, judges that the anomaly is functional to the marketer's goals of deception and fraud, and believes that the agent had adequate discretionary control over the presentation to produce the anomaly intentionally. The consumer notices an anomaly by comparing the information presented to what would be expected. This requires that the consumer has a clear mental template of what should and should not be, or is likely or unlikely to be, in a marketing presentation of this sort if clear, complete nondeceptive communication was being attempted. If an anomaly is spotted, a consumer generates and tests alternate hypotheses as to why that particular anomaly occurred in this case. Is the discrepant cue consistent with an interpretation of intentional deception? If not, then the consumer could interpret it as a mistake due to fatigue, slipups, lack of attention, or insufficient knowledge by the ad's creator or the salesperson. Finally, the consumer evaluates whether this is a big or small deviation from the mental template for a clear and complete good-faith marketing presentation like this. Big, intentional deviations from honest complete full disclosure are treated as detected deception tactics, and that triggers deception neutralization activities.

Doing skillful neutralization allows a persuasion target to further reduce uncertainties about the deceptive elements of the persuasion attempt, to draw on social resources by asking others what they make of the persuasion attempt, or to wait for and take advantage of serendipity, as when the unsought, coincidental and revealing discovery of other parts of the same overall persuasion campaign occurs. An especially useful deception neutralizing skill is to discipline yourself to seek controlled reexposure to the persuasive message on your own terms. You learn to diligently take the time to reread, immediately or later, text passages in marketing messages, or to read the entire message later under information-processing conditions of your own choosing. Rereading enables someone to do all sorts of effortful information processing tasks more effectively. When interacting with a salesperson, telemarketer, or Internet marketer, you learn to regularly discipline yourself to ask for repetitions and/or rephrasings of what the marketer says in the planned and scripted persuasion attempt. This is a simple skill to understand conceptually, and by late adolescence people have the cognitive capacity to do it. However, the real skill development lies in becoming able to do it reliably during everyday marketplace persuasion. A related skill is learning to, during the neutralizing period, starve a persuasion attempt of the added favorable cognitive inputs that it needs to be successful. For example, McGuire's (1968) information processing model of persuasion postulates simply that to be successful a persuasion attempt must induce people through a sequence of cognitive activities: attention to favorable message content, comprehension of that content, storage in memory of beliefs consistent with that content, and so forth. To accomplish successful deception neutralization, consumers develop skill in tactically engineering disruptions of this multimediator process so that nothing further happens in their mind that works to the marketer's advantage while the consumer is giving the deceptiveness hypothesis full examination. People can also develop skill in doing overt actions that help neutralize a persuasion attempt. They can learn to disrupt its preplanned flow by being misleading themselves in what they show to and say to a salesperson. This requires a learned skill by a consumer, we suspect, because lay people are accustomed to behaving courteously and unguardedly during many social interactions. Consumers can, for example, learn to strategically act confused, to digress and sidetrack, to filibuster, to obfuscate by talking abstractly to a salesperson, to insert distracters (strange facial expressions or surprising gestures) into the salesperson's delivery, or to withhold facial feedback by blankly staring. People can also develop skill in executing actions to redefine the agent's persuasion game from one where they are a target to one where they are the "deception detective," for example, naming aloud the deception agents' tactics, labeling the agent's process unfair, and explaining to the agent or others how it would be fairer. Each of these is a simple thing for a person to conceive of doing, but it requires practice to develop poise-under-pressure in doing it smoothly when socially engaged with a sales or service agent.

We conceive of active resistance to a deceptive persuasion attempt as an attack on the agent for having attempted to deceive. It thus goes a step beyond neutralization. Neutralization often will produce a game-suspended outcome. Skillful active resistance to a deception attempt actively confronts and attacks the deceptiveness by the marketer. It includes all the cognitive attacking a person does that is driven by a judgment that the agent was indeed acting maliciously to deceive and to thereby contaminate one's belief system and taint one's buying decision. However, we do not think there is a bright line between what we conceive as deception neutralization and what some may think of as resistance. Neutralization will sometimes lead into resistance. Further, neutralization could be seen as passive resistance, giving deception a slow death.

As discussed in Chapter 2, psychologists have not studied people's active resistance to deceptive persuasion as a specialized type of acquired expertise. However, many of the cognitive mechanisms associated with persuasion resistance can be viewed as acquirable skills. Individuals can learn through practice to perform these activities more reliably and effectively. To our knowledge, prior accounts and studies have not treated them as acquirable skills. For example, the much researched mechanism of counterarguing (Petty, Ostrom, & Brock, 1981; Wright, 1981) has been tied to the act of resisting a persuasive message. Counterarguing is typically conceived very generally as thinking about the topic of the persuasive message that runs counter to the favorable arguments or information on the topic presented in the message. Counterarguing can be viewed as a skill that one has to practice and develop in order to apply it flexibly, regardless of the particular message topic, or as a skill that is topic-specific (e.g., skill in counterarguing health-related marketing messages). However, we have not seen it discussed or studied in skill acquisition terms in the persuasion and attitude change literatures. As another example, traditionally the properties of someone's existing attitude on the specific topic addressed by a persuasion agent (e.g., the existing attitude's strength or accessibility) are thought to confer resistance (Petty & Krosnick, 1995; Tormala & Petty, 2004). This mechanism produces resistance coincidentally; it depends on having already prepared one's topical attitude to be strongly grounded and held with certainty. However, learning to prepare one's important attitudes to have these resistance-conferring properties could be viewed as an acquired skill that requires practice to master. Another type of resistance mechanism involves selectively recalling information supportive of one's existing attitude or selectively reweighting one's beliefs (Ahluwalia, 2000). Taking a skill-acquisition perspective on this, people could develop their skills in doing these specific cognitive gymnastics reliably and effectively.

The metabeliefs that people harbor about their own deception resistance capabilities and preferences (Brinol, Rucker, Tormala, & Petty, 2004; Tormala & Petty, 2004) are another component of persuasion resistance skills. To put these into play in a real-world context, a person must first have developed significant capacity for metacognitive thinking, and to have also learned to use that capacity for the specific task of developing personal persuasion-related metabeliefs, which are elements of a self-concept. Similarly, people may learn to correct for perceived biases in their own judgments exerted by what they believe are the external causes of such biases, according to their lay theories of deception and influence. (Wegener & Petty, 1997). For that to happen, adolescents and adults must first acquire sufficient skill in metacognitive analysis to construct a personal lay theory of social bias relevant to a persuasion situation (what types of deceptions exert how much distorting influence on judgments and decisions?). Then, they must also develop skill in recognizing specific biasing factors in a situation, and in cognitively adjusting for that. Presumably, some consumers develop more skill earlier in life than others in generating and drawing on metacognitive beliefs about their deception protection efficacy.

Psychological theories of resistance are largely about internal resistance. They identify the cognitive maneuvers by which someone resists, without doing anything behaviorally that accomplishes or contributes to resisting. Doing covert neutralizing or resisting masks these actions from observers, including a persuasion agent if he or she is present, and therefore provides flexibility across social settings; it gives the appearance of being courteous and avoids social embarrassment, but masks the ongoing deception protection thoughts and emotions. The skillful consumer practices strategic deception of deception agents and observers for their own purposes. However, MDP skills broadly conceived also include developing skill in doing specific overt actions that bolster immediate neutralization or resistance, even when private cognitive resistance skills have temporarily failed. Youngsters and other neophytes in deception protection can therefore develop skill in performing actions we call "resistance bluffing." Resistance bluffing facilitates deception neutralization and ultimately may enable production of more determined and solidified resistance to the deception attempt. Examples are learning to say simple variants of the oft ridiculed "Just say no!" (e.g., "No way," "I'm not listening to another word," "Buzz off," or the ever-useful "That's BS."). These are useful situational deception-protection actions to master because someone can do them, and thereby appear resistive to themselves, conferring on themselves a resistive attitude, even if what they say or do does not yet have substantive cognitive roots.

There is a general principle of deception protection lurking in the adage "What's sauce for the goose is sauce for the gander." We call it the "turning-the-tables principle of deception protection": Whatever tactics deceptive persuasion agents can use to bamboozle a consumer, a consumer can learn to use to thwart an agent and self-protect from the agent's machinations. To illustrate, consumers can convert the devious "disrupt-then-reframe" (DTR) persuasion tactic (Chapter 6) into a useful deception-neutralizing tactic of their own. Whenever a consumer suspects that something deceptive is happening or simply feels out of control while coping with a marketing presentation, they can express aloud or subvocally something strange, puzzling, or nonsensical that disrupts the misleading train of thought engineered by the marketer before it gains momentum or reaches closure. We will label this the "disrupt-then-reframe counter-deception heuristic." Having inserted one's own disruptor into the flow overtly or via subvocal thought, the consumer regains control and then reframes what is happening in blunt deception mockery, for example, "You are so BUSTED!!" If a consumer expresses their disrupter aloud, that probably magnifies its neutralization value and certainly disrupts a salesperson's scripted flow. A consumer can choose one or two favorite non sequiturs that work reliably to confuse a salesperson, or that entertain and mock the agent covertly. The stranger and more unsettling it is, the better; for example, saying "It's crackers to slip a rozzer the dropsy in snide" (a longtime *Mad* magazine inanity) aloud, then chuckling, will disconcert and befuddle most salespeople, and reframe the event for the consumer as having fun, entertaining oneself, and discouraging the deception. Indeed, there is no reason why a consumer needs to have an audience present for this DTR counter-deception heuristic. While reading a misleading advertising brochure or inspecting a Web site, saying something nonsensical aloud as a deception disruptor to interfere with and mock the deception attempt can be effective. Indeed, mocketing (making fun of heavy-handed, awkward, silly and nasty marketing tricks) is in general a useful approach to neutralizing deceptive marketing. And, for that matter, good old consumer bullshit has practical value in the consumer's deception neutralization arsenal; spouting BS, talk for the sake of talk, a ramble that occupies the time, regardless of its relevance or meaningfulness, works to disrupt and neutralize a marketing presentation suspected of underhandedness.

Proactive Coping Skills: Preparing for Battle Before It Begins

Consumers must learn to recognize when as-yet-undefined deceptive persuasion attempts are approaching and to act ahead of time to prepare for or forestall such events. Proactive coping involves advance preparations. It involves consumers' accumulation of resources and acquisition of skills that prepare them for staving off the stresses caused by the recurring array of deception attempts that marketers will send their way over time. Aspinwall and Taylor (1997) define psychological coping in general as activities to master, tolerate, reduce, or minimize environmental or psychic demands that represent threats or cause harm. They define *anticipatory coping* as preparing yourself usefully for the stressful experience of coping with a specific event once that event is certain and imminent, and its specifics apparent. Persuasion and deception attempts represent threats like that because they can, if unchecked, invade and alter one's beliefs, attitudes, and decision. Not all persuasion and deception attempts will represent threats or cause stress. So we expect consumers to be more concerned about potent persuasion and deception attempts that deal with important personal choices, and less concerned with transparent deception attempts concerning the many unimportant marketplace choices.

However, what Aspinwall and Taylor call *proactive coping* is more relevant for our purposes. Proactive coping precedes anticipatory coping. Proactive coping involves the accumulation of resources and the acquisition of skills that are not designed necessarily to address any one particular stressor situation but to prepare in general. This requires different skills than extant coping. Proactive coping requires the ability to identify potential sources of stress before they occur. When consumers have done successful proactive coping, they may not show or experience much stress during persuasion attempts. And, if they are successful at averting and minimizing deceptive persuasion's effects, their successful proactive preparations may go unsuspected by observers.

Proactive coping with deceptive marketing messages will, according to Aspinwall and Taylor's (1997) model, entail a number of self-regulatory activities. The first of these is resource accumulation. The consumer builds a reserve of time, social resources, financial resources, and skills for dealing with the recurring problems of deceptive persuasion regarding important life choices. This requires getting resources built up and then using them sparingly, judiciously, and wisely for some, but not all marketplace deception attempts. This stockpiling enables a person to use their deception protection resources preventively in future time periods to offset not-yet-predictable future net losses of these resources from unexpected emergency situations (deception attempts) before a truly important deception protection situation begins. This resource accumulation skill helps offset time pressures and fatigue which may, when the threatening moment arises, keep the consumer from recognizing the warning signs of deceptive persuasion that go below her radar. It also keeps her from fretting about the vague future stream of deception attacks in her world, because she feels prepared. It keeps her fresh to do situational adaptations, and prevents her from having to prematurely resort to using packaged System 1 deception protection heuristics that are not adapted to a deception situation.

A second proactive coping skill (Aspinwall & Taylor, 1997) is managing selective attention and threat recognition. Consumers learn to screen the environment for signs of impending exposures to potentially persuasive and deceptive marketing messages and campaigns. They develop a skill for foreseeing when such marketing exposures are forthcoming. They become sensitive to their own internal suspicions that suggest a significant deceptive persuasion threat may soon arise. This involves gaining predictive insights about what types of marketplace situations are potentially most stressful to deal with, about one's likelihood of facing such situations, and about one's own ability to deal with upcoming deception protection demands. A basic subskill here involves learning how to schedule and reschedule deception protection tasks, so as to complete important ones before another starts, or to realize when insufficient time means setting new priorities about which deception protection task to confront immediately and which to cancel or postpone. As consumers build this skill, they must also develop a capability for regulating their concerns over imminent deception attempts so that they avoid being hypervigilant.

A third proactive coping skill (Aspinwall & Taylor) involves initial situational appraisal. Individuals develop their skills for initially identifying "What is this social message all about? What will it become? Will it turn out to be a persuasion or deception attempt even though it starts out as entertainment or as an educational message? Should I keep an eye on how this message unfolds for shifts in goals and giveaways of tactics?" So, consumers hone their initial appraisal skills to generate appropriate vigilant processing. These skills depend on their learning to reliably notice salient, dramatic, proximal, and relevant cues that evoke within them relevant deceptive marketing schemas. Becoming good at psyching oneself up is a key subskill; being able to reliably generate or self-prime a mental state of deception protection readiness is a valuable consumer skill. A fourth proactive coping skill (Aspinwall & Taylor, 1997) is preliminary coping. Resourceful consumers plan for a foreseeable upcoming exposure to a threatening but important marketing message so they are not caught off guard. They learn to always seek information from others in advance about the type of product that the potentially deceptive marketing presentation will promote. They get skillful at taking preliminary actions to help themselves encounter a threatening deceptive message on their own terms, when they are ready.

If someone has indeed developed good proactive coping skills, they will probably have also developed a strong self-confidence in their own deception protection self-efficacy. High perceived self-efficacy at the outset of a threatening deception attempt may reflect their (a) having stockpiled resources to apply, (b) having had prior experience and practice with deception protection challenges akin to this one, (c) having done cognitive simulations beforehand of what they will do mentally when they confront the upcoming deceptive persuasion attempt; and/or (d) having a lot of context-specific beliefs to draw on. In essence, they are confident that they have developed their persuasion and deception knowledge, topic knowledge, and agent knowledge so that they can confront and harness this particular marketing message. The emphasis in proactive coping is on identifying the specific skills to learn, learning what environments to seek and create to foster these skills, taking personal responsibility for getting practice done, and especially for recognizing environments that help oneself do proactive coping and avoiding those that prevent or inhibit that.

Resource Management Skills

Friestad and Wright (1994) proposed that another skill that people develop with experience is how to strategically use all the time available for processing ads. Consumers can learn that they need not accomplish all their processing of a particular ad during a short discrete time period (e.g., the start and end of a 30-second television ad). They can learn to skillfully take advantage of posttransmission periods, coupled with memory retrievals, to create for themselves added opportunity to think about things said, seen, or implied in an ad and about omissions, distractions, and other deception tactics. They can use this time period adaptively to do counterfactual analysis of how this marketer could have presented a more fair and honest message or how they themselves could have dealt with the message more perceptively. Some marketplace communication situations create a useful learning and comparison environment that can facilitate deception detection. For example, even a standard television advertising environment presents people with multiple chances to review the same ad, and hence to gain better insights about the ad's deception tactics during subsequent exposures. Further, standard television and print advertising practices place different advertisers' competing ads for the same type of product in close proximity to each other. This creates a potentially rich learning environment for consumers, as they become more and more skillful in using the stream of repeated exposures to the same ads, and easy comparisons between competing ads, to their advantage in doing deception protective thinking. Now, simply finding oneself immersed in a marketing-rich environment may activate deception protection tendencies. For example, Koslow (2000) found that a person's general feeling of reactance and skepticism increased as they simply watched more and more ads. Koslow argued that as advertising floods someone's mind, that in itself gradually primes a vague suspicion that somehow, somewhere, one or more of these ads will try to deceive me. The same may occur as someone scans over a set of monthly bills and credit card statements, filled with mysterious language and unclear itemized changes, gradually growing more and more upset ("I know these companies are putting something over on me somehow, somewhere, in this barrage of obfuscation"). Our viewpoint, however, is that skilled consumers proactively put themselves in a deception protection mindset without waiting for that to be triggered, or not, by a situational barrage of possible deceptions.

People must learn to judge when to take deception protection risks, how to judge such risks, and how to efficiently allocate their coping skills and resources across the persuasion episodes of everyday life. In order to learn new things and adaptively grow, individuals must periodically open their minds to potentially deceptive persuasion attempts, especially in the marketplace domain. Doing so is inherently risky because beliefs, attitudes, and decisions may thereby be altered in unforeseeable ways. However, whenever someone does try to do significant deception protection, their effort depletes cognitive resources, leaving them vulnerable to upcoming persuasion attempts (Brinol, Rucker, Tormala, & Petty, 2004; Wheeler, Brinol, & Hermann, 2007). In this book we focus mainly on marketplace deception. However, people must learn to cope with the full array of deceptive persuasion attempts directed at them during everyday life. They encounter the many instances of marketplace deception dispersed among the many instances where friends, family, coworkers, and others attempt to persuade them about something.

Therefore, we propose that people must develop an overarching *resource management skill* in judging how to efficiently allocate their deception protection investments across the persuasion episodes of everyday life. Wegener et al. (2004) analyzed in theoretical terms the information processing effort entailed by a variety of psychological mechanisms that produce resistance to persuasion. Following that line of thinking, one skill development task involves a person's learning how much of their self-regulatory resources it takes to effectively execute various deception protection mechanisms, and becoming proficient at taking resource-demands into account in making situational how-to-protect-myself choices. An important related concept is that someone's overall self-regulatory resources are scarce and valuable so that using them for persuasion resistance impairs subsequent attempts to resist persuasion. Any exertion of self-regulatory willpower or self-control for deception protection purposes, when one's default or natural tendency is to mindlessly acquiesce, could reduce self-regulation efficacy on subsequent deception protection tasks (Muraven, Tice, & Baumeister, 2000; Vohs, 2006). This resource management skill can be seen as a portfolio management skill; that is, maintaining a balanced portfolio of more or less risky investments in deception control and prevention. Individual consumers can gradually get better at doing that over their lifespan, but it requires them to periodically update their metabeliefs about the effort it (now) takes them to execute different deception protection activities, as they move toward automatizing some of those.

A person learns to invest over time in some high-effort, high-importance, high-risk-of-failure deception protection ventures balanced with many other low-effort, high-chance-of-success deception protection cases, and even some unprotected persuasion cases. In assessing the risk of confronting different deceptive persuasion attempts, consumers are likely to take into account the importance of the topic to them, their recent and expected deception protection investments, and their metabeliefs about their own MDP skills in the context at hand. If deception protection is indeed effortful- and resource-depleting, youngsters will ideally learn first to do it most skillfully when a persuasion attempt is most threatening, intrusive, and powerful. One view is that at the collective level, evolutionary pressures drive us toward early development of refined coping skills for the most potentially powerful influence tactics. But evolutionary pressures could also work to preserve the general effectiveness of the most powerful deception tactics, leaving youngsters still vulnerable to those during childhood and early adolescence, because youngsters still benefit from being influenced by adults, even via deception, more so than later in life when independence is established. If so, youngsters will be slow in learning to cope with some highly powerful tactics until late adolescence, when their skill in this would then accelerate. In any case, because potentially powerful tactics are also likely to be the most widely attempted tactics, even by novice marketers, youngsters will have abundant opportunities for practicing MDP skills honed to such tactics.

Marketplace Deception Protection Self-Efficacy

We propose that consumers develop a belief about their efficacy in doing marketplace deception protection self-efficacy (MDPSE). This is a metabelief about how well they do the tasks of deception detection, neutralizing, and resistance needed to achieve effective self-protection from deception in encounters with marketers' persuasion attempts and tactics. Generally speaking, a person's self-efficacy is a situation-specific set of beliefs they develop about their skill and success in doing a particular type of task or doing whatever group of tasks are called for in a particular type of situation (Bandura, 1987). Self-efficacy beliefs are a form of metabeliefs. They reflect self-confidence in having a sufficient array of procedural knowledge and skills to do essential tasks needed for success in a particular task domain, under specific (common) conditions. We have not developed and tested a measure of MDPSE. Marketplace deception protection self-efficacy could be measured summarily, for example, by items such as "I am really good at detecting marketers' deception tactics and making sure those do not influence me." Alternately, MDPSE could tap someone's specific beliefs, such "I can reliably spot a telemarketer's attempt to flood my mind with details so I cannot think about the product's drawbacks."

A person's self-efficacy beliefs about doing marketplace deception protection may or may not closely match the person's actual performance. Self-efficacy metabeliefs regarding deception protection may be especially inaccurate when a person's experience in trying to do that is limited and when it is hard to tell whether one was successful or not in such situations (Kardes et al., 2005). If people have high self-confidence about their marketplace deception protection skills, but are in fact still inexperienced in, untrained in, and unreliable in detecting, neutralizing and resisting such messages, their misplaced self-confidence makes them vulnerable targets of marketers' tactics. Their vulnerability stems partly from their limited deception protection knowledge and skills, but is magnified by overconfidence which can mute their motivation to keep learning and improving those skills. For example, an adolescent's self-perceived invulnerability can leave them stuck at a lower level of self-protection skill development than some peers, for a longer time in their lives than is desirable, and repeatedly cause them to miss good chances to upgrade their skills when the opportunity arises, as from a training program (Sagarin et al., 2002).

Researchers have discussed various forms of self-efficacy. To make clear how MPDSE differs from prior concepts, we discuss these earlier concepts in some detail. People may over their lifetime develop very general self-efficacy beliefs concerning their overall competence to perform as effectively as required across a wide variety of achievement situations. Someone with high general self-efficacy beliefs might believe things like "I will be able to achieve most of the goals that I set for myself"; "I am confident that I can perform effectively on many different tasks"; "I can always manage to solve difficult problems if I try hard enough"; and "I am confident that I could deal efficiently with unexpected events." (Mukhopadhyay & Johar, 2005). These broad beliefs represent a composite record of a person's mastery experiences, their mental bookkeeping account of personal triumphs and failures. A key finding in research on people's general self efficacy beliefs is that such beliefs about life in general bear little relation to someone's beliefs about their self efficacy in particular activity domains, nor to their actual behavior in particular activity domains. So, a consumer's general self-efficacy beliefs do not indicate what they believe about their deception protection or persuasion protection skills in the marketplace.

General social self-efficacy has been studied as a moderator factor in numerous persuasion and compliance studies, including marketing contexts. The following belief scales illustrate how researchers (e.g., Bither & Wright, 1973) have conceptualized general social confidence (GSC), or social self-esteem. Someone with high GSC would hold self-efficacy beliefs such as "I feel capable of handling myself in most social situations"; "In group discussions I rarely fear my opinions are inferior"; "I always make a favorable first impression on people"; and "When confronted by a group of strangers, my reaction is never one of shyness and inferiority." These items tap broad beliefs about self-efficacy in vaguely defined interpersonal situations; the situations described are not ones that necessarily involve persuasion or deception attempts; and beliefs about efficacy in performing specific deception-protection or persuasion protection skills are not measured. The nature of the relationship found between general social self-confidence and response to a persuasion attempt has varied a lot from study to study. McGuire (1968) proposed what he called a "pretzel-shaped" model to reconcile these divergent findings in terms of different, sometimes compensatory, relationships between self-confidence levels and different information processing activities basic to persuasion (attention, compre-hension, resistance/yielding). His prediction about linear relationships under some conditions and nonmonotonic relationships in other condi-tions has been generally supported. In a marketing context, for example, Bither and Wright (1973) found a linearly increasing relationship between general social-self confidence beliefs and message resistance/acceptance when people processed a TV advertisement while undistracted, but a non-monotonic (humpbacked) relationship when people had to also deal with visual distractions in the ad. Bither and Wright's review of related research showed that the linear relationship was common when subjects responded to persuasion attempts in situations that afforded high-response opportu-nity for everyone, and the nonmonotonic relationship was common when people tried to cope with (and resist) persuasion attempts while response opportunity was strained. Moving slightly closer to consumers' skills for coping with marketing campaigns, Wright (1975) assessed information processing confidence as a hodgepodge of beliefs related to coping with persuasion (e.g., "I am totally confident about my ability to judge messages coming from the mass media"; "When I hear an argument being presented, I am quick to spot the weaknesses in it"), to self-regulatory skills ("I have less trouble concentrating then most people"; "I am certainly able to think quickly"), and to verbal skills ("My thoughts do not race ahead faster than I can speak them"; "I am never at a loss for words"). Wright (1975) found that both social self-efficacy and information processing self-efficacy were related to counterarguing against an ad's claims.

Smith and Betz (2000) conceived of social self efficacy as a person's confidence in their ability to engage in the social interaction tasks needed to initiate and maintain interpersonal relationships. In this view, people who have low social self-efficacy would act shyly and feel a lot of social anxiety and awkwardness. So Smith and Betz defined different realms of interpersonal activities relevant to the social lives of adolescents and young adults: making friends (e.g., how comfortable and skilled I am in asking a potential friend out for coffee); social assertiveness (e.g., how comfortable and skilled I am in joining a lunch or dinner where people are already sitting and talking); public performance (e.g., how comfortable and skilled I am in expressing my opinion to a group of people discussing a subject of interest to me.); groups and parties (e.g., how comfortable and skilled I am in going to a party or social function where I probably won't know anyone) and giving and receiving help (e.g., how comfortable and skilled I am in asking someone for help when I need it). Again, these self-efficacy domains do not focus on persuasion-protection or deception-protection skills and achievements or on situations involving the marketplace domain of communication.

The skills required for marketplace deception protection involve self-regulation processes. Self-regulation is those processes, internal and transactional, that enable a person to guide his or her goal-directed activities over time and across changing circumstances and contexts. It entails one's modulation of thought, emotion, affect, behavior, and attention via one's deliberate or automated use of specific mechanisms and supportive metaskills. For example, one important self-regulation skill is attentional control. This is a person's skill at focusing on a given task, controlling and regulating external distractions and internal distractions, and working single-mindedly toward a desired goal. Self-regulatory behavior is sequential in nature and includes, in addition to attentional control, skills in planning, evaluating actions, correction of behavior, and termination of activities. A person with strong positive beliefs in their own general self-regulatory efficacy would believe (Diehl, Semegon, & Schwartzer, 2006) such things as: "I can concentrate on one activity for a long time, if necessary"; "If an activity arouses my feeling too much, I can calm myself down so that I can continue with the activity soon"; "If I am distracted from an activity I don't have any problem coming back to the topic quickly"; "It is easy for me to suppress thoughts that interfere with what I most need to do"; "I can stay focused on my goal and don't allow anything to distract me from my plan of action." These self-regulatory beliefs can be divided into beliefs about my competence to start and perform specific regulatory processes, to control and adjust them, and to execute them when contingencies occur that challenge me.

Bearden, Hardesty, and Rose (2001) moved self efficacy more directly into the domain of consumer self-protection. They defined a person's overall consumer self-confidence as the extent to which an individual feels capable and assured with respect to his or her marketplace decisions and behavior. They propose that this meta-appraisal is fairly accessible to an individual because consumer activities pervade everyday life. Bearden, Hardesty, and Rose (2001) defined overall consumer self-confidence as a function of decision-making confidence and protection self-confidence. Decision-making confidence reflects a person's appraisal of his or her purchase-related information acquisition and information processing skills, skill at forming consideration sets of products, and skill at making purchase decisions that satisfy personal goals and social goals. Of most relevance here, Bearden, Hardesty, and Rose (2001) defined a consumer's protection self-confidence as her or his appraisal of own skill in protecting self from "being misled, deceived or treated unfairly." This appears to be marketplace deception protection self-efficacy, pure and simple. However, they defined protection self confidence in terms of a person's general beliefs about their persuasion knowledge: "ability to understand marketers' tactics and to cope with those tactics [and] to understand the cause and effect relationships that determine marketers' behavior and to deal with attempts to persuade." Bearden et al. (2001) also defined a companion type of protection confidence, called *marketplace interfaces confidence*. They operationalized marketplace protection self-confidence by these items: I know when an offer is too good to be true; I have no trouble understanding the bargaining tactics used by salespersons; I know when a marketer is pressuring me to buy; I can see through sales gimmicks used to get customers to buy; I can separate fact from fantasy in advertising. From our perspective, these capture some parts of persuasion protection skills, boiled down to beliefs about one's overall skill in detecting bargaining tactics of all sorts; detecting the tactic of exerting pressure; judging overexaggeration tactics; detecting sales gimmicks of all sorts; and detecting advertising elements that are not realistic. Bearden et al. (2001) defined marketplace interfaces confidence as the ability to stand up for one's rights and express one's opinion when dealing with others in the marketplace (e.g., store employees; salespersons), including asking for product demonstrations, refusal to purchase, and demands to remedy defective purchases. This was measured by these items: I am afraid to ask to speak to a manager; I don't like to tell a salesperson something is wrong in the store; I have a hard time saying no to a salesperson; I am too timid when problems arise while shopping; I am hesitant to complain when shopping. Note that these activities are all overt ways of handling problems that arise in a store or a sales presentation. None are psychological activities that a consumer can do to detect, neutralize, resist or penalize marketers' deceptive behaviors.

Obermiller and Spangenberg (1998) conceptualized advertising skepticism as a state of enduring disbelief about the quality and validity of the content and claims in advertisements. They developed a nine-item scale to assess this constellation of beliefs. Note that these are not metabeliefs about one's own skills or knowledge in critically analyzing or resisting ads, or detecting and coping with deception tactics. Advertising skepticism is more like a chronic suspicion that advertising in general is not believable, useful, and honest. The Ad Skepticism Scale items are:

We can depend on getting the truth in most advertising.
Advertising's aim is to inform the consumer.
I believe advertising is informative.
Advertising is a reliable source of information about the quality and performance of products.
Advertising is generally truthful.
In general advertising presents a true picture of the product being advertised.
I feel I've been accurately informed after viewing most advertisements.
Most advertising provides consumers with essential information.

This ad skepticism measure has been used in a number of recent studies as a possible indicator of a person's enduring disposition toward self-protective vigilance, or motivation to disbelieve all advertisements.

Wegener, Petty, Soak, and Fabrigar (2004) developed what they called a Resistance Preference Scale. They conceived resistance preference as an enduring tendency to resist persuasive messages by using one of two resistance methods: (a) counterarguing or (b) attitude bolstering. As they discussed, counterarguing and attitude bolstering are only two of the plausible mechanisms of resistance available to people. To measure counterarguing tendency, their scale used these items: When someone challenges my beliefs, I enjoy disputing what they say; I take pleasure in arguing with those whose opinions are different from my own. Wegener et al. (2004) measured someone's attitude bolstering tendency with these items: When someone gives me a point of view that conflicts with my attitudes, I like to think about why my views are right for me; When someone has a different perspective on an issue, I like to make a mental list of the reasons in support of my perspective. Note that these items pertain only to protecting an already-formed attitude from counter-attitudinal attacks. Thus, this measure is somewhat narrow, for example, counterarguing might equally involve one's dispassionate critical analysis of the logic of an argument in a message or the quality of the evidence presented even when you have no well formed prior attitude to preserve. It is a mechanism consumers can use when, for example, they examine marketing messages about unfamiliar products and services. The attitude bolstering measure here closely resembles what has traditionally been called *support argument*.

Nevertheless, assessing metabeliefs about one's own chronic tendencies to use (and perhaps skill in using) particular types of persuasion protection methods is a promising step. A logical extension is a measure that includes metabeliefs about one's disposition to use, and skill at using, specific deception protection methods. As is evident, researchers are moving closer and closer toward measuring the specific deception protection beliefs consumers harbor regarding the broad marketplace domain and regarding specific task domains within the marketplace.

8
Developing Deception Protection Skills in Adolescence and Adulthood

Overall, marketplace deception protection skills involve component skills in detecting deception in specific situations, neutralizing the effects of that deception, resisting deception, and making decisions about whether and how to penalize the deception agent. It also involves an overarching self-regulatory metaskill, in which someone gradually learns how to efficiently conserve and allocate their cognitive deception protection resources across the different persuasion episodes they encounter in everyday life. In this chapter, we discuss the process of acquiring marketplace deception protection (MDP) skills by examining the research on children's understandings of and responses to advertising, and their development of beliefs about persuasion and deception. We also examine how they develop domain-specific beliefs and skills regarding various social situations and the difficulty of transferring these skills to other contexts. Finally, we discuss how adolescent cognitive development and an overloaded learning environment affect the acquisition of marketplace deception protection skills.

An individual's acquisition of deception coping skills is, we believe, a lifelong process. People continue refining and adapting their MDP skills throughout their lifespan. Our analysis of the skill acquisition processes applies to consumers of all ages, including adults and the elderly, as they try to improve and expand their MDP skills. However, we will focus mainly on the period of life before full-fledged adulthood for several reasons. First, adolescence is a complicated developmental period during which there are several processes involved in developing persuasion protection skills. These processes include a person's maturation in both cognitive and physiological functioning, and their diverse attempts at learning new skills across a number of social interaction fronts. Second, little persuasion-related research has been done on youngsters in early and midadolescence.

Paradoxically, the vast majority of persuasion experiments have dealt with people still in what developmental researchers define as late adolescence (ages 18 to 22). Many of those individuals are just learning how to handle themselves in adult social domains where they encounter the full repertoire of adult persuasion and deception expertise and tactics. We know little about how well developed these adolescents' deception coping skills are. Third, few developmental psychologists have studied persuasion-related or deception beliefs or skills among adolescents. We hope to motivate more interdisciplinary research on this topic by developmental psychologists and consumer behavior scholars.

MDP skills depend in the early years on both the development of basic cognitive and executive function capabilities and on the experience an individual accumulates in doing specific types of deception-coping activities. So we present an overview of how these skills may develop over roughly the first 25 years of life. This spans the periods that contemporary developmental psychologists (Smetana, Campione-Barr, & Metzger, 2006) define as childhood (birth to 9 years old), early adolescence (ages 10 to 13), middle adolescence (ages 14 to 17), late adolescence (ages 18 to 22), and emerging adulthood (through the mid-20s). Framing deception protection activities as skills has several advantages. It distinguishes these skills from simple declarative beliefs about deception and persuasion. It elevates them as valuable and essential parts of the human development process. Beyond that, the hallmark of all communication-related skill acquisition is that improvements in performance require significant amounts of task-specific, context-specific practice (Anderson, 1993; Greene, 2003). So to understand the overall course of MDP skill development up to adulthood, we need to take into account opportunities for getting significant amounts of context-specific practice in detecting, neutralizing, resisting, and penalizing specific forms of misleading advertising and marketing.

The point of skill development is that individuals eventually come to do a specific task reliably again and again. A well-skilled young adult, for example, would successfully reapply their MDP component skills whenever they face a telemarketing call, an Internet Web site, a salesperson, or a mass media advertisement. So we move beyond discussing the state of adolescents' declarative (conceptual) knowledge about persuasion and deception tactics, their deception coping (i.e., what they know they could do), and even beyond what they may actually have tried doing occasionally and ineffectively. We consider what they do or do not become skillful in doing consistently and effectively to detect, neutralize, and resist specific forms of marketplace deception and persuasion. Ultimately, a well-skilled adult would be able to fluently and judiciously transfer MDP skills between different marketing contexts (e.g., transfer skills honed to the television advertising context to the Internet context or the telemarketing context); and such an adult would be able to distinguish between different deception protection social domains, and will not mistakenly apply deception protection methods from another domain (e.g., friendship) to the marketplace domain.

Growing Up Targeted

American children and adolescents grow up targeted for persuasion. They are targets of advertising and marketing activities that saturate their lives, and they also grow up targeted for persuasion by the adults in their everyday lives (peers, parents, teachers, coaches, and even strangers.) So learning to cope with persuasion in general, and with marketplace deception in particular, is a key part of preparing for adult life. The modern marketplace is a special domain of human social interaction that requires domain-specific skills from consumers. When prior generations grew up, marketplace persuasion was not nearly as complicated and omnipresent as it is today. Between starting school and becoming an effective adult consumer, an early twenty-first century youngster must try to learn to navigate competently through marketplace persuasion contexts that encompass television advertising, Internet marketing, advergames, personal selling, point-of-sale displays, print advertising, telemarketing, direct mailings, service relationships, ambient marketing (via schoolbooks, cars, stores, peers' clothing), product placements, stealth endorsers, digitized alterations of and insertions into televised events and photos, cross-merchandising by corporate media conglomerates, packaging, character merchandising, Internet "sock puppets," public relations, event marketing, viral or buzz marketing, interactive communication, purchase disclosure statements, product usage instructions, and warnings. Virtually no research has been done on how adolescents or young adults develop marketplace deception knowledge, and build their deception coping skills.

There have been useful studies on various advertising-related topics such as children's ad-evoked cognitive responses (Brucks, Armstrong, & Goldberg, 1988), changes over time in adolescent beliefs about the psychological effects of ad tactics (Boush, Friestad, & Rose, 1994), the relative effects of advertising and product use on children's product attitudes (Moore & Lutz, 2000), the joint effects of ads and peers on adolescent smoking intentions (Pechmann & Knight, 2002), how adolescents integrate advertising into their daily lives (Ritson & Elliott, 1999; Bartholomew & O'Donahue, 2003), and the relationship between advertising and adolescent materialism (Goldberg, Gorn, Peracchio, & Bamossy, 2003). However, these studies have not focused on deception protection beliefs and skills. In her integrative review of consumer socialization research, John (1999) noted that research on adolescents' persuasion and deception coping skills was quite scarce. A decade later, it still is quite scarce. Finally, we presume that a child's knowledge about the domain of marketplace persuasion develops gradually toward an adult-like understanding. So, adult-like understanding represents a benchmark. It also represents what a child's mind is striving toward. Hence, a logical starting point for research on children's understanding of marketplace persuasion would be a comprehensive working model of the structure and content of adult advertising knowledge and deception protection skills. The only meaningful way to calibrate children's attainments in advertising literacy is in comparison to the skill levels that young adults can and do achieve. Certainly that comparison lies at the heart of policy debates about special regulation of advertising to children, or about educational programs to improve children's advertising literacy. Our analysis of MDP skills in Chapter 7 is complete enough, we hope, to serve as a benchmark model for gauging youngsters' progress.

Children's Beliefs About Television Advertising

Before they reach adolescence, children develop some conceptual understandings of persuasion and advertising. One source of evidence for this is the body of research on youngsters' beliefs about television advertising done mainly from the early 1970s through the late 1980s, before today's kids were born. At best, therefore, that research can only reflect what the parents of the current generation of children knew about advertising when they were kids. However, everyday knowledge on marketplace persuasion continuously evolves. This is true about all of children's societal understandings, including their domain-specific understandings of economics (Webley, 2005), politics (Berti, 2005), or the legal system (Ceci, Markle, and Chae, 2005). Everyday knowledge about advertising and persuasion is socially diffused from one generation to the next (Boush, 2001; Friestad & Wright, 1994, 1999), so descriptive data about children's advertising knowledge attainments from thirty or more years ago should be treated the same as any other decades-old secondary data. Its applicability to current policy decisions should be questioned, both for its current validity and its correspondence to recent models of everyday marketplace persuasion knowledge.

Young (1990), in a landmark analysis of that pre-1990 research, discussed how the work had evolved as a product of heated societal and regulatory debates, rather than as a subject of dispassionate cumulative scholarship. In particular, he bemoaned the theoretical sterility and conceptual disarray in much of that pre-1990 research, stating that "this has led to some muddled thinking and conceptual confusion during the years when most of the research was published" (p. 39). When we analyzed this body of research for ourselves in some detail recently (Wright, Friestad, and Boush, 2005), we found that the conceptual variance across the studies makes reviewing and interpreting the body of empirical work daunting. A general conclusion can be drawn that children learn important things about advertisers' goals and tactics between their toddler years and the time they graduate from high school. But at a more specific level, the findings are not obviously cumulative. There are frustrating differences from study to study in the ways in which children's advertising knowledge has been conceived, as well as in the measurement methodologies used.

Despite the unevenness of the empirical work, there was some excellent theorizing. In their seminal work, Robertson and Rossiter (1974) analyzed what a child watching television at that time needed to understand in order to attribute a specific type of communicative intent to advertising messages. They dealt solely with children who were exposed to television advertising in the standard format of that period, that is, discrete ads of standard short lengths that appear at predictable intervals in program breaks. Their model identified five subskills that together enable children to discern a television ad's intent in that environment. These are the capabilities to discern the television commercials as discrete messages distinct from regular television programming; to recognize a sponsor (in general) as the source of an advertising message; to grasp the idea of an intended audience for the advertising message; to understand the symbolic nature of the product, characters, and contextual representations in television ads; and to discriminate, via concrete examples, between products as advertised on television and products as the child has personally experienced them. Ward, Wackman, and Wartella (1977) proposed a more abstract economic component of children's advertising knowledge, which included an understanding that advertisers want to sell products in order to make economic profits. They highlighted this economic knowledge about marketplace institutions and transactions as part of a child's overall socialization as a consumer. It remains unclear if or why this economic knowledge is an essential component of marketplace persuasion knowledge. Others (e.g., Young, 1990) have commented that understanding the concept of selling, selling intent, and profit gains should best be treated as a separate aspect of a child's knowledge, rather than as critical to the child's skill in interpreting and coping with advertising. Certainly, such economic knowledge requires a high level of abstraction and societal understanding by a child about distant events and institutions. Even in this early era of research on children's understanding of television advertising, Robertson and Rossiter (1974) recognized that longitudinal research on changes in individual children's knowledge over time is the only valid way to learn much about the separate and interactive roles played by general cognitive development and domain-specific learning in the development of advertising literacy. Other researchers have echoed the need for this type of research (Boush, Friestad, and Rose, 1994), but even 20 years later there still had been very little longitudinal research on the processes underlying a child's development of advertising knowledge.

In the next decade, Roberts (1983) argued that in prior research a confounding existed between children's knowledge about the perceived selling intentions or business motives of advertisers, and their knowledge about marketers' persuasive intentions and goals. He proposed that a child's understanding of persuasive intent is the critical skill, and formulated a model of adult-like comprehension of persuasive intent that designated four persuasion-related insights. The first insight is that the message source has other perspectives and hence other interests from those of the receiver. The second and third insights are that the source intends to persuade, and that all persuasive messages are biased. The fourth insight is that persuasive messages demand different interpretational strategies than do messages that are intended to be primarily informational, educational, or entertaining.

Brucks, Armstrong, and Goldberg (1988) examined the key question of knowledge-in-use, as opposed to knowledge-in-mind. They examined if and when children access their advertising knowledge and/or product knowledge while processing an advertisement. This type of research moved the study of children's advertising knowledge directly into a consideration of memory processes, cognitive resources, and message processing tasks, which aligned it more directly with models of adult persuasion processes. These researchers also discussed children's "cognitive defenses" in more specific terms than had previously been the case, also in keeping with models of adult message processing. For example, they conceived of children generating advertising-directed counterarguments or product-directed counterarguments. They also emphasized a child's need to develop skill in retrieving advertising knowledge from memory during ad processing, and the value to a child of some explicit cue in the ad or environment to provoke that retrieval during or soon after message exposure.

Developing Persuasion Knowledge

Friestad and Wright (1994) discussed in some depth the different types of persuasion-related knowledge and skills that children, adolescents, and young adults gradually develop to cope effectively with marketers' and others' strategic attempts to influence them. They discussed how such knowledge develops from a simplistic set of beliefs into an integrated, complex structure of implicit beliefs, which are automatically activated in everyday contexts. Their persuasion knowledge model (PKM) did not focus exclusively on children, nor did it propose age-specific stages that classify children's and adolescents' emerging persuasion knowledge. Rather, the PKM focused broadly on how people develop and refine persuasion knowledge continually over their life span. However, developmental propositions about children's and adolescents' understanding of marketplace persuasion abound in Friestad and Wright's (1994) discussion; we modify those propositions here to reflect how they could be applied to the development of marketplace deception protection beliefs and skills. First, from early childhood through adulthood, an individual develops knowledge relevant for the two deception-related tasks of everyday life: coping effectively with others' deception attempts and effectively executing one's own deception attempts. A youngster's marketplace deception knowledge develops from scratch into an increasingly interrelated and valid structure of causal–explanatory beliefs about (a) the psychological events that advertisers may try to influence (intended psychological goals); (b) deceptive advertising tactics that advertisers may use, separately or in combination, to accomplish particular psychological effects; (c) deception-coping tactics that the youngster can use to self-manage or control an advertisement's effects on internal processes and overt actions; and (d) deception-control goals that can be pursued when processing an ad. As a youngster's marketplace deception knowledge matures, he or she develops more understanding of the temporal course of the deception process and the relative effectiveness and appropriateness (fairness) of particular deception tactics. A child's development of deception coping expertise depends strongly on how much practical experience is gained in recognizing, evaluating, and responding to the specific deceptive advertising tactics that are observed most often. Hence, the specific advertising tactics prevalent during an individual's childhood and adolescence will be those that are dealt with most effectively through adolescence. A person's motivation to learn how to effectively cope with marketers' deception attempts will increase considerably through late adolescence and early adulthood. This motivational change occurs because marketplace deception knowledge becomes increasingly valuable to more and more everyday tasks and goals, such as making increasingly significant and numerous buying decisions, establishing and maintaining an independent identity, managing more complex social relationships, and facing more diverse and subtle deception tactics than in early adolescence.

As a person's experience in coping with deceptive marketing methods increases, their deception protection activities grow increasingly automatized and effortless to execute. However, this shift into automatization may be gradual because learning effective deception protection skills is difficult. People's deception beliefs eventually become more implicit, refined, complete, and valid. They slowly learn to more quickly and effortlessly (a) access marketplace deception beliefs from memory; (b) recognize when a deception attempt is happening; (c) note situational cues about what a marketer's specific tactics and goals are in the particular campaign or situation; (d) construct and execute their own self-protective message processing tactics; (e) store in memory information about the deceptive tactics used in specific ads, and (f) access that information later to help recognize similar ploys. However, the path to automatized deception protection belief activation and skill execution is a slow one. As practice in processing advertisements increases, adolescents gradually develop some abstract understandings about advertising in general, although a youngster's deception coping proficiencies and strategies will often remain highly context-bound, geared to the same specific instances and forms of advertising tactics in the same media as those already encountered.

From childhood through early adulthood, a person also gains skill in using their deception and persuasion knowledge in concert with two other knowledge structures that are critical resources in processing advertising: agent knowledge and product knowledge. General models of persuasion depict people as learning how to thoughtfully or heuristically access these types of knowledge during message processing, in order to elaborate on aspects of an advertising message or to rely on simpler "peripheral" cues from the ad. Learning to efficiently juggle and blend their product, advertiser, persuasion, and deception knowledge is challenging to adolescents and adults alike. First, a youngster must gain experience in simply retrieving and using any one of these types of knowledge when processing advertising. Second, each type of knowledge is itself changing gradually in accessibility and complexity, as the individual encounters new ads. For example, in a 12-year-old adolescent's first encounter with a particular ad for a specific video game, his or her game knowledge (product knowledge) or knowledge about that particular advertiser (agent knowledge) may be more or less developed, and hence more or less useful, than knowledge about advertising tactics and deception tactics. A year later, if the youngster's product knowledge about the video game or about specific deception tactics has increased, he or she will rely on a different mixture of knowledge structures to process and cope with ads in that same advertising campaign than a year before. Learning to juggle cognitive resources effectively, when those very resources are rapidly changing in validity and accessibility, will not be easy. One implication of this is that an adolescent or early adult may at different times cope better with some types of ads than others, cope better with ads for some types of products than others, and cope better with some deception tactics than others.

Friestad and Wright (1994) singled out as a key event the change-of-meaning that occurs periodically when a person first realizes that some aspect of an advertising message may well be there as an advertiser's intentional deceptive persuasion tactic. We hereby label this as a "critical deception insight." Before this critical deception insight, the person had not construed the presence of that ad feature as having any deception-related meaning; it was simply there in one or more ads. But once the individual realizes that this aspect of an ad might be intentionally put there to deceive, they would begin to significantly reinterpret other ads that contained this same element. These critical deception insights will occur at different moments and situations for different individuals. When one occurs, its immediate effects on a person's subsequent ad processing are difficult to predict, because the person is not yet sure how to respond to its presence. Ultimately, the person figures out a stable way of responding to that deception tactic. A bottleneck to the development of deception protection beliefs is the rate at which youngsters develop insights about psychological states and activities that mediate persuasion. Adults harbor a rich conception of the many different ways that ads might influence internal psychological events that seem instrumental to persuasion (Friestad

& Wright, 1995). However, children's conceptions of these psychological events will be less complex and centered on the first few types of internal events they gain insights about (e.g., belief, attention, liking, desire). Afterwards, their understanding of tactics will increase in proportion to the further expansion in their understandings of the range of psychological events that are of interest to advertisers and other persuasion agents. In research on youngsters' beliefs about persuasion or deception, there have been only a few attempts to examine the development of these beliefs, or to compare older people's beliefs directly against those of younger people. Boush, Friestad, and Rose (1994) identified eight possible psychological effects that children and adults may believe advertisers intend to produce via advertising (e.g., grab attention; learn about product; like the ad; like the product better; remember the ad; trust what the ad says). They also identified eight types of advertising tactics that people may think advertisers use to produce those psychological effects (e.g., show a popular TV or movie star; use humor; show people similar to you; compare one product to another). Finally, they asked young and older adolescents what they believed about the specific psychological effects that advertisers intend to achieve via each of those tactics. Using these data, they examined if youngsters develop increasingly adult-like mental representations of how tactics in ads generate psychological effects.

Martin (1997) presented a thoughtful meta-analysis of the assorted empirical studies and findings on the relationship between children's chronological age and their understanding of general advertising intentions. She found that, across all studies, the average correlation between age and "more advanced" beliefs about advertisers' intentions was a significant, but modest, .37. That means that, on average, age alone explained only about 10% of the variance in children's advertising knowledge. She also found that age-related differences were much more pronounced in studies reported before 1974 than in studies from 1975 to 1989, and that in the one case during the period 1991 to 1996 the correlation was very small. The lower this correlation, the weaker is the relationship between chronological age distinctions and knowledge of advertising intentions. One reason for these findings may be that over the years, the advertising knowledge of younger children has grown more similar to that of older children. However, that speculation remains to be directly tested. Such a change across generations may be due to a general social diffusion of advertising knowledge within the culture, to recent advertising literacy teachings, or to helpful effects from legislative changes that have altered the advertising exposure environment and enhanced children's ability to learn about advertising from experience. Martin (1997) concluded that drawing conclusions about age-related differences in current children's advertising knowledge from this overall set of studies is problematic because of the differences across studies on so many factors. In another overview John (1999) summarized empirical findings on children's advertising knowledge into several succinct age-stage propositions about understanding of advertising intent, use of advertising knowledge in processing ads, and general attitudes toward advertising. John's model of overall consumer socialization is important because it embedded the development of advertising knowledge firmly amid the other diverse and challenging consumer skills that youngsters are concurrently struggling to develop.

Moore and Lutz (2000) discussed in depth how children at different age levels vary in their skill at integrating their brand beliefs generated from ads with their own personal product usage experiences, either before or after ad exposure. Their analysis suggested that younger children may have more difficulty than older children in accessing whatever advertising-created knowledge they possess, either during or after ad exposures. And that a personal product usage experience may dominate ad exposure effects more strongly among younger children than among older children. They suggested that as children mature they develop both more advertising knowledge and more expertise in using it when needed, and also develop more motivation to reconcile the world as presented by advertising with the world of product performance (because they are more involved in buying decisions). Hence, younger children may be less likely than older ones to successfully access ad-generated memory traces in contexts beyond the immediate ad exposure situation. Finally, Webley, Burgoyne, Lea, and Young (2001) discussed children's understanding of advertising within the larger context of children's and adolescents' economic socialization. They reviewed the range of tasks everyone tries to master to navigate competently through the varied economic decisions and institutions that fill everyday life across one's lifespan. An adolescent must learn to make sense ultimately of all the communicative aspects of the commercial and economic world, including advertising, point-of-sale displays, packaging, financial disclosures, money handling, money acquisition, product usage instructions, warnings, and so forth. Over time and overall, research on children's and adolescents' understandings about advertising and persuasion has been a sometime-thing, and research on their deception beliefs and marketplace deception protection skills is nonexistent, as far as we know.

Developmental Psychology and Theory of Mind

In contemporary developmental psychology there is no single, widely accepted theoretical framework to draw on for answers about the development of understandings about marketplace deception (Moses & Baldwin, 2005). Piagetian theory was dominant until the mid-1980s and that theory or its extensions have strongly influenced the literatures on children's beliefs about advertising and consumer socialization. However, in the last two decades, questions about the validity of Piagetian theory have emerged (Moses & Baldwin, 2005). In particular, current researchers believe that classifying kids into universal stages is not meaningful because a child's abilities often differ markedly across different domains of knowledge and skills. Moses and Baldwin (2005) argue that the set of specific understandings and skills youngsters need to cope with advertising, even just a single form such as television advertising, develop at different ages for specific children in specific cultural contexts. Moreover, after these conceptual abilities emerge, children will need time to become proficient in using them. Moses and Baldwin propose that a domain-specific approach to skill acquisition, integrated with more general information processing accounts, is needed in explaining how children and adolescents learn to cope with advertising.

Research on a youngster's development of a fundamental theory of mind is pertinent to their understandings of deception, persuasion, and advertising, although concepts from this theoretical approach have not generally penetrated the consumer behavior literature.

Theory of mind (TOM) refers to a person's coherent body of beliefs about the mind and the mental states that are used to interpret, predict, and explain human action and interaction. TOM research has mushroomed in the last 15 years (Carpendale & Lewis, 2006; Moses & Carlson, 2004). Moses and Baldwin (2005) argue that the TOM work implies that children develop understandings essential to appreciating advertising earlier than previously believed. For example, toddlers aged 2 to 4 demonstrate perspective-taking, and appreciate that other people have different emotions, perceptions, and desires from their own. Moses and Baldwin's (2005) review establishes the following. Young preschoolers aged 4 to 5 start acquiring notions that individuals act on the basis of their own private mental representations, show understanding of the nature of motivational states and intentions (i.e., the existence in people's minds of goals and desires), and then start to understand epistemic states (i.e., beliefs or knowledge). Older preschoolers understand the mind as a kind of representational organ that can take in information (sometimes partial or faulty), form representations of the world based on that information, and then generate actions based on those representations. From ages five to seven, they develop an understanding of the existence of "second order" mental states (i.e., that someone's mental states may be embedded within other mental states) such as "He thinks that she thinks that that toy is cool." During that same period, kids shift to a constructivist or interpretive theory of mind, which lets them start appreciating the interpretive diversity among people. Once that begins, a child comes to appreciate the subjectivity in people's thinking and communicating, including the concepts of personal preferences, communicator biases, or social prejudice. Regarding advertisers' intentionality, Moses and Baldwin (2005) argued that preschoolers should easily distinguish television ads from program content, because they can already make sophisticated distinctions among categories such as between mental and real things (a thought about a toy versus a real toy), fantasy and reality, appearance and reality, as well as between television images and real objects. Further, preschoolers readily infer what parents and peers want them to do, and that parents and peers are trying intentionally to get them to do it. So young preschoolers should be able to recognize that advertisers want people to buy their products and are trying to get them to do so.

Perhaps the most basic concept in understanding deception is that some things are true and other things are not true. Moses and Baldwin (2005) summarized the developmental path as follows. Children develop an ability to distinguish true factual statements from false ones at about the age of three or four. Young children may attempt to deceive without fully understanding the way deception is designed to affect behavior. Learning when to lie and when to tell the truth is viewed as a major developmental task. Children in many circumstances also can discriminate between lying and fantasy by age four. By age five children realize that thoughts can be biased by the perspective of the viewer. This is important because perspective-taking combines with the knowledge of truth and falsehood to create an understanding that other people can express false (mistaken) beliefs, which are not lies if they are stated in good faith. The ability to make such judgments is nearly general by age seven or eight. Many deceptive tactics involve inducing people to make incorrect inferences, so understanding how deception works is aided by the knowledge that beliefs can be acquired by inference rather than by direct experience. This cognitive development occurs before age six (Moses & Baldwin, 2005). Finally, around ages 10 to 12, youngsters grasp how to mask their feelings, and that others will mask feelings to deceive. Thus, most of the understandings basic to start grasping marketplace deception are in place by those ages. However, it is doubtful that many early adolescents have progressed far in learning about specific types of marketplace deceptions or about the idea that deception in marketing is a panoramic process that takes place over time and across various messages from a marketer.

Moses and Baldwin (2005) concluded that young and older adolescents' inability to cope with advertising is not a conceptual failure but primarily a task performance failure, due in large part to their immature executive function skills. They explained that some executive function skills are relatively mature by early adolescence but the full set of executive function skills continues to be refined and consolidated throughout adolescence and into the early twenties. Undeveloped executive control leads to poor self-control, impulsivity, poor judgment in decision-making contexts, failure to organize and plan ahead, difficulty integrating knowledge with future goals, difficulty implementing strategies, perseverance of inappropriate behavior, difficulty sustaining attention, and difficulty simultaneously processing multiple sources of information. Immature executive functioning skills may leave children and adolescents perceptually seduced by salient and pleasing but irrelevant audiovisual effects in ads (no inhibitory control and resistance to interference), and attentional inflexibility may make them unsuccessful at switching attention to more relevant, less salient, information in ads (Moses & Baldwin, 2005).

Domain Specific Skills and Cross-Context Transfers

The idea that human social thought is domain-specific to a significant degree has become quite influential. In this view, youngsters acquire domain-specific "if–then" regulatory mechanisms that selectively and contingently prepare them for the diverse features of social life. Bugenthal (2000) called these collections of "if–then" knowledge structures "social algorithms." From her impressive review of the literature on developmental, cognitive, social, and evolutionary psychology, social psychobiology, and behavioral ecology, Bugenthal proposed that distinctions can be made between the algorithms by which children and adolescents organize five historically critical domains of their social life: (a) attachment during infancy in the service of safety (attachment domain); (b) use and recognition of social dominance (the hierarchical power domain); (c) identification and defense of "us" versus "them" in group coalitions (coalitional group domain); (d) management of reciprocal obligations and benefits for communal life, also known as the reciprocity domain; and (e) selection and access to sexual partners (mating domain). She argued that these domains differ on a number of factors, including the key problems to be solved and the developmental course of acquiring domain-relevant information.

Several aspects of this view seem relevant in understanding how youngsters acquire marketplace deception protection (MDP) skills. First, domain-specific social skills depend in some unknown proportions on evolutionarily supplied social algorithms for survival-related social interaction problems; socially supplied rules, vocabulary, and heuristics; and subjective interpretations of personal life experiences. So, MDP skills should reflect each of those influences to varying degrees, creating substantial individual variability in what develops when. Second, the specifics of the "if–then" persuasion-related social algorithms someone acquires for each domain probably differ. That is, people develop detailed, but different, deception detection, neutralizing, and resistance heuristics for mating problems versus hierarchical power problems (e.g., parents), and coalitional group formation problems (e.g., peers and peer groups). Third, there could be some fundamental cross-over of deception protection rules and skills that allow early learning about some general deception tactics that one must be prepared for, and coping skills to apply, across multiple domains and relationships. Some of that information could be passed on genetically, for example, if some robust influence-related skills have been practiced and refined for centuries, and their cross-domain resourcefulness becomes deeply encoded in the human mind (Bugenthal, 2000). Alternatively, we believe that a key development in each individual's deception protection development is their realization that specific "if–then" information pertinent to those skills in one social domain (e.g., attachment domain) transfers usefully to another domain (e.g., mating domain), or that such a transfer (e.g., to the marketplace domain) is dysfunctional. Learning to make such transfers effectively will, we believe, come slowly.

The marketplace does not correspond neatly to any one of the five problem domains Bugenthal (2002) discussed. Therefore, the application of social rules and understandings from these major historic problem domains into the marketplace context is, we believe, problematic for youngsters. It presents them with a nontrivial cross-over transfer challenge in either (a) learning how to parse the diverse realm of marketplace encounters and relationships, and match these with particular social algorithm problem domains, or in (b) learning how to merge together in their minds parts of different social algorithms into a set of skills directly suited for the modern marketplace. To us, the marketplace falls at the cusp of the reciprocity domain and hierarchical power domain. The reciprocity domain's central problem is facilitating coordinated, matched, and mutually beneficial actions between related and unrelated individuals. Reciprocity problems require youngsters who are functional equals to become competent in keeping track of past benefits from specific others and later on extending in-kind exchanges, using some type of cost-benefit mental accounting capacity. The hierarchical power domain's central problem mandates that children and adolescents gain skills in negotiating for their own self-interests within a hierarchical interaction. Youngsters learn how to negotiate benefits and escape harm from those in control of resources and outcomes, and how to negotiate compliance from others when they themselves have a resource or dominance advantage. Interestingly, learning indirect forms of resistance is particularly important here because children and adolescents may have opportunities to gain skill in negotiating with, bargaining with, or persuading parents, teachers, and coaches to modify their demands. Both the reciprocity and hierarchical power domains require gaining skills in assessing the other party. In the reciprocity domain there is continuous mutual monitoring and correction, while in the hierarchical domain, skill at accurately monitoring others is more vital for those with less resources and power.

If the marketplace does bridge these two domains, then youngsters must somehow merge early-learned social algorithms for reciprocity with those for hierarchical power to achieve marketplace deception protection competency. In relationship terms, it requires that youngsters adapt their deception protection skills developed for parent–child, child–child, and child–sibling relationships to the marketplace's assortment of relationships with adult strangers. Also, if our speculations are approximately valid, they underscore that developing marketplace persuasion coping skills may be a gradual process, compared to developing interpersonal social skills. Many of the persuasion, compliance-gaining, and deception tactics that parents and peers use on children and adolescents are inappropriate or inapplicable to marketplace persuasion. Therefore, what a youngster learns to do to detect, control, or resist deception in the contexts that dominate early life could become *psychological baggage* when the youngster's mind turns to marketplace coping. Further, even if some of one's parents' and peers' tactics are also prevalent in marketing, the executions of those by parents and peers have probably been less sophisticated and skilled, or taken different forms, than the executions found in most sophisticated marketing campaigns. So it may be that the deception protection skills that a person acquires from interpersonal domains are only honed to the least sophisticated of marketing attempts. Finally, although marketplaces are not new to human thought, it is plausible that there has been so much change in the contents of the modern marketplace over the past century that it impedes a youngsters' capacity to draw heavily on bioevolutionary deception-protection heuristics. This could be because the form and details of the modern marketplace do not map well into the marketplace domain representations of past generations, or it could also be more of an overload effect because of the sheer amount of detailed information youngsters today must wade through to understand the modern marketplace they will eventually need to cope with as adults.

In addition to the problem of learning to adapt one's deception protection skill from other social contexts to the marketplace, consumers may also have difficulty successfully transferring their deception protection skills from one marketplace context to another (e.g., from television advertising to the Internet). Research shows that applying the skills learned in one context to a different context is not easy (Barnett & Ceci, 2002; Speelman & Kirsner, 2005). Doing successful cross-context transfers of skills itself requires a skill, which takes time and practice to develop. Barnett and Ceci (2002) argued that, unsurprisingly, the success of such transfers depends on just how similar the new application context is to the original learning context. They propose that new application contexts may differ from original learning contexts in many ways (e.g., concrete versus abstract; closed-space problems versus fuzzy problems; different memory demands; different physical contexts; different functional mindsets; different modalities and media). Therefore, Barnett and Ceci (2002) argue that as the number and size of these differences between contexts increase, the likelihood of making a successful transfer decreases, and the skill needed to do a successful transfer increases. Analogical learning models also provide an account of cross-context knowledge transfers, and thus these models are relevant to the development of deception protection skills. Gregan-Paxton and John (1997) presented a sophisticated model of consumer learning by analogy (the CLA model) to explain how someone deploys their beliefs about a familiar product to understand a novel type of product. They explain the four stages of analogical transfer as (a) the access stage, in which a newly encountered product activates someone's prior mental representation of a familiar (base) product; b) a mapping stage, in which the person tries to construct one-to-one correspondence between representations of the two products' elements; (c) an actual transfer stage; and (d) in some cases, a schema-creation stage in which the person generates more abstract knowledge as a byproduct. The CLA model is presented as an account of product-to-product learning transfers. However, the same type of multistage processes could occur in trying to transfer a deception protection skill learned in one specific persuasion context to a different persuasion context (e.g., from television advertising to telemarketing or Internet advergames). This analogical transfer process could be done skillfully or inappropriately. An inappropriate transfer would occur, for example, when someone transfers, *without modification*, a deception protection skill they learned for one context to a different context, where that specific skill is not as effective or is downright dysfunctional. Given that marketplace persuasion contexts such as Internet marketing, television advertising, and personal selling differ from each other in many ways, it is likely that consumers' transfers of deception protection skills from one of these contexts to another is error-prone.

Adolescence and Marketplace Deception-Protection Skills

In this section we provide an overview of factors that shape and influence the development of MDP skills during adolescence (approximately ages 10 to 22). We cannot specify the exact role of each of these separate factors. Rather our goal here is to outline an overall picture of their probable combined effects on how the specific task of developing MDP skills fits into the adolescence experience. Adolescence is characterized by skill-learning overload. Teenagers are awash in a sea of new things to learn, practice, and master. Pechmann, Levine, Loughlin, and Leslie (2005) provide a remarkably accessible and authoritative discussion of the neurological bases for adolescent brain functioning, and discuss how brain development and other adolescent behavioral tendencies may affect youngsters' general susceptibility to advertising for addictive or harmful products. Pechmann et al. (2005) do not discuss MDP skills per se; however, we can draw on what they say and on other accounts of adolescent development (e.g., Amsel, Browden, Contrell, & Sullivan, 2005; Arnett, 2004; Berti, 2005; Galotti, 2005; Klaczynski, 2005; Luna, Garver, Urban, Lazar, & Sweeney, 2004; Smetana, Campione-Barr, & Metzger, 2006; Zelazo, Astington, & Olson, 1999) to identify the following aspects of an adolescent's life experience that should affect their success in developing MDP skills.

According to these accounts of adolescent development (Pechmann et al., 2005), from early through late adolescence the brain's cortex undergoes massive structural changes and is affected by the significant hormonal changes that occur during puberty. A person's fundamental executive function capabilities continue to develop in important ways throughout their adolescence and into their early twenties. These executive function capabilities include inhibitory control, attention flexibility, planning, self-regulation, impulse control, resistance to interference, error detection and correction, selective attention, focused attention, and working memory. Slow development of these basic control capabilities is directly tied to immaturity in someone's prefrontal cortex, as is slow development into adulthood of a person's metacognitive capabilities, including metaprocedural skills and metacognitive monitoring skills. Because of the continuing cortical, hormonal, and executive control changes, adolescents display pronounced impulsivity, an inability to delay gratification, sensation-seeking behaviors, social self-consciousness, imagined embarrassment, and poor risk assessment skill. Further, throughout adolescence personality traits are gradually emerging and stabilizing. Individuals in mid-adolescence often have low social self-esteem and self-confidence, although they may gradually develop higher self-esteem and social self-confidence during later adolescence. Adolescents are intently focused on learning to handle a particular subset of complex social interaction problems: parent–adolescent conflicts, sibling relationships and conflicts, peer pressures, and romantic relationships. They are also trying, to some extent, to develop the entire set of consumer socialization skills (John, 1999), which include (in addition to advertising and persuasion coping skills) shopping skills and skills for making purchase decisions (information search, product evaluation, decision-making skills). And, obviously, throughout this period adolescent guys think about girls and adolescent girls think about guys a significant part of the time.

Finally, adolescents are also trying to acquire important societal-level understandings about such things as economics, financial institutions, politics, the media, the education system, the legal system, social class, gender, and the broader world. At the same time they are trying to master complex academic subjects (e.g., algebra, life sciences, literature), technical skills (e.g., using computers, car maintenance, driving) and recreational skills (e.g., sports and games). Modern American adolescents spend considerable time doing multitasking, much of which involves a variety of electronic and digital technologies for entertainment, interpersonal, educational, and marketplace purposes. Adolescents are also slowly developing a host of communication skills (e.g., verbal and nonverbal conversational fluency, friendship skills, teamwork skills). Many adolescents achieve only modest proficiency in these communication skills. And as late adolescence unfolds (ages 18 to 22), new arenas of life such as college and the workplace introduce a diverse set of new topics to learn about and skills to tackle.

Thus, the executive function skills of adolescents are challenged by the substantive cognitive, hormonal, and social changes going on in their lives as they are trying to acquire a host of diverse understandings and task skills for the first time. Therefore, what adolescents can accomplish in developing skills for detecting, neutralizing, and resisting the diverse forms of marketplace persuasion must be, we suspect, fairly limited. Further, MDP skill development requires that an adolescent somehow has the opportunity to do repeated practicing of specific tactic identifications and associated neutralization and resistance activities. However, the real-world environment does not facilitate the sort of focused task-specific practice needed for rapid skill development. For example, an individual might go weeks between opportunities to try to detect, control, or resist a specific deception tactic being attempted, because these opportunities depend on the coincidental content of the diverse array of social and marketplace messages the person encounters.

9
Teaching Marketplace Deception Protection Skills
Prior Research

In this chapter we discuss what we know about teaching youngsters and adults to improve their marketplace deception protection skills. We review and describe in some detail the small set of studies in which researchers designed and tested methods for teaching consumers to cope with deceptive persuasion. These studies are published in diverse places and examining them provides insights about how to design and test more effective deception protection tutoring programs. The studies we focus on examined how to teach people to cope with implied claims (Bruno & Harris, 1980; Harris, 1977; Harris & Monaco, 1977; Harris, Trusty, Bechtold, & Wasinger, 1989), omitted information (Kardes, 2006), corrupted persuasion tactics (Sagarin, Cialdini, Sherman, & Rice, 2002), telemarketing fraud scams (AARP, 2003), alcohol advertising tactics (Goldberg, Niedermeier, Bechtel, & Gorn, 2006), and tobacco advertising tactics (Pechmann, Zhao, Goldberg, & Reibling, 2003).

Deception protection beliefs and skills concern a complex social domain, where the normatively correct way to self-protect is not crystal clear, and where other people's values, agendas, alliances, and self-interests affect the coaching they are willing to pass on to others. Deception protection knowledge and skills give consumers power, and power is something that older individuals tend to withhold from younger ones, or more expert individuals tend to withhold from less expert peers. Because of this, the educational process regarding deception protection is neither rapid nor smooth. However, we believe that coaching can accelerate learning about how to self-protect against deceptive marketing, and that designing effective teaching programs is an exciting challenge.

Our analysis of marketplace deception protection (MDP), skill acquisition, and knowledge in Chapters 7 and 8 suggests that MDP skill development during adolescence and early adulthood is gradual, with or without coaching. It is highly variable in its rate and course across individuals, and within an individual it is variable across specific marketing communication contexts and tactics. To develop refined and flexible skills in detecting, neutralizing, and resisting marketplace deception, youngsters must build conceptual understandings of a concise set of important persuasion and deception tactics, develop sufficient self-regulatory and executive function capabilities to guide focused practice in trying initial MDP skills in real-world situations, and find or create opportunities to do repeated MDP skill practice within their everyday lives, which are already filled to overflowing with new and challenging learning tasks. There is much for a consumer to learn as they go through adolescence and adulthood. There is no convenient lock-step, age-and-stage model that specifies what people are likely to know about or be able to do to protect themselves from marketplace deception at certain ages. Therefore, baseline assessments of what components of MDP beliefs and skills the target audience has mastered are helpful, even essential, in designing and calibrating MDS teaching materials and lessons. Moving someone along a path toward enhanced MDP skills requires teaching both understandings and skills along the way. However, teaching understandings and skills that a learner has already mastered can give them a false illusion of efficacy and self-satisfaction, which may deter future progression on their own or from the training. Teaching (reteaching) skills that a youngster has already learned and automatized may actually cause that person to regress for a while. And, finally, teaching students questionable, oversimplified lessons elicits resistance and apathy from those who are already knowledgeable or skilled.

Coping With Implied Claims

Harris and his colleagues have conducted a pioneering research program on how consumers deal with advertisers' implied claims, and how consumer education efforts might change that (Harris, 1977; Harris, Dubitsky, Connizo, Letchner, & Ellerman, 1981; Harris, Bechtold, Trusty, & Wasinger, 1989). They analyzed consumers' processing of implied claims as follows: First, memory is constructive, so there is alteration of information during encoding and storage, based on inferences made when storing or retrieving information noted in an ad (Harris, 1981, Harris & Monaco, 1978). Therefore, consumers treat strongly implied (probabilistic) claims as equivalent to directly asserted (certain) claims, as they store the claims in memory (Bruno, 1980; Bruno & Harris, 1980; Harris, Dubitsky, & Thompson, 1979). Harris (1977) analyzed the effects of giving consumers instructions to avoid interpreting implied claims as asserted facts. He found that trained subjects reported stronger disbelief in implied claims than untrained subjects under conditions where the ad processing was a low memory-load task, and there was immediate posttraining testing. However, when consumers had to watch a series of ads, thereby creating a high memory-load task, there was no beneficial effect of prior training. Harris et al. (1979) examined the effect of a more elaborate and lengthy 15-minute training session and found significant beneficial effects on disbelief of implied claims. Bruno and Harris (1980) continued this research program by comparing immediate training effects versus those observed for 2 days, 7 days, and 9 days later. These training session effects persevered over the extended posttraining time intervals. In those studies, the training about implied claims had used the same ads and same implied claims in both the training and test sessions. Dubitsky et al. (1981) tested transfer effects to new ads, not to the same ones. They contrasted training versus no training effects on subjects' coping with implied claims in either the same form or different forms across immediate, 2-day, 7-day, and 9-day time periods. This training program was more rigorous than in their prior studies, with four training sessions over 10 days, each lasting 35 minutes. In the first session, subjects got instruction on how to discriminate implied claims from direct claims. They then discussed 12 advertising slogans that used hedge words, identified the hedges, and restated the claim directly to contrast the difference between implied and asserted claims and to show that claims are sometimes directly asserted. The training also extended to include recognition and interpretation of juxtaposed imperatives, negative questions, or statistical misuse. Training effects were assessed immediately after training and after delays. In each later session, the trained subjects were reminded about how to interpret the implied claims. In this study, training decreased the perceived truth of implied claims more than asserted claims, and there was a general beneficial effect across sessions and types of ads. Further, in the final session there was a beneficial training effect that transferred from the ads that were used for instruction to new unfamiliar ads that employed comparable implied claims. Finally, Harris, Trusty, Bechtold, and Wasinger (1989) revisited the phenomenon in which people's memories get transformed from the original, relatively weak implied claim in an ad to stronger inferences (Bruno & Harris, 1980; Russo, Metcalf, & Stevens, 1981). Continued studies had shown that strongly implied claims evoke the same inferences by consumers as directly asserted claims, especially when the ad-processing environment is demanding or tiring. Harris et al. (1989) studied the effect of instilling in subjects a self-relevant shopping goal to motivate them to think carefully when processing implied claims. However, this involvement-enhancing instruction had no beneficial effects. Harris et al. speculated that the instruction to get involved was strong, but that it may require even more focused intentional-learning or intentional critical thinking mindsets to induce consumers to discount implied claims.

Coaching Consumers to Detect Omitted Information

Kardes et al. (2006) define "omission neglect" as a person's insensitivity to missing information about unmentioned product attributes, relevant issues, and/or products other than the advertised product. It occurs because consumers often rely heavily on whatever information the marketer chooses to include in the materials. When people rely only on what a marketer presents, without realizing that other relevant information is being withheld and that the omitted information may well be unfavorable to the product, they form overly favorable impressions of the marketer's product on the basis of the incomplete and biased information. Kardes et al. (2006) designed coaching techniques to increase people's sensitivity to missing information. Prior research shows that people grow more aware of what is missing from marketing materials when the person is highly knowledgeable about the product category or when cues are provided in the immediate situation that prompt a person to consider what information is missing and why it has been left out. In one training study, before subjects got information about a particular car model, they were explicitly asked to think about which attributes of cars are most important to them to consider in evaluating cars. The researcher gave them a list of nine car attributes, and asked them to rank order the attributes from most important to least important. The task of rank ordering is engaging because it forces a consumer to compare each attribute against each other attribute. This requires more thought than simply rating some attributes as highly important, some as moderately important, and some as less important. In addition, each subject then wrote out a brief explanation for their ranking of the attributes. This procedure was meant to focus each subject's mind directly on their mental template of the relevant attributes, as a prelude to processing marketing materials about a specific car. The subjects who did this preparation generated more moderate judgments about a car described by incomplete information than did uncoached control subjects. Apparently, the coaching intervention caused subjects to place less weight on the presented attributes, thus displaying cautious sensitivity to the incompleteness of the information. This suggests that coached subjects had rehearsed, and thus made salient, their own mental model of their preferred choice or judgment procedure, or of what a full disclosure marketing presentation would include, thereby increasing their awareness of what was left out of the car ad they inspected.

In a second study, Kardes et al. changed the coaching procedure so that the task to prime which attributes to consider came only after exposure to the car message. This was akin to a person pausing to systematically review what things they had learned about the product and what things they had not been told. Further, each subject's chronic "need for cognitive closure" was measured (Kruglanski & Webster, 1996). In general, people with a chronically high need for cognitive closure tend to make snap judgments based on easily processed information about products. Kardes et al. reasoned that these types of consumers might need extra strong coaching to make them sensitive to what information is not disclosed in a message. In a third study, some subjects got incomplete camera information already formatted in an easy-to-use list of attributes. Others got similarly incomplete information that was presented via a complicated prose narrative text, akin to the way advertising presentations are often made. The narrative version said, "Imagine you are planning a vacation to beautiful Hawaii. With your XXX camera you now have 3 megapixels of picture resolution at your fingertips. The XXX is compact and lightweight (10 oz.), which means you can carry it with you almost anywhere. With its long flash range (15 feet) and long battery life (450 shots), it is easy to take many beautiful pictures of palm trees, beaches, and all the wonderful sights you would expect to see in a tropical island paradise." In this study subjects were more sensitive to what was left out of the ad when they were prompted to consider what they felt was important right after processing the ad (but before they produced a final overall evaluation of the product) compared to control subjects. Further, when the ad format used a low cognitive-load format, subjects were more sensitive to what was left out. Finally, the coaching effect was more pronounced among the subjects who characterized themselves as typically wanting to "rush to judgment." The coaching interrupted and altered their usual superficial ad processing style. In contrast, the subjects who described themselves as typically cautious and thorough did not benefit as much from the coaching, presumably because they were spontaneously less prone to omission neglect. It's important to note that the ad narrative in this study was a high cognitive-load narrative text that can be seen as an example of the use of high cognitive load as a deception tactic. It invites a person into elaborative favorable mental simulations by asking them to imagine hypothetical concrete scenarios. It combines specific quantitative information with vague verbal assertions. It closes with a lengthy thirty-four word sentence, two-thirds of which must be processed right after the last attribute disclosure is made. And, it presents the façade of an ad that is full of information because of the flowery, verbose language used, even though only five camera attributes were disclosed.

Coaching Consumers to Detect and Resist Corrupted Persuasion Tactics

Sagarin, Cialdini, Sherman, and Rice (2002) conducted experiments on teaching late adolescents to better cope with corrupted "authority tactics" in advertising. A corrupted persuasion tactic is a misleading execution of an otherwise fair, and potentially effective, method of social influence. Abundant research on source credibility effects demonstrates that consumers may be more readily persuaded when they are presented information by someone they believe is an actual expert or authority on the topic. Consequently, advertisers and marketers have long used actual experts and authorities in their campaigns, as well as imposters or pseudo experts who aid them in creating the illusion of expertise and authority. The Sagarin et al. (2002) studies are pioneering experiments on an important topic, and we can derive insights about the ingredients to an effective coaching program from a critical examination of the coaching method they executed. These studies and the thinking behind them provide a starting point for future researchers to learn from and move beyond. In addition to their studies, Sagarin and his colleagues present a thoughtful discussion about how to teach consumers informed resistance to deceptive advertising (Sagarin et al., 2002). In terms of our framework of deception protection skills, these researchers studied how to coach late adolescents to detect an advertiser's corrupted use of an imposter expert on the advertisement's topic, to evaluate the use of an imposter expert unfavorably and the use of a legitimate expert favorably, and to therefore strongly discount and/or carefully scrutinize any ad that features an imposter authority. They set several self-imposed practical constraints on the program they constructed, and those constraints affected the approach they took.

Sagarin et al. (2002) limited themselves to a brief (8 to 10 minute) one-shot coaching episode. They therefore focused on teaching subjects a simple classification rule that might be easy to learn and apply. They reasoned that this simplicity might increase the likelihood that subjects could master the rule quickly and then use it when faced with rapid-fire mass media advertising (e.g., traditional TV advertising). Further, they hoped to construct an intervention that could be easily incorporated into a variety of educational contexts. Significantly, in the actual materials used for teaching purposes, the task was framed as discriminating ethical versus unethical behavior by a marketer. Teaching an ethics lesson rather than just teaching deception detection added a layer of abstraction to the coaching program that should be noted. Three experiments were conducted. In each, the same basic method was used to teach subjects a discrimination rule the researchers believed was appropriate. Subjects in the coaching treatment first read a six-page discussion about the researchers' prescribed rule for evaluating the use of experts in advertisements, accompanied by six exemplar print ads. Subjects in the control condition in the study read a six-page discussion of the use of color and tone in ads, which used those same six exemplar ads as illustrations for that topic. The rule-teaching discussion used the following instruction: "How can we tell when an authority figure is being used ethically or unethically? For an authority to be used ethically it must pass two tests. First, the authority must be a real authority, and not just someone dressed up to look like an authority. Second, the authority must be an expert on the product he or she is trying to sell."

To illustrate this rule four of the six exemplar ads were meant by the researchers to illustrate what they considered to be unethical practices. These were a Web site ad for the *Wall Street Journal* showing a man dressed in a business suit; an ad for Rolex watches featuring former test pilot and race car driver Chuck Yeager; an ad for the National Milk Processor Promotion Board featuring celebrity Ivana Trump; and an ad for Hitachi Electronics that featured actor Craig T. Nelson. The coaching materials asserted that the Rolex ad featuring Chuck Yeager and the milk board ad featuring Ivana Trump were unethical practices that violated their rule because the researchers believed that the authorities were not experts on the products the ads were trying to sell. The materials further argued that the *Wall Street Journal* ad was an unethical practice because the man in the ad might or might not be a stockbroker, and that the ad did not provide a name or information about any credentials. Thus, the researchers concluded that the ad failed their first test and was therefore unethical because the model could be "just dressed up to look like an authority." The coaching materials also included two print ads that the researchers considered examples of good ethical practices because the researchers thought they used actual experts. These were an ad for Chubb Financial Services that featured Marcel Cockaerts who was described in the ad as the president of a major bank, and an ad for Northwest Airlines that reported survey data from J.D. Power and Associates, a firm that conducts consumer surveys.

The coaching materials argued as follows regarding the Chubb ad: "Here we see a man dressed in a nice suit standing in front of what looks like a very old building. ... Apparently he is the authority being used in the ad. But is this ad ethical? To answer that question, let's see if it passes the two tests. ... If we look at the caption next to him, we see that this is Marcel Cockaerts, president of Kredietbank, Brussels. He's got the credentials that let us know he's a real authority. ... This guy's for real. Does it pass the second test? Well, the ad is trying to sell insurance for banks. It makes sense that the president of an international bank would know a lot about bank insurance. ... Marcel Cockaerts is an expert on the product. Is this an ethical use of authority? The answer is yes."

In the first experiment Sagarin et al. (2002) coached subjects, using the rule they were taught, became more sensitized to, and discriminated with about ethical (legitimate, uncorrupted) versus unethical (illegitimate, corrupted) uses of an authority appeal in immediate judgments about the test ads' manipulative intent and persuasiveness. Compared to control subjects, the coached subjects judged the test ads that the researchers had picked to represent ethical practices to be less unfairly manipulative. The coached subjects also judged the ads thought by the researchers to be unethical to be slightly more manipulative and less persuasive than the controls; however, this downgrading effect was weak. The coached and control subjects did not differ much in judgments about the ads the researchers had deemed to be unethical. In a second experiment, an attempt was made to both replicate the results of the first experiment and track whether the coaching program effects extended over several days and generalized to a different context of advertising response than that of the training program. In the second study (Sagarin et al., 2002), the coached subjects again displayed more favorable immediate ratings than control subjects of test ads that the researchers picked as ethical authority appeals. However, in this study the coached subjects did not downgrade the supposedly unethical ads any more than the control subjects. After a 1 to 4-day delay, some of these same respondents were asked, in a classroom task, to rate two possible ads that might appear in the campus paper. One featured a doctor described as Dan Shroktel of the Minnesota Pain Institute, who discussed Excedrin, a pain reliever. The researchers considered this stimulus ad to represent an ethical, nondeceptive execution of an authority appeal. The other ad featured actor Jeff Goldblum, who discussed IBM Internet Television Services. The researchers created this ad to represent an unethical, deceptive authority appeal. Subjects rated their attitudes toward one or the other of these two ads, but they did not rate how manipulative or deceptive it seemed. There was a significant but weak carryover effect of the training session on these delayed ad evaluations such that on five-point scales, the control subjects and coached subjects differed by about 0.3 scale points in their ratings of the two ads.

In a third experiment, Sargarin et al. (2002) examined the possibility that these college students saw themselves as invulnerable to advertising, and thus they were blasé about learning the deception protection lesson by doing a pilot survey. In this study, the researchers added an intervention to heighten the subjects' acute feelings of personal vulnerability and to moti-vate them to more deeply internalize the self-protection rule. Two versions of the intervention to convince students of their vulnerability were tested. Further, the researchers examined if coaching encouraged people into a simplistic mindless mode of message processing or a more elaborative cautious scrutiny of message content. Sargarin and his colleagues called the two approaches to elevating perceptions of personal vulnerability the "assessed vulnerability" approach and the "demonstrated vulnerability" approach. In the assessed vulnerability approach, subjects received a mod-ified version of the coaching materials used in the first two experiments. This material inserted some new language in several places to prompt a person to reflect on his or her vulnerabilities. For example, it said, after discussing that *Wall Street Journal* ad, "When you looked at this ad, did you notice that this stockbroker was a fake? Did you ask yourself whether you should listen to this so-called 'expert'? If you didn't, then you left your-self vulnerable to the advertisers that are trying to manipulate you." In the "demonstrated vulnerability" version, prior to any coaching, subjects were instructed to examine a sample ad on their own and rate how convinc-ing they found it. The ad was one that used (according to the research-ers' rules) an illegitimate authority appeal. The large majority of subjects rated that ad as at least "somewhat convincing" on a seven-point scale. Follow-up questions asked them to write down which two aspects of the ad were important in making their judgments that the ad was convincing. Then they received the same materials as the subjects in the "asserted vulnerability" condition, except that this time subjects were told to look back at their initial response to the first ad: "Take a look at Ad 1. Did you find the ad to be even somewhat convincing? If so, you got fooled." And, later, "Take a look back at your answer to the second question. Did you notice that the 'stockbroker' was a fake?"

In the third experiment (Sagarin et al., 2002) the researchers again created two test ads for subjects to examine, one meant as an example of an ethical (undeceptive) authority tactic and the other as an example of an unethical (deceptive) authority tactic. The ethical test ad, for Excedrin pain reliever, used a Dr. Daniel Schroeder, identified as director of the Minnesota Pain Institute, who was quoted as endorsing the product's pain relief effectiveness. The test ad created to represent a deceptive authority tactic was an ad for Internet Television Direct that quoted Arnold Schwartzenegger, movie star and governor of California, endorsing the superior technological sophistication of that product. Both ads also contained other claims about product features. The experimental design varied the number of claims and the relative strength (relevance, importance) of these claims. The results from this study showed that both asserting and demonstrating the subjects' potential vulnerability to being fooled by a questionable authority figure increased perceived manipulative intent ratings and decreased perceived persuasiveness ratings of the Excedrin ad (compared to uncoached control subjects). These results paralleled the effects found in the first and second experiments, which had been achieved without any special effort to elevate subjects' acute sense of vulnerability. However, for the first time in these studies, there was evidence that the coaching episode caused subjects to downgrade the use of an illegitimate authority in an ad. The subjects whose vulnerability to being fooled was demonstrated to them penalized the Schwartzenegger ad for Internet television services. They rated that ad's perceived persuasiveness lower than the other subjects did (including subjects who had been told, but not shown, that they were vulnerable to being fooled). However, the coached subjects' ratings of perceived manipulative intent apparently did not show this same effect. The data analyses also showed that in this study the subjects who received coaching on the ethics of authority tactics in ads did not rely solely on their perception that the person in the ad was or was not a legitimate authority, but also considered the ad's specific claims about the product.

In the context of deception coaching, this research highlights the importance of an individual's beliefs about their personal vulnerability to being misled. A sense of personal ineptitude or uncertainty about one's own deception protection skill heightens attention to the teaching interventions. The importance of people's perceptions of their own vulnerability has been cited for decades in the context of responses to health practices persuasion. Finding evidence that perceived vulnerability to marketers' deceptions moderates the impact of deception detection coaching is a valuable step. Sagarin et al. (2002) recommended that when feasible, an explicit demonstration to students of their susceptibility to being deceived be used, one that is unambiguous, proximal, and highly relevant. They cautioned, however, that doing this convincingly is often impractical or even unethical itself because it requires being deceptive to convince the subjects they are vulnerable to deception (e.g., giving them false feedback about their own prior performance or naivety). Further, prior research on self-efficacy beliefs indicates that someone's self-efficacy beliefs about a task domain will usually not be easily altered. We suggest that adolescents and young adults, like those in the Sagarin et al. (2002) studies, do not really have strongly held, entrenched beliefs about how good or bad their deception-protection skills are, but merely a façade which masks an underlying sense of insecurity.

Some choices Sagarin et al. (2002) made in designing their coaching program suggest to us ways to improve teaching materials in future consumer education studies and programs. The self-imposed constraint of a brief, one-shot teaching attempt drove these researchers to select a simplistic rule to teach to their subjects. This choice was made for reasons of practicality and convenience, but it does not allow the full use of explanation, interaction, practice, and feedback, all of which are vital to teaching skills to be applied in different real-world contexts. Nor does it facilitate teaching of somewhat complex but realistic conditional if–then judgment rules that help students navigate through different situations. Finally, it also risks understating or masking potential treatment effects. Further, choosing good examples for teaching and testing purposes is important. If real–world ads are to be used as teaching examples of a specific deceptive tactic, they should be chosen carefully to be unequivocal examples, not weak or questionable examples. This is especially tricky for illustrating a specific supposedly misleading communicator characteristic, like a person impersonating an expert or authority. Advertisers use people in ads for all sorts of reasons. Everyone in an ad is not there to impersonate an expert. In our judgment, some of the coaching ads and test ads in the Sagarin et al. (2002) experiments were questionable examples of marketers trying to mislead by having someone impersonate an expert. In some of those ads, the celebrities (e.g., Ivana Trump;

Chuck Yeager) were probably used mainly as an attention-getting tactic, not as a pseudo-expert on the topic. For example, the Ivana Trump ad was just one ad in a long-running (and award-winning) campaign by the milk board in which over 200 celebrities have appeared, including Elton John, Jackie Chan, Sheryl Crow, Danny Devito, Britney Spears, Muhammad Ali, the band Kiss, and Elvis Presley impersonators. Two-dozen cartoon characters have also been featured, including Batman and Bart Simpson. Clearly there was no intent to fool people that these entertainers and imaginary characters are experts or authorities on milk or nutrition. Also, sometimes in ads the person shown is meant to exemplify the target market the product is meant for, not to pose as a fake expert. The Chuck Yeager ad for Rolex watches was an example of this, as it was one execution from a long running campaign that had consistently featured Yeager. Indeed, Rolex designed and sold a model known as the Yeager watch. In fact, as a renowned Air Force test pilot and speed racer who actually wore Rolex watches during combat missions, Yeager's credentials as an authority on the durability and accuracy of precision electro-mechanical equipment seem fairly high. He is not a watch-making expert but he appears to have higher relevant expertise on the type of equipment advertised than do many other product endorsers featured in ads. As another example, in the ad about financial services that was used as an example of deceptive (unethical) impersonation of an authority, the person in the ad was simply someone dressed in a business suit, whose role there was so ambiguous that even the instructions that this was a deception said "we can't really tell who that person is." The danger in using questionable examples for teaching is that this muddies the concept being taught and can undermine the lesson's perceived validity. It can easily evoke counterarguing from students against the instructional lesson, those who readily realize that the celebrities and other people used in the exemplar ads are not being deceitfully presented as experts or may indeed actually have relevant expertise. Any ambiguity like this may disrupt the effectiveness of the teaching, and even cause students to wonder about the teacher's expertise.

Framing teaching about detecting deceptive tactics as teaching the students ethical lessons also adds unneeded baggage, and we suspect that the ethical framing attempted in these studies weakened the effectiveness of the coaching. Ethical judgments derive from abstract belief systems, and are contingent and complicated. When a teacher simply offers up his or her own personal belief about what is or is not ethical, that alone will not and should not be convincing to late adolescents. Other aspects of the procedures used by Sagarin et al. (2002) should be noted when future researchers continue the line of research. The stimulus ads used as exemplars for teaching dealt with low-involvement products to these students, and the situation itself muted involvement in making a personal choice about the product. These students were not in the target markets for many of these products, and so were detached. In addition, the control subjects here were focused on critiquing the uses of color and tone in ads, so they represented both an untutored audience and a distracted audience, not just an untutored audience. Further, the subjects in the treatment conditions gave the tactics in the test ads low perceived manipulative intent ratings in general, so these tactics were not something they judged to be a bad action by the advertiser, or at least the tutoring failed to persuade them of that. Choosing more threatening tactics and marketing communication contexts for teaching purposes seems desirable.

Finally, we must take note of the teaching situation in the third experiment, where the ads were made up by the researchers, but then apparently presented to the students as if they were real ads. The fictional doctor in the "legitimate expert" Excedrin ad never really appeared in such an ad or said the things in the ad. Similarly, Arnold Schwartznegger never appeared in an ad for DIRECTV nor did he make the statements attributed to him by the researcher-created ad about technological issues. There are clear advantages to constructing ads for teaching purposes that illustrate what one wants to illustrate, rather than choosing messy real ads that may be murky examples. But still, it is ironic to be giving students an ethics lesson that using fake experts is unethical while presenting them fake stimulus ads that fake the use of fake experts. In designing teaching interventions about deception detection, researchers should consider candidly telling the students up front that an ad they constructed for teaching purposes is in fact a made-up ad. We propose that doing this will not weaken the teaching effect and may actually strengthen it. In any case, doing so avoids the irony of using deception to teach deception protection. We know Sagarin et al. (2002) were sensitive to this issue, and we highlight it here to bring it to the attention of less experienced researchers as they pursue research on this topic.

Coaching Adolescents to Cope With Deceptive Alcohol Advertising

Goldberg, Niedermeier, Bechtel, and Gorn (2006) designed, delivered, and tested an intervention program to help adolescents cope with the deceptive persuasion tactics used in advertisements promoting alcoholic beverages. Goldberg et al. described their program's goals as teaching adolescents that alcohol advertisers intentionally and recklessly target their ads at children and adolescents, and that they try to psychologically pressure youngsters into only doing one-sided, pro-drinking thinking. Other goals were to help adolescents develop their counterarguing and critical thinking skills regarding the claims and tactics in alcohol advertising, and to correct adolescents' mistaken beliefs that drinking is more prevalent among their peers than it actually is. Goldberg et al. constructed an elaborate coaching program adapted from Watson, Davis, Tyner, and Osborn's (1993) Adsmarts program, which the current researchers saw as having a media literacy focus that spent considerable time on issues such as the meaning conveyed by different camera angles. Goldberg et al. created a shorter program with five 50-minute sessions that could be administered within a 1-week period. They focused on teaching strategies for coping with alcohol advertising using the motivational elements found in the Adsmarts program, as well as elements derived from the persuasion knowledge model (Friestad & Wright, 1994). The program was implemented in fifteen 6th-grade classes.

The first day's session (Goldbeg et al., 2006) emphasized teaching students that alcohol advertising tries to deceive adolescents into believing that everyone drinks a lot; that alcohol advertisers target kids by placing ads where kids will see them and deceptively using young-looking actors in ads who the advertisers know will be aspiration-models to younger teens; and that ads aim to limit an adolescent's psychological freedom to decide for themselves whether or not to drink. The second session focused on teaching that alcohol ads present only "partial truths" that omit a lot of information unfavorable to the ad's pro-drinking theme. It gave students practice in mentally generating counter-scenarios, for example, when ads imply that drinking makes partying more fun, students tried imagining themselves getting sick and vomiting, missing school or work, letting other people down while hung-over, hurting themselves and others by driving drunk, doing out-of-control, unwanted, and unsafe sex, and abusing someone else physically or sexually. The third day's session taught about other deceptive persuasion tactics, such as attention-getting "hooks" (sex appeal, pop music, popular celebrities, humor), and "rub off" which is a simplified notion of the tactic of repeatedly associating drinking with positive things shown in the ads to make these associations accessible in adolescent's minds. The fourth day's session focused entirely on coaching the students to build their skills in counterarguing. This used analogical learning by first discussing how youngsters readily think of contrary ideas (e.g., by saying "yes, but" when parents ask them to do chores), and then teaching the subjects to simply transfer that same vigilance and contrariness to what alcohol advertisers try to get them to do. The last session provided even more practice in counter-seductive thinking. Students brought in alcohol beverage ads from magazines, then created their own "counter-ads" to run on an adjacent page that would persuade someone a year younger than themselves not to drink alcohol when they become a teenager.

The subjects' beliefs about ad tactics and self-efficacy in coping with alcohol advertising were measured either 2 hours or 7 days after the final coaching session (Goldberg et al., 2006). Control group subjects who had not received the coaching program completed these measures on the day of the last coaching session. More specifically, measures were taken of the program's effects on the 6th-graders' beliefs about deceptive persuasion tactics in alcohol advertising and their skill in recognizing (and countering) the tactics that had been discussed in the coaching program. The answers to ten questions on beliefs and tactic-recognition skills were scored as correct or incorrect, and summed into a persuasion knowledge score for each student. These overall persuasion knowledge scores were analyzed and reported, while the question-by-question accuracy scores were not presented in the published report. The results showed that the coaching intervention increased these sixth-graders' persuasion knowledge scores in the immediate and delayed measurements compared to the control group. The increase in accurate beliefs about alcohol advertising tactics was most pronounced among the students who had already started drinking alcoholic beverages. However, the increase in accurate beliefs was not especially strong overall. Students in the control group, with no program exposure, got about half the ten belief questions correct, while the coached students got seven questions correct. Goldberg et al. (2006) also measured the students' coping self-efficacy beliefs by asking subjects how much they agreed with two statements: (a) "When I am watching TV at home and I see ads for beer or other alcohol, I stop and analyze them carefully," and (b) "When I hear or see commercials now, I want to talk or argue back to them." The mean of the combined answers served as the measure and showed that on a four-point scale the coached subjects (mean = 2.5) held more confident beliefs about these coping activities than the uncoached subjects (mean = 2.1). Finally, we offer one speculation about the program's design, and that is that it may have aimed too low. As best we can tell, the program's lessons were not based on preliminary testing of what the uncoached students in this population already knew or believed. Given that the uncoached students got 50% correct on the postcoaching beliefs test, it appears that many of the ideas being taught were already well known by these students. Preliminary tests of specific deception tactic beliefs and deception detection skills in the product and advertising context(s) seem vital in order to decide what lessons to include and what to leave out of a coaching program aimed at a specific population.

Coaching Adolescents to Cope With Deceptive Cigarette Advertising

Pechmann, Zhao, Goldberg, and Reibling's (2003) study about the effects of exposure to antismoking television ads on adolescents adapted Roger's (1993) protection motivation theory framework to analyze the effectiveness of different message themes used in television messages meant to coach teens not to smoke. In Chapter 2, we discussed how protection motivation theory identifies the key factors that increase motivation or intention to self-protect from something harmful. This theory proposes that people do a threat appraisal and a coping appraisal in judging how much effort to invest in any form of self protection within specific domains. So a consumer's deception-related threat and coping appraisals influence the effort that will be expended in trying to learn better deception protection skills and applying those skills to a particular persuasive message. Accordingly, a consumer's motivation to invest seriously in deception protection is influenced by beliefs about (a) the severity of the harm from being deceived, misled, or unfairly persuaded; (b) their own vulnerability to (likelihood of) being deceived, misled, or unfairly persuaded; and (c) the benefits of doing successful deception protection. Further, a consumer's motivation to learn to do deception protection is also affected by beliefs about (a) already-attained self-efficacy in performing specific deception protection skills relevant to the immediate persuasion attempt, (b) the maximum level of protection that might be achieved in the immediate case from successfully performing one's repertoire of deception protection activities (response efficacy), and (c) the cognitive costs of trying to do that in the situation at hand. Pechmann et al. (2003) noted that real-world messages have often been used as stimulus messages in studies of protection motivation, and using that same approach, they examined 194 real-world, antismoking television ads that had been used in various states' antismoking communication programs from 1986 to 1997. They coded these ads according to seven main themes the ads employed. These themes were disease and death, endangers others, cosmetics (bad breath, yellow teeth), smokers are losers, refusal skills, selling disease and death, and deceptive marketing tactics. The last three of these categories are of special relevance here because they relate in theory to deception protection and persuasion protection beliefs and/or skills.

More specifically, the refusal skills antismoking messages in these ads showed adolescents overtly stating their refusal to smoke and stating aloud their attraction to and admiration for the person who refuses to smoke. Pechmann et al. described the message content of the refusal skills ads this way: "Attractive role models do not smoke because they view it as highly unappealing, and they refuse others' cigarette offers." One possible, but secondary, goal of the refusal skills messages could be to teach adolescents specific acts of resistance and to raise their perception that they can easily execute acts of resistance. However, the researchers point out that significantly altering people's entrenched self-efficacy beliefs can require intense coaching experiences that permit practice and mastery of the specific focal skills (Bandura, 1997).

The theme of "nasty" marketing tactics stressed that tobacco firms use powerful marketing tactics such as image advertising and targeting children, women, and minorities. In one such ad, cigarettes rain down on a schoolyard while a tobacco executive says: "We have to sell cigarettes to your kids. We need half a million new smokers a year just to stay in business, so we advertise near schools, at candy counters ... " Another ad features a former tobacco lobbyist who says, "Maybe they'll get your little brother or sister, or maybe they'll get the kid down the block, but one thing is perfectly clear to me, the tobacco companies are after children." Pechmann et al. (2003) interpreted these ads as attempts to teach adolescents new persuasion knowledge about cigarette marketing tactics. This knowledge, they speculated might cause adolescents to interpret cigarette ads quite differently than they had before seeing the ad; and perhaps motivate them to attempt to exert more control over such ads' effects on them in the future. However, Pechmann et al. (2003) doubted that these "marketing tactics" ads could actually enhance deception coping or persuasion coping skills, because these ads, much like the "refusal skills" ads, provided only passive demonstrations, not skill development coaching and opportunities. Finally, the "selling disease and death" ads argued that tobacco companies use deception to persuade people to buy their products, which are known to cause serious diseases and death. Pechmann et al. (2003) characterized these ads as stressing the severe health damage from smoking. They also speculated that these ads had the potential to enhance persuasion knowledge and feelings of self-efficacy at resisting cigarette ads. One such ad featured a former cigarette-advertising model with throat cancer who says, "I was a model in cigarette ads, and I convinced many young people to smoke. I hope I can convince you not to." A second ad shows a man whose brother portrayed the notorious Marlboro Man in cigarette ads and later died of lung cancer. The man says, "The tobacco industry used my brother ... to create an image that smoking makes you independent. Don't believe it. Lying there with all those tubes in you, how independent can you be?" Pechmann et al. (2003) proposed that such ads might increase self-efficacy beliefs among adolescents, although they noted that these ads were mainly focused on dramatizing the severity of harm caused by smoking.

Subjects were seventh graders and tenth graders from public middle schools and high schools located in middle and lower-middle class, ethnically diverse neighborhoods. Subjects were assigned to view a videotape that showed them all eight of the anti-smoking ads that used the same particular theme; for example, one group of subjects saw a group of eight "refusal-skills" ads, another group saw a set of eight "selling disease and death" ads, and so forth. Each ad was repeated twice on the videotapes (Pechmann et al., 2003). Additionally, one group of subjects saw a videotape that included an example of *each* of the seven different types of message themes. A control group saw a tape of anti-drunk-driving ads. All subjects were shown the videotapes in a classroom setting, and then completed a survey. The entire procedure took about fifty minutes. The dependent measures included a three-item measure of perceived self-efficacy at *refusing cigarette offers*. It asked how confident they were that they could say no, walk away, or change the subject if other people pressured them to smoke. A parallel, two-item measure of self-efficacy at *resisting tobacco marketing* asked how confident they were they could resist being fooled by cigarette advertisements and cigarette promotions. We believe that this measure is better interpreted as a measure of deception protection self-efficacy because it asks directly about "being fooled by" marketing activities. There was also a nine-item measure of perceived vulnerability to the health risks of smoking. However there were no measures of the adolescents' perceived vulnerability to the risks of being deceived, misled or unfairly persuaded by cigarette ads and promotions.

Pechmann et al. (2003) predicted that the ads would not have much effect on these subjects' perceived self-efficacy, and their data showed that none of these message executions affected the adolescents' perceived self-efficacy at refusing cigarette offers from others, or at protecting themselves from being fooled by cigarette ads or promotions. However, these ad exposures were not totally ineffective some of the message themes affected the subjects' beliefs about health risks and social approval, as well as their general smoking intentions. In addition, these researchers reported in a footnote that they had also measured some aspects of these adolescents' persuasion knowledge regarding tobacco marketing. They found that the "marketing tactics" and "selling disease and death" ads significantly increased persuasion knowledge compared to the control group. Further, watching the videotape that showed an example of each message theme also significantly increased persuasion knowledge; although as we would expect, this gain in declarative knowledge by itself had not bolstered subjects' feelings of self-efficacy at being able to skillfully resist tobacco marketing. Connie Pechmann told us that the study's authors had considered these gains in persuasion knowledge important and had included a full report in an initial version of their study. However, the journal reviewing process had relegated them to a footnote. The authors graciously sent us their measure of knowledge about tobacco marketing tactics. It asked subjects how strongly they believed that cigarette companies "aim their messages at children, aim their messages at minorities, aim their messages at women, hook customers by making smoking look desirable, need to look for new smokers to replace dead ones, lie to the public, make unsafe products, are not concerned that smoking can injure your health, just want to make money, and that cigarette marketing (ads, promotions) encourages you to smoke." So, the exposure to anti-smoking ads that coached youngsters about marketers' deception tactics and motives did affect beliefs about deception tactics and motives. To us these are notable findings that imply that exposing adolescents to even brief messages like these can help them grasp things about marketers' deception tactics, such as that youngsters who have weak deception protection skills are being targeted or that marketers sometimes lie and are motivated to deceive.

The "Off the Hook" Program to Reduce Participation in Telemarketing Fraud

Under the sponsorship of the American Association of Retired Persons (AARP), an interdisciplinary team of researchers conducted a unique program of six field experiments to learn how particular intervention tactics might increase vulnerable adults' resistance to telemarketing scams (AARP, 2003). This research team included a prominent social psychologist, Anthony Pratkanis, along with law enforcement specialists, social services caseworkers, volunteer peer counselors, and professional telemarketers. The basic idea was to design effective scam-protection coaching messages that could be transmitted to high-risk telemarketing victims over the phone, thereby creating a "reverse boiler room" akin to telemarketers' "scam boiler rooms" which are filled with people making fraudulent telemarketing sales pitches. This research was conducted out of the Telemarketing Victim Call Center (TVCC) in Los Angeles. These studies provide a unique example of one approach to doing research-aided training of consumers to improve their personal detection and protection skills. Readers may not be aware of these studies because they were not published in the mainstream academic literature, therefore we will discuss these studies in some depth because they provide a number of interesting insights.

The studies took as a practical constraint that the training messages could not take more than about 15 minutes to deliver (AARP, 2003). The subjects in all six experiments were real people whose names had been taken from actual "hot prospect" lists found in raids on financial-scam boiler rooms by the Federal Bureau of Investigation (FBI). These were people who had given personal information to a criminal marketer, and had been pre-qualified by scammers as likely targets. Experiment 1 tested a forewarning + fear type of coaching message where subjects first received either (a) a forewarning phone call or (b) a control phone call from someone at the TVCC. They were then called within five days by telemarketers working with the researchers who pitched a "rare coin investment" scam to them. The TVCC callers received a full day of training, and then made the training-program calls. The forewarning + fear messages told the subjects that the caller was calling from the TVCC as part of an FBI program to warn people "like yourself" whose names were found on telemarketers' lists of targets. The introduction thus sought to establish authority and to raise the person's acute sense of vulnerability. There was an initial rapport-building chat (Have you gotten any calls lately? What do you tell them?). Then, in order to reinforce their vulnerability, subjects were told that telephone frauds have cost victims huge amounts of money and typically target people named on prospect lists. Then subjects were told directly about specific "rare coins" scams being used that offered free gift enticements. They were instructed never to make an investment on the phone and given some general scam-detection tips. These training calls took 5 to 15 minutes. Control group subjects from the same prospect lists took part in a shorter

TVCC call asking about favorite TV programs. The subsequent telephone scam messages were made by professional telemarketers, who were told to ignore personal ethics and make the strongest pitch possible. Some novice telemarketers doing this for the first time also participated. The telephone scam message was designed to seem authentic and was based on actual telemarketing fraud scripts found by the FBI and the advice of an experienced scammer. It incorporated several persuasion tactics discussed in the persuasion literature, such as a foot-in-the-door, scarcity, appeals to reciprocity norms, and mental simulation requests. The scam participation rates for control and experimental subjects differed with thirty-seven percent of the forewarned subjects convinced to sign on to the scam versus about seventy-five percent of the unwarned control group subjects. Even more telling was that the professional telemarketers who made the pseudo scam calls convinced ninety-two percent of their control-group targets to take part versus only fifty percent of the forewarned subjects.

The second experiment (AARP, 2003) focused on charity fraud scams, with the initial call forewarning subjects about phony charity scams related to the September 11 terrorist attacks. These messages gave subjects two specific questions to ask of all charity telemarketers: (a) What is this charity's registration number? and (b) What percentage of donated money is given to charities? Finally, in the forewarning call the subjects were told not to donate money if a telemarketer cannot or will not answer both questions. The ensuing scam telephone pitch for a phony charity emphasized tactics such as scarcity, foot in the door and incentives. In this case, the telephone scammers convinced only fifteen percent of the trained subjects to donate to the phone charity versus fifty percent participation among the untrained control subjects. The training message in this experiment produced the biggest self-protection effect of the six tested. But, interestingly, none of the experimental subjects who refused the charity scam actually asked the two specific questions they were urged to ask; they all simply just hung up the phone. The authors' suggested some explanations for this message's high impact in getting subjects to resist the deception. First, at the time of the study this sort of scam was being discussed in the news media, and so it may have been generally more salient to the potential victims than is typically the case. Second, suggesting specific buffering tactics bolstered subjects' general feelings of self efficacy, even if they did not execute the suggested tactics but simply took a more aggressive escape (exit-the-phone-call) action. We note that these subjects were simply told about these two buffering tactics, but they did not practice executing them as part of the training intervention. Without some rehearsal and practice executing the tactics (asking these questions out loud), no tactic-performance skill development and procedural learning occurred as part of the intervention. So the subjects' subsequent failure to actually perform these specific buffering tactics (ask the two specific questions) when the deception attempt occurred is not surprising.

The third experiment (AARP, 2003) contrasted several different training message strategies. First, in a vividness approach, the TVCC caller asked the subjects to imagine a stranger knocking on the door wearing a ski mask whenever a telemarketer called. And the caller next asked them to imagine themselves hanging up the phone, just like they would not open the door to the masked stranger. These subjects also received a follow-up letter that repeated and reinforced this "masked stranger" analogy to telemarketers. A second experimental message used the same "masked stranger" script, and then also invited the subject to join an active fraud-fighter program that included receiving a kit and certificate, monitoring and reporting incoming telephone fraud calls, and talking to others about fraud resistance. The third experimental message used the "masked stranger" script, and added an active skills-rehearsal part at the end where the caller asked the subject to think about what he or she would say to resist a telephone scammer. Subjects were then asked to verbally respond to the following questions: What would you say on the phone? What would you do to get the scammer off the phone? What would you say to test if a telemarketer is a fraud? The subject thus self-generated specific verbal actions to take in their mind and had the opportunity to practice expressing these aloud to the caller. In this experiment, fifty percent of the control (no tutoring) subjects complied with the scammer, and subjects who got either the "masked stranger" call or the "masked stranger plus active fraud fighter" call had similar participation rates to the control group. Hence, those two message strategies did not increase scam resistance behavior. However, only twenty-three percent of the subjects who got the "masked stranger plus generate-and-describe your own buffering and resistance tactics" treatment were seduced into participating in the scam. The effectiveness of this treatment was probably due to engaging the subject in personal procedural learning, in which they self-generated a concrete set of actions and expressed/rehearsed the actions. By taking ownership of those tactics and making them memorable and personally executable, these subjects increased their own self efficacy and skill development.

In the fourth experiment (AARP, 2003) the warning message focused on resisting identity-theft telemarketing scams. It included what the authors called a "gotcha" tactic to try increasing the subjects' acute sense of vulnerability to an identity-theft phone call. Before the TVCC caller delivered the forewarning script used in the first experiment, they said, "All I need is for you to answer a few questions, OK? … Wait! Don't answer that question. Here's why. Answering it is the first step in [an identity theft scam] … I'm actually an FBI volunteer. We're warning people that giving out just a little bit of information such as I asked for gets you scammed … ." This gotcha tactic is meant to reduce a person's blasé sense of personal invulnerability by showing the person how readily they can get suckered. However the gotcha message did not increase resistance to the ensuing telephone scam call above that created by the forewarning message itself. These researchers speculated that these subjects might not have really had a sense of being personally invulnerable to identity theft, making this gotcha message superfluous. It may also be that this message was simply not effectively executed, either because it was not realistic enough to evoke much elaborative thought about one's own vulnerability, or because the immediate continuation of the caller's spiel suppressed such thinking (as described in Chapter 3).

Motivating consumers to want to improve their marketplace deception protection skills is critical to the success of skill-coaching programs. Motivating people to learn how to protect themselves from harm is, as it turns out, a well-studied topic. Historically, much of the relevant research has been done in the context of getting people to learn how to take actions that protect themselves from getting a disease or being injured. However, learning to self-protect from significant marketing deceptions should be no different from learning to self protect from smoking, unsafe sexual practices, dental diseases, breast cancer, heart attacks, and so forth. However, the deception protection coaching programs we have reviewed have not yet benefited much from explicit consideration of this research on self-protection in health care contexts. It may be that the relevance of that body of research has not been recognized, its application to deception protection training has not been apparent, or perhaps protecting people from being seriously deceived by marketers has just not seemed as important as protecting them from poor health practices.

Our analysis indicates several things directly applicable to designing deception protection teaching programs and message. Strong vulnerability appeals used with effective coaching messages and programs that build high self-efficacy beliefs and competency skills are the most effective methods for teaching self-protection. On the other hand, strong vulnerability appeals used with overly brief, unconvincing, weak, and ineffective methods of building coping skills and self-efficacy merely lead people to avoid or resist the coaching message itself. One criterion to use in analyzing deception protection coaching programs is: Did the program lead off with a strong, imaginative (and honest) method to make people feel acutely vulnerable to a specific threat of marketplace deception? And, did the program follow up that strong motivational method for increasing vigilance with a convincing, useful, learnable, customized program for teaching deception-protection skills?

10
Societal Perspectives
Regulatory Frontiers, Societal Trust, and Deception Protection Education

In this chapter we discuss some societal factors that influence and are influenced by marketplace deception. These include significant changes in communications technologies and marketing practices that affect consumers' self protection capabilities; challenges facing regulatory protections; deception effects on societal and marketplace trust; and societal efforts to teach consumers deception protection skills.

Changes in Communication Technology

New media always provide marketers with new opportunities for deception and give consumers new deception protection problems because of the particular skills needed to negotiate them. The pace of change in media has been dramatic. We provide a brief history of the whirlwind of media evolution to dramatize the acceleration over the last 10 years. From Roman times through the Middle Ages commercial messages were handwritten on walls or proclaimed by public criers. The birth of mass media occurred in the late 15th century after Gutenberg's invention of the moveable type printing press. Coincidentally or not, during that same period Nicolo Machiavelli, an undistinguished civil servant, authored a short treatise titled *The Prince*, which was published after his death, and which made Nicolo famous and "Machiavellian" a cultural synonym for cunning social influence and deceptive behavior. Printing technology saw some improvements over the next several hundred years but the spread of printed information was facilitated more by political and economic developments such as secular universities, libraries, and the growth of the merchant class (Sampson, 1974). Yet even into the 19th century, an apprentice stationed outside a retailer's door asking "What do you lack, sir?" was a large component of a company's total media budget. By the early 20th century in America, lavish print ads were common in adult magazines and children's magazines; the authors' collection includes a 1910 issue of the popular *Youth Companion* magazine that had as its front cover a full-page ad for Colgate toothpaste. The technology that really boosted mass communication occurred in the 1920s, when radio became widely available. The telegraph and telephone had preceded radio but they are exclusively one-to-one media. Radio hugely accelerated the development of mass markets and national brands. It has been described as the original WWW (worldwide wireless) (Hanson, 1998). The diffusion of television in the 1950s in America and then Europe advanced the trend toward mass markets. In the 1970s cable television increased the number of television channels, permitting finer segmentation and better targeting of particular markets.

On the eve of the 21st century, networked computers gained wide distribution. In 1994 the National Science Foundation ended both its subsidy of the Internet and the "acceptable use" policy that prohibited all but the most indirect commerce via the Internet (Hafner & Lyon, 1996). Within five years an estimated 160 million users were online and at this writing over 1.1 billion people have Internet access worldwide. As that only constitutes 17% penetration, (Internet World Stats, 2007), there is room for enormous growth. The Internet also allows deceptive attempts aimed at a large number of potential victims with no geographical restrictions at extremely low cost. Online message production technologies make marketplace media much more widely accessible both to buyers and sellers than ever before. Today, people with little or no special training can produce professional looking videos and post them in places where they can be accessed by millions of others. Making digitized alterations of photos and videos is something 12-year-olds can now do. Consider for comparison, the small number of sellers with the resources to make a production-quality television commercial that could be seen in a million households in 1965, compared to today. More noteworthy, consider the capacity to fake video now, compared to then. The speed of communication has also accelerated, with consequences for the speed of deception. Previous attempts to defraud people out of their life savings traditionally required days. Targets had to go to their banks, physically withdraw money, and hand it over to the scam artist. The online version of this requires only that they mistake a bogus financial information request for the real thing. In moments their accounts can be drained.

We highlighted earlier that when prior generations of consumers in America and other societies grew up, marketplace persuasion was not nearly as complicated and omnipresent as it is today. This is problematic to consumers' deception protection activities because the coaching they get from wise old adults may be ill-suited for today's media environments, and because it magnifies the task of making successful cross-context, cross-media transfers on their own of deception protection tactics and skills they have developed. To repeat ourselves and dramatize, between starting school and becoming an effective adult consumer, an early 21st-century youngster must learn to navigate competently through television advertising, Internet marketing, computer advergames, personal selling, point-of-sale displays, print advertising, telemarketing, direct mailings, service encounters and relationships, ambient marketing (via schoolbooks, vehicles, peers' clothing), stealth product endorsers, product placements, digital alterations of televised events and photos, brand extensions, blog marketing, cross-merchandising by corporate media conglomerates, viral or buzz marketing, public relations spin, character merchandising, event and sports marketing, interactive computer chatrooms, product usage instructions and risk warnings, lengthy purchase contracts, and so forth.

Rapid societal changes in the media and technological deception methods used by marketers place consumers in the position of continually having to learn to detect and cope with new forms, or seemingly new forms, of deceptive persuasion. When a marketer uses a deception tactic in a new-to-the-consumer communication medium, the consumer may not initially be effective in detecting and coping with that tactic in this unfamiliar context, even if they have dealt well with it in a more familiar context. For example, someone who has become wary of television ads in which actors are falsely portrayed as "experts" about a product may not be as suspicious and discerning when he or she first encounters people masquerading as "experts" in, say, Internet chat rooms or Web site visits, blogs, telemarketing calls or service relationships. The change of media and context put a person out of touch with deception protection skills they have developed in other situations. As the number and variety of marketing persuasion media and contexts grows, the more cross-context adaptations a person has to keep making to remain competent in handling misleading marketing. Regulatory institutions try to slowly adapt to keep pace with communication technology. When the Internet became commercial in 1994, regulators found that the existing legal framework was poorly equipped to handle the new online opportunities for deception. This led to the creation of such things as the FBI Internet Fraud Complaint Center and the OECD Guidelines on Cross Border Fraud. Further, continual innovation in product technologies places consumers in the position of continually having their product knowledge made obsolete. Consumers can no longer get by using their "craft knowledge," that is, their fairly accurate understanding of how products are made. For example, a consumer finds it very difficult to keep fully informed about or understand new developments in medical care practices and procedures, health care programs, and drugs. And, the complexities of health care plans, medical procedures and equipment, and the manufacturing of pharmaceuticals baffle most consumers. Detecting deceptiveness is especially challenging when someone has outmoded and inaccurate product knowledge.

Regulatory Protections

Patent medicine advertising full of deceptive claims was the leading product category advertised throughout the 19th century. Some people got sick on these medicines and some died, but mostly they parted with a great deal of money ($75 million by 1905; Young, 1967). But the seeds of societal efforts at consumer protection were sewn. Some magazines, notably the *Ladies Home Journal*, began to refuse patent medicine advertising (Norris, 1990). In 1906 Congress passed the Pure Food and Drug Act, which prohibited statements on the labels of proprietary medicines that were false or misleading. In this period the *Saturday Evening Post* ran a series of lengthy articles over several years that revealed to readers how advertisers, salesmen, con artists, and retailers in the "new world" of commerce went about influencing and fleecing customers. Textbooks and how-to courses explained the psychology of advertising and selling in terms surprisingly similar to what similar books and courses say today. Throughout the 20th century a series of laws and regulations further challenged unbridled caveat emptor. The Federal Trade Act (1914) established the Federal Trade Commission, the agency that would eventually play the largest role in regulating deceptive practices in the U.S. marketplace. Although the original provisions of the act were aimed at regulating unfair competition rather than at protecting consumers, the FTC soon began prosecuting companies for deception. In 1938 the act was amended to make its consumer protection role more formal, broadly prohibiting all marketplace unfair and deceptive acts or practices. The movement that became known as "consumerism" gained momentum in the last part of the 20th century.

Two events deserve particular mention. First, a 1962 speech to Congress by President John F. Kennedy outlined four basic consumer rights, which later became known as the Consumer Bill of Rights. These included the right to be informed, the right to safety, the right to choose, and the right to be heard (Evans, 1980). The first, the right to be informed, most directly addresses deception through protection against misleading information. Several laws of the 1960s and 1970s in the areas of financing, advertising, labeling, and packaging were aimed at this right. The second development that encouraged the consumerist movement was the publication of *Unsafe at Any Speed* (Nader, 1965), a book about the Chevrolet Corvair. Issues of consumer safety (another of Kennedy's consumer rights) are frequently implicated along with deception.

While the trend in regulation generally has been in favor of consumer protection, some recent legal developments tilt toward the seller. In the mid-1970s the Supreme Court established for the first time that commercial speech is afforded some First Amendment protection. False or misleading speech is not protected, but some more recent cases have shifted the burden of proof. For example, some FDA regulations requiring substantiation for questionable health claims have been overturned in the federal courts. These concern dietary supplements which, unlike drugs and food additives, are ordinarily marketed without prior FDA screening. Dietary supplements make such claims as decreasing the risk of cancer or heart disease. At this writing, such supplements can legally claim benefits that have not been scientifically proven as long as the claims are accompanied by "clarifying" disclaimers (Vladeck, 2000), disclaimers which themselves often appear to mislead and deceive. Courts can issue cease and desist orders and can fine offending companies for deceptive practices. Class action lawsuits for deceptive practices can result in a company having to make restitution to consumers who may have been harmed by a deceptive practice. Companies also can be ordered to provide corrective advertising, a remedy that has received particular attention from consumer researchers because its effectiveness rests on complex information processing mechanisms. Corrective advertising presumes that the effects of false or deceptive information can be undone by providing truthful information. The law does not try to regulate all forms of marketplace deception. For example, there is no attempt to keep a salesperson from pretending to be the customer's dearest friend. There is no prohibition against a salesperson giving poorly supported opinions about product quality in an authoritative tone of voice. The absence of regulation suggests that some kinds of deception cannot be regulated efficiently, that they are regulated by mechanisms other than the law, or that they are harmless or even beneficial (Alexander & Sherwin, 2003).

In particular, the current practices that are collectively called "stealth marketing" are problematic from a legal perspective (Goodman, 2006). E. P. Goodman educates consumer researchers about why consumers cannot expect to rely on societal protections from stealth marketing, and implicitly builds the case for why consumer researchers should step up and do the needed research. Understanding more about how consumers can cope with these inherently deceptive tactics is an important and challenging research opportunity. Goodman explains that American mass media law has long been hostile to stealth marketing via radio and television. For example, "payola" is illegal (unreported payment to get airplay of specific content or programming, directed toward employees of broadcast stations, program producers or program suppliers, via money, service, or any other valuable consideration), as is "plugola" (the on-air use of or promotion of products and services in which the person responsible for including the promotional material in the broadcast has a financial interest). Goodman (2006) argues that stealth marketing harms by damaging the quality of public discourse and the integrity of the media institutions that support and shape this discourse. She explains the advantages of explicit sponsorship disclosure requirements regarding any form of what is otherwise stealth marketing, as a way to mitigate this harm to trust and provide consumers with valuable deception protection information. Advertising in traditional print and broadcast media requires sponsorship disclosure except where that sponsorship of a marketing message is obvious to consumers. However, existing sponsorship disclosure laws fail to operate in the newer electronic media that claim most public attention. Existing law conceives of stealth marketing as a single set of practices. Goodman discusses the tradeoffs between creating a technology-neutral functional approach to required sponsorship disclosure and creating cumbersome media-specific laws.

We highlight these emerging issues about stealth marketing to prompt research on consumer self-protection capabilities in the current marketplace and future environments where covert deceptive practices will multiply. Legal protections will not do the job. And legal protections will not even be forthcoming if the legal community judges that those are too costly or ineffective, and that consumers can and should do skillful deception protection themselves re stealth marketing. Consumer research would presumably show that some forms of stealth marketing have different potential impacts, and are more or less easy for consumers to detect.

Research on consumer MDP skills related to stealth marketing tactics is an exciting and timely opportunity. These tactics include stealth forms of branded entertainment, branded journalism, and integrated marketing; messages embedded into what is or appears to be independent editorial content; unattributed news releases supplied by corporations; paid-for mouthing by journalists of corporate marketing messages; advertainment programming, such as paying and coaching broadcast networks to include messages helpful to a marketing campaign in the scripts and plots of sitcoms and dramas, and especially of "reality TV" programs and the now-ubiquitous product placements, some done so seamlessly that even savvy audiences will not detect them as such.

The "sophisticated consumer" concept has entered contemporary legal writings, especially regarding trademark law. Beebe (2005) introduced the concept of "search sophistication," which he describes as the consumer's capacity to distinguish between similar trademark uses and to recognize that specific mark uses designate different sources, thereby avoiding inferential confusion. Beebe also discussed the legal implications of "persuasion sophistication," which he defined as a consumer's opportunity to resist commercial persuasion attempts. Beebe (2005) derived the persuasion sophistication notion directly from work by consumer researchers on the persuasion knowledge model (Friestad & Wright, 1994); he refers to the PKM and related research as having important legal implications. Courts do try to consider degree of consumer sophistication. They do so via lay wisdom and intuition as substitutes for drawing on specific and persuasive evidence about consumer behavior, regarding issues of sophistication, skills, and knowledge. When there is a dearth of programmatic research on consumers' MDP skills, courts must continue to rely on lay intuitions. Turning that around, research on consumer MDP skills has the potential to become important input to regulatory and court proceedings, and thereby contribute in helping society do its share of deception protection, in complement to whatever consumers achieve from own personal deception protection activities.

The federal agency most responsible for monitoring deceptive practices in the U.S. is the Federal Trade Commission (FTC), especially its Bureau of Consumer Protection (BCP). The BCP conducts investigations, sues companies and people who violate the law, develops rules aimed at protecting consumers, and educates consumers and businesses about their rights and responsibilities. The BCP tries to be proactive and current in setting enforcement priorities, publishing reports, holding workshops, and proving the public with educational information. Much of what they do is directly aimed at helping to prevent deception. The BCP, like other under-financed under-resourced consumer protection institutions, sets priorities regarding the most troubling marketplace problem areas. Recently, in the early 21st century, health, nutrition, consumer finances, mortgage disclosure and identity theft problems are prominent. The BCP is also concerned with helping consumer segments that may need some special protection, especially children and the elderly, and to some degree Hispanic consumers for whom English is a second language. The BCP continues to pursue telemarketing and direct mail scams, but new online communication technologies are priorities both for enforcement and for education.

Consumer researchers who are trying to frame their own research questions about marketplace deception protection can get inspiration from learning more about the deception protection problems of most concern to the BCP's insightful deception sentries. Visiting the BCP's Web site is a good start. Among the research, educational, and enforcement goals currently important to the BCP are:

1. Combating deceptive advertising of fraudulent cure-all claims for dietary supplements and weight loss products
2. Monitoring and stopping deceptive Internet marketing practices that develop in response to public health issues
3. Monitoring and developing effective enforcement strategies for new advertising techniques and media, such as word-of-mouth marketing
4. Monitoring and reporting on the advertising of food to children, including the impact of practices by food companies and the media on childhood obesity
5. Monitoring and reporting on alcohol and tobacco marketing practices
6. Shutting down high-tech Internet and telephone scams that bilk consumers out of hundreds of millions of dollars a year
7. Ending deceptive telemarketing or direct mail marketing schemes that use false and misleading information to take consumers' money
8. Stopping fraudulent business opportunity scams
9. Stopping violations of the Do Not Call and CAN-SPAM consumer privacy protections

The consumer education topics currently highlighted are: (a) how best to provide consumer deception-protection advice online regarding automobiles, computers and the Internet, credit and loans, diet, health and fitness, education and scholarships, energy and the environment, ID theft, privacy and security, investments and business opportunities, and telemarketing and telephone services; (b) how best to educate consumers about protecting against identity theft and guarding their social security numbers; (c) how to help consumers cope effectively with the insidious, often deceptive practice of "negative option" marketing; (d) how to design better disclosure forms to reduce the deceptiveness of consumer mortgage disclosures; and (e) how to design disclosures about testimonials featured in ads to reduce consumer deception. The BCP also provides lengthy well-researched reports that consumer researchers concerned with deception will find educational. Examples include reports of the FTC's annual surveys of consumer fraud and identity theft in the U.S., and explanations of the background, rationale, and details of regulations on truth-in-lending, consumer leasing, equal opportunity credit, electronic funds transfers, college scholarship fraud, and Internet spam and spyware.

Readers should be pleased to learn that the FTC's instructions to companies about how to meet legal standards for non-deceptive behavior reflect many of the concepts discussed in this book. For example, the FTC's electronic document, "Dot Com Disclosures: Information About Online Advertising," states that online disclosures to prevent an ad from being misleading must be clear and conspicuous. In evaluating whether disclosures are likely to be clear and conspicuous in online ads, advertisers should consider the placement of the disclosure in the ad and its proximity to the relevant claim. Additional considerations are the prominence of the disclosure; whether items in other parts of the ad distract attention from the disclosure; whether the ad is so lengthy that the disclosure needs to be repeated; whether disclosures in audio messages are presented in an adequate volume and cadence, and visual disclosures appear for a sufficient duration; and whether the language in the disclosure is understandable to the intended audience. To make an online disclosure clear and conspicuous, advertisers are instructed to place disclosures near, and when possible, on the same screen as the triggering claim and to use text or visual cues to encourage consumers to scroll down a Web page when it is necessary to view a disclosure. When using hyperlinks to lead to disclosures, online marketers are told to make the link obvious; label the hyperlink appropriately to convey the importance, nature, and relevance of the information it leads to; use hyperlink styles consistently so that consumers know when a link is available; place the hyperlink near relevant information and make it noticeable; take consumers directly to the disclosure on the click-through page; and assess the effectiveness of the hyperlink by monitoring click-through rates and make changes accordingly. Online marketers are instructed to display disclosures prior to purchase, using disclosure placements well before and/or on the order page; prominently display disclosures so they are noticeable to consumers, in terms of the size, color, and graphic treatment of the disclosure in relation to other parts of the Webpage; ensure that other elements—text, graphics, hyperlinks, or sound—do not distract consumers' attention from the disclosure; make repeat disclosures, as needed, on lengthy Web sites and in connection with repeated claims; display visual disclosures for a duration sufficient for consumers to notice, read, and understand them; and use clear language and syntax so that consumers understand the disclosures. If a seller uses email to comply with an FTC disclosure rule requirement, the seller should ensure that consumers understand that they will receive such information by email, and provide it to them in a form that consumers can retain. Finally, from a regulatory perspective, "direct mail" solicitations include email. If email invites consumers to call the sender to purchase goods or services, that telephone call and subsequent sale must comply with the Telemarketing Sales Rule requirements. However, the FTC has insufficient resources to actually monitor and discipline all the companies whose marketing disclosures do not meet the FTC guidelines.

Deception in financial markets is rampant. The different perspectives on regulating deception in that specialized domain are interesting to consider. Until the 1970s the Securities Exchange Commission (SEC) prohibited futuristic disclosure as inherently unreliable and misleading. Subsequently, the SEC's stance steadily changed, buttressed by evolving academic finance theory, to require future disclosures that focus on material risks of future adversity. In the 1990s earnings reports that specified expectations and corporate pro forma figures that expressed "hopes" became common (Cunningham, 2005). The representational forms varied a lot, often using obfuscation techniques, omissions, and giddy future scenarios (simulations). Then, the Sarbanes–Oxley Act of 2002 cracked down to some degree. Forward-looking disclosure proponents choose to cater to the sophisticated, rather than ordinary investor, thus creating a charade that both investment professionals and lay consumers have equal "futuring" abilities, including deception protection. However, many observers believe that ordinary investors in the stock market and other investment markets simply trust in the managers' simulations of future financial returns. They argue that lay investors do not appreciate how much uncertainty there is in forecasting what will happen in a company's future and how much the forecasters are motivated to be unrealistic and deceptive (Cunningham, 2000). Managers may be so adept at concealing true value that potentially informed consumers find it prohibitively costly to generate their own value-relevant information. So this assures that the true value of stocks is not revealed through consumers' personal analysis informed by effective deception protection skills geared to financial forecasts (Pardes, 2003; Subrahmanyam, 2004). Hanson and Kysar (1999) reviewed behavioral evidence on the manipulability of probabilistic judgments and concluded that exploiting cognitive biases represents a profit-maximizing opportunity to firms and that marketers must excel at deception in order to stay apace of competition!

Deception's Effects on Societal and Marketplace Trust

At the societal level, pervasive marketplace deception could contribute to erosion of societal trust. A marketplace where nothing can be believed makes it impossible to reward marketers for offering better products than competitors, and erodes trust on a larger scale. A marketplace where instances of egregious deception seem to go unpunished and where deceptive marketers simply fold up shop, assume a new corporate identity, and reappear under a new disguise, doing the same scam and fraud tactics, frustrates and angers consumers. It is common in theorizing about trust to state the obvious idea that deceit somehow influences trust, but beyond that the trust literature says little about how variations in deceptive practices undermine or build trust between consumers and marketers. Deception could affect at the level of the individual consumer, for example, as their initial trust of a marketer erodes or builds while processing a potentially deceptive message or series of messages from the specific marketer, or from marketers in the same industry. Further, a marketing organization's internal level of trust among its employees—its culture—can be affected by the level and nature of employees' participation in marketplace deceptions, and the organization's apparent reliance on, tolerance for, and rewarding of managers' marketplace deceptions. Sanctioning deception or expecting marketing managers, salespeople, and front-line service employees to do deception as a job requirement will over time influence the internal deceptiveness of the employees with each other and the job satisfaction of employees. However, these possibilities remain to fully analyzed and studied.

Trust is a much discussed but still ambiguous concept. There seems to be a lot of definitional debate in the trust literatures, and many definitions of trust appear to reflect general lay knowledge and common sense notions. Rotter (1980) defined trust as a generalized expectancy held by an individual that the promises and statements of another individual or group can be relied on. Sociologists commonly define trust as a property of groups, linked to interrelationships between people, rather than measurable within an individual (Lewis & Weigert, 1985). Luhmann (1979) describes trust as a functional prerequisite for the very possibility of society. That is, without a certain level of trust all the social groups that we take for granted could not exist. Seen from this perspective trust is a form of social capital and is most noticeable where it is lacking (Fukuyama, 1995). A view popular with economists is that trust arises out of rational calculations, efficient rules of thumb, and knowledge of previous transactions. People rationally compute the probable costs and probable benefits for putting themselves at risk (Williamson, 1993). Transactions are organized to trade off the forces of opportunism and bounded rationality. Consumers have to guard against the hazards of opportunism while at the same time economizing on bounded rationality—avoid being cheated without working at it too much. Formal governance through many formal rules and contractual arrangements discourages opportunism but adds costs (like legal fees and costs of maintaining a bureaucracy). At the other extreme, informal trusting relationships lower costs as long as no one abuses the other's trust. In the marketing management literature general definitions abound, for example, trust exists when one party has confidence in an exchange partner's reliability and integrity or is willing to rely on an exchange partner in whom one has confidence, that is, someone who is trusted (Morgan & Hunt, 1994). Trust is thought to reduce complexity of market exchanges more quickly, economically, and thoroughly than making specific predictions about a specific marketer's likely behavior (Lewis & Weigert, 1985). Each person is able to trust based on the assumption that others in the social world do the same. Everyone trusts in the assumption that others trust (Luhmann, 1979). Cook, Hardin, and Levy (2005) explain what they call encapsulated trust as an effort-saving mechanism by which consumers simply trust that others in society are taking care of things and protecting the consumer's best interests. This argument for a cognitive leap of faith seems to be wrapped up with strong feelings and deeply held values. For people who have internalized the norms of close-knit communities certain behaviors and options become unthinkable. On the other hand, few decisions are expressly noncalculative. Even if they are, the decision to avoid calculation may itself be calculative. Williamson asserts that this kind of nearly noncalculative trust exists only in close personal relationships that would be seriously degraded if calculation were permitted, but that noncalculative trust does not and should not be predominant in commercial relations.

A number of authors have discussed possible antecedents of trust in buyer–seller relationships (Atuahene-Gima & Li, 2000; Doney & Cannon, 1997; Ganesan, 1994; McAllister, 1995; Sirdeshmukh, Singh, & Sabol, 2002). For example, trust levels may be affected by the degree of two-way communication, even to the point of involvement in each other's business or personal plans (Andersen & Weitz, 1992), commitment and sacrifice (Morgan & Hunt, 1994), and long-term orientation (Ganesan, 1994; Noordewier, John, & Nevin, 1990). Doney and Cannon (1997) proposed that trust development can entail a calculative process, a prediction process, a capability assessment process, an intentionality assessment process and a transference process from one trusted source to another. Aiken and Boush (2005) found that issues of privacy and security dominate online trust. Marketplace trust also has been studied in the context of mixed motive games (Heide & Wathne, 2006; Montgomery, 1998; Schurr & Ozanne, 1985).

Despite the abundant literature of trust, we found little analytic discussion of deception as a mediating factor in the development of trust. Beyond the general notion that suspected or apprehended deception probably erodes interpersonal trust, there is hardly any theoretical analysis or empirical research on the psychological processes by which consumers' deceptiveness judgments regarding different forms of observed deception tactics cause them to so severely punish marketers as to significantly undermine marketplace-level or societal trust. The relationship between perceived deception and the growth of distrust is, we suspect, complex. For example, what deceptive tactics under what conditions, if detected, anger and disappoint consumers so much that they penalize the perpetrator severely, vowing never again to trust that marketer? Do numerous instances of perceived deceptiveness by individual marketers really undermine someone's trust in the marketplace as an institution, or in the society within which that marketplace is embedded? What beneficial effects are there on a consumer's development of generalized distrust of increased self-efficacy beliefs in own marketplace deception protection skills? Do increased public consumer education programs that focus directly on building deception protection skills ameliorate growing marketplace distrust, through their effects on skill levels and/or the signal they give to consumers?

David Michaels (2008) recently discussed and documented a pervasive form of corporate deception in contemporary American society that seems threatening to societal trust. Michaels is an epidemiologist, director of the Project on Scientific Knowledge and Public Policy at George Washington University School of Public Health and Health Services, and was assistant Secretary of Energy for Environment, Safety, and Health in the Clinton Administration. He thoroughly exposes corporate and industry campaigns, aided by captive legislators, to create what we called in Chapter 3 "murk, uncertainty, and doubt" (MUD) regarding scientific findings and criticisms of industry products and practices. We cannot do justice to this impressive review. Anyone who has read our book to this point should absorb Michaels' full treatise. Two types of deceptions leap out. One is the attempt to cloud all scientific studies done by, or used by, critics of a company's products, mainly by hiring company-funded academic researchers to micro-critique the methodology in all such research, while ignoring the methodology used by the company itself in its own studies of product efficacy and safety. The second is the artful and deceptive ways in which company-funded researchers design the company's studies to generate deceptive findings, and the artful and deceptive ways in which companies then cherry-pick or frame their research results when presenting them as part of a marketing campaign. Michaels' analyzes these practices in many industries. The pharmaceutical industry's shenanigans are an example.

According to commentaries by distinguished scientists, pharmaceutical companies' commonly used methods for deception in designing studies of drug products include (a) testing the company's drug against a treatment that is well-known not to work or not to work very well; (b) testing a company's drug against too low a dose of the comparison drug because that will make the company's product appear more effective; (c) testing against too high a dose of the comparison drug because that will make the company's product appear less toxic; (d) publishing and presenting the results of a single multicenter trial many times in many places because that will suggest that multiple studies reached the same conclusion; (e) publishing or presenting only that part of a drug trial that favors the company's drug, and burying the rest of the results; (f) funding many studies but publishing and presenting only those that make the company's product look desirable, and (g) data dredging, sometimes called Texas sharpshooting: fire a bullet at a blank wall, draw a circle around it, and then claim that you got a bull's eye. In this case, a company's researcher dredges through data long enough and creatively enough to discover something spin-able, and the company's marketers showcase it.

Michaels says that most consumers and many researchers are astonished to learn that the drug companies can get away with these sorts of deceptions. He states from experience that the FDA ignores research reports a company submits to scientific journals because the agency knows these can be badly incomplete or dominated by spin, not substance. This still leaves physicians who rely on the medical literature deceived and misled in making treatment choices, and consumers who rely on physicians and on their own understanding of misleading presentation of studies in ads and marketing materials doubly deceived.

Societal Education on Deception Protection

For better or worse, adult communication is critical to youngsters' understanding of persuasion tactics and development of persuasion coping skills. So, the quality of the adult communication to youngsters looms large. Our impression from inspecting the academic and popular literatures on persuasion is that the popular vocabulary is so diverse that it will mainly confuse youngsters trying to develop their understanding of advertising and persuasion tactics. Further, much of what gets passed along via word of mouth or even well intended media literacy and life-skills educational programs for adolescents will not be very helpful to MDP skill development. Over the last quarter century there was a sharp increase in educational programs devoted to media literacy.

Media literacy is defined broadly and abstractly. It encompasses competence at critically analyzing the media-supplied messages of everyday culture, and at creating one's own well written messages in print, audio, video, and multimedia forms, as well as the ability to analyze and appreciate respected works of literature. Participants in media literacy debates have wide-ranging disciplinary backgrounds in such fields as media studies, the fine and performing arts, history, sociology, psychology, education and literary analysis, and include academics, high school English teachers, public health experts, screenwriters, advocates for children's television, communication policy specialists, elementary school teachers, video artists, musicians, the religious community, youth counselors and technology experts (Hobbs, 1998). Two things about this diversity of players seem important to us. First and foremost, consumer behavior scholars have not participated, by and large. This is unfortunate because it is in K-12 media literacy classes that youngsters start acquiring their formal education about advertising and marketing practices. Whatever media literacy teachers currently have to say to students reflects only limited awareness of the perspectives and knowledge of the consumer behavior academic community. Second, consensus is just beginning to emerge about a basic analytic framework for media literacy. Hence, there remains a significant opportunity for consumer behavior scholars to get involved in shaping the framework and helping with program design and materials.

Alternatively, it is useful to think outside the box of current K-12 media literacy programs and consider how our own field can effectively do the required research and then create specially designed programs and materials to tutor adolescents in MDP skills. This "our own way" route is highly appealing because media literacy programs are already crowded with topics. For example, media literacy programs discuss the economic and political structures that govern various types of media; provide training in analyzing and interpreting varieties of media content; and use hands-on media production activities as a learning tool (e.g., producing a newscast). They all teach about "media content" (i.e., what ideas, values, ideologies, characters or roles, behaviors, themes, topics, or persuasive appeals are "within" a message) regardless of whether it is on TV, in a magazine article, in a novel, or in public speech. Students are taught how to decode the intended explicit message; to explore intended or unintended implicit messages; to be aware of different content genres; and to be aware of the cultural, economic and institutional forces that cause certain types of messages to be transmitted and others to be avoided. Some programs teach about "media grammar" by discussing how production variables can be technically manipulated to alter people's perception of message content in print media (e.g., typeface designs; spacing; paper texture; text/graphic layouts), and in TV or film (e.g., visual fade outs; zooms; speed changes; electronic volume and tone). Some literacy programs also cover the implications within a society of choosing one medium versus another for a particular message, such as an e-mail invitation to a party versus a telephoned invitation; a political debate on radio compared to TV; being educated in a "print culture" versus an "electronic culture." However important all that is, it leaves scant room for teaching practical MDP skills effectively. Existing media literacy programs' treatment of advertising and marketing is, as well as we can tell, fairly superficial. Curriculum materials and teacher training do not reflect currently available knowledge about consumer behavior and make virtually no effort to help youngsters understand advertising in terms of basic psychological processes. Hence, the framework offered to students excludes information that is fundamental to the thinking of the marketers and to a person's natural development of knowledge about persuasion and advertising.

There is, we believe, a widespread implicit view among social scientists that teaching resistance to persuasion is a bad thing, because resistance to persuasion implies closed-mindedness, which is a barrier to education. Resistance connotes (even in dictionaries) anti-authority, anti-establishment behavior. When *"Viva le resistance!"* is shouted, the resistance being cheered is resistance to authority by people outside the establishment. While academics may think of themselves as mavericks, and other people persistently believe that academia is full of liberal thinkers, academics still want to preserve their authority and their mandate to change other people's minds. To be sure, academics advocate teaching students critical thinking skills, but those skills are not synonymous to practical deception protection skills. Books on teaching critical thinking barely mention anything to do with teaching deceptive detection, neutralizing or resistance skills.

A pro-deception value or at least a love–hate ambivalence about deception is deeply embedded in the American culture, in which national growth was based on deceptive land grabs, our nation's namesake (Amerigo Vespucius) was known to be a conniving scoundrel, and cultural heroes such as Huck Finn, Scarlett O'Hara, Harry Potter, Indiana Jones, Butch Cassidy, and Ulysses are applauded for being devilishly deceptive. Our American culture, like other human cultures, celebrates the use of deception in romance and courting, effective everyday parenting, and gracious peer and spousal interactions. Deception is depicted approvingly as clever and humorous throughout pop culture (television programs, movies and novels) and is in fact taught, practiced, and applauded in all levels of competitive sports and in games playing (board games and video games). We all seek out and pay for exposures to showings of deceptions, feints, surprise endings, exciting legal skirmishes, dramatic suspense and surprise plot twists, and theatrical performances. We enjoy paid-for escapism and willing suspensions of disbelief, and the suspense and surprise generated by entertaining deceptions (misdirection, omissions, concealments, impersonations) that we value and approve of, except when they are badly done and fail to deceive audiences successfully enough or "as promised," or sometimes when they are disapproved of for violating a sport's or art's implicit rules of deception.

Over the past 25 years, there has been an outpouring of writings that explain to persuasion professionals what psychologists have learned about doing successful persuasion. This pass-along of practical know-how on being an effective persuasion agent is a natural part of the continuing process by which expertise is transferred from the social sciences community to segments of the general society. And it is a potentially healthy process unless it is decidedly asymmetric, unless it favors one segment of society to the disadvantage of another, as it does now. Unfortunately for consumers, and for the general health of the marketplace, these teachings on persuasion and influence by influential psychologists have so far had much more impact on the behavior of persuasion professionals in society—such as marketers, salespeople, attorneys, and consultants— than on the behavior of individual consumers who are the targets of marketing campaigns. Selling one's expertise in how-to-do successful persuasion is apparently an age-old profession. For example, Campbell (2001) describes how Socrates' trainees converted themselves into well-paid consultants on how to persuade and deceive others. Today's marketplace is loaded with how-to-persuade books and tutorials from people whose vocation is professional persuasion. There are very few countervailing tutorials and self-help writings on how to recognize and resist deceptive persuasion.

Academic researchers are in part responsible for this imbalance. Social psychology and consumer behavior textbooks and courses on persuasion and influence can have three different emphases: (a) emphasizing what the research implies for how-to-practice persuasion successfully; (b) emphasizing how to persuade successfully while taking great precautions to assure your persuasion attempt is not misleading and deceptive; or (c) emphasizing how to self-protect yourself from other people, especially well-organized and well-coached marketers, who try to persuade and deceive you. If we inventoried such books or course syllabi, we would undoubtedly find a strong imbalance toward teaching persuaders how to persuade, with minimal teaching of how to persuade without misleading or deceiving, or of how to protect yourself from other people's deceptive persuasion tactics. To be sure, there is some weak value for self-protection learning purposes in simply describing to students how others execute effective persuasion, that is, how the deception agent thinks, but that stops far short of teaching adolescents or adults how they can operationally detect, cope with, and resist these tactics. Practical persuasion protection skills give people power, and power is something that older individuals tend to withhold from younger ones, more expert individuals tend to withhold from those who are less expert, and "tribes" of hunters with more understanding and skills want to withhold from prey. So it is not hard to understand why the societal process of educating people in MDP skills has been slow and sporadic.

It is time for countervailing research programs. One of the central goals of the transformative consumer research philosophy (Mick, 2006), and a central goal in this book, is to provoke more research on how people can learn deception protection skills. Developing a body of scientific knowledge on this will motivate us all to find ways to educate broad consumer segments in useful self-protection know-how to counter-balance, in part, the professional training of marketplace persuaders. Researcher-educators can and should play a more pro-social, pro-consumer role regarding deceptive marketing. Highlighting the behaviors of educators in models of marketplace phenomena is uncommon. However what the people in a culture believe about persuasion and deception is historically contingent—it changes over time. What people believe about deception and persuasion, and what they can learn to do with that knowledge, is affected by classroom teachings that continuously diffuse new research findings and alter popular conceptions, and (if available) by formal education programs in schools and universities that teach consumers how to skillfully cope with marketplace deception.

Then, there is selling of research expertise and services to directly aid in marketers' deception efforts regarding the public, the courts, and third-party observers. One example is the selling of research expertise to pollute survey findings, which become the fodder for misleading advertising claims or for defending scoundrel corporations from regulatory or civil court actions to prevent or punish their deceptions. We research professionals are highly trained in how to construct research procedures and questionnaire designs that generate unbiased results, or as unbiased as possible. We teach our students how to do valid and unbiased research. However, this expertise is turned on its head by consultants who apply it in-reverse to knowingly construct survey procedures that encourage responses favorable to a client company's marketing campaign or to a defendant corporation's case that it is not guilty of misleading and deceptive marketing. For example, in our experience, researchers designing surveys funded by companies or industry groups often build priming questions and priming effects into the study's procedures, to bias the answers consumers give to subsequent questions in ways that help the client's later deception efforts.

We recently reviewed the body of research on children's and adolescents' knowledge about advertising and persuasion (Wright, Friestad, & Boush, 2005). We concluded that this work, which occurred mainly in the 1970s and 1980s, is hard to interpret because of conceptual and methodological issues, and because at best it could only tell us what the parents of today's youngsters believed when they were youngsters. We wound up offering some general ideas about how to do better research on youngsters and advertising in the future. Then, we wrote this book to add some meat to those ideas.

There is a general dissatisfaction emerging, we believe, with how little we know about how to effectively educate people about marketplace

persuasion and deception practices. Sagarin and Wood (2007) summarized
the appallingly limited research on teaching or instilling resistance to persuasion. In doing so, they had to content themselves with inventorying some
general thoughts and recommendations about effective resistance by prominent persuasion researchers. Here are examples: Pratkanis and Aronson
(2001) suggest that consumers and others "monitor your emotions ... If
you feel that your emotions are being played on, get out of the situation
and then analyze what is going on" (p. 342). Similarly, Cialdini (2001) rec-
ommends that people be alert to the "rush of arousal" (p. 231), then "we
can take steps to calm the arousal and assess the merits of the opportunity
in terms of why we want it (p. 231)." Pratkanis and Aronson (2001) also
recommend that consumers should "think rationally about any proposal
or issue" (p. 342). "Attempt to understand the full range of options before
making a decision" (p. 342), and "Always ask yourself: What are the arguments for the other side?" (p. 344). Sagarin and Wood (2007) point out that
this amounts to telling people to switch from System 1 to System 2 processing. Pratkanis and Aronson (2001) recommend that people "Explore the
motivations and credibility of the source of the communication" (p. 342),
and "Avoid being dependent on a single source of information" (p. 345).
Pratkanis and Aronson (2001) and Sargarin & Wood (2007) suggest that
consumers try to separate the marketing and persuasion from the entertainment in media transmissions. Pratkanis and Aronson (2001) also recommend that we all should "support efforts to protect vulnerable groups
such as children from exploitative persuasion" (p. 344), "write companies
asking for proof of advertising claims" (p. 347), "support and extend efforts
to squelch deceptive advertisements" (p. 347), and "... eliminate misleading
labels and other deceptive practices" (p. 347). Cialdini (2001) suggests simply that consumers can protect themselves by asking themselves whether a
purported authority is truly an impartial expert; distinguishing situations
where social proof evidence is valid from those where it is not; trying not
to like a salesperson too quickly; being alert to favors that are actually part
of a compliance gaining tactic; and paying attention to feelings that they
are being duped "It occurs right in the pit of our stomachs when we realize
we are trapped into complying with a request we *know* we don't want to
perform" (p. 91).

It is disappointing that after four decades of intensive research on persuasion and consumer behavior, vague notions like those above are the
best that we can offer to help current and future consumers skillfully self-
protect from marketers' deceptive persuasion attempts. This dramatizes
the complete imbalance in the "science of persuasion and influence" as of

the end of the first decade in the 2001 millennium. The newer and next generations of consumer researchers and conscientious social scientists can and should seize the opportunity this void left by their elders presents. Pratkanis and Aronson (2001) recommend that we educate children about the techniques of influence and propaganda, and Sagarin and Wood (2007) echo this. We argue in this book that we need to go way beyond merely informing about the tactics of persuasion, and teach people effective skills to execute in detecting, neutralizing, resisting, and penalizing these deceptive persuasion tactics.

The key idea is to actually teach *adaptive* deception protection, in which people learn skillful situational thinking rather than a facade of blanket cynicism. Laypeople's cognitive psy-curity systems are typically "M&M" systems; like the well-known candy, they have a thin shell of outer protection that covers up a soft squishy interior core. Strengthening that interior core of knowledge and skills is what meaningful MDP education should be about. Theory-building, theory-based research that defines helping consumers to help themselves as its main long-term goal will make our field decidedly more prosocial and egalitarian, help the overall health of the marketplace, and make researchers feel good about themselves. Studying how people cope with and protect against deceptive persuasion in the marketplace and other social domains is an intellectually exciting research frontier. Wouldn't it be great if a decade from now abundant research has been done on how to help consumers acquire deception protection skills, and this research is widely applauded for its prosocial benefits?

References

Aaker, J., & Lee, A. (2001). "I" seek pleasures and "we" avoid pains: The role of self-regulatory goals in information processing and persuasion. *Journal of Consumer Research, 28,* 33–49.

AARP Foundation (2003). *Off the hook: Reducing participation in telemarketing fraud.* AARP Foundation: Washington, DC.

Adams, P. J., Towns, A., & Gavey, N. (1995). Dominance and entitlement: The rhetoric men use to discuss their violence towards women. *Discourse & Society, 6,* 387–406.

Ahluwalia, R. (2000). Examination of the psychological processes underlying resistance to persuasion. *Journal of Consumer Research, 27,* 217–232.

Ahluwalia, R., & Burnkrant, R. E. (2004). Answering questions about questions: A persuasion knowledge perspective for understanding the effects of rhetorical questions. *Journal of Consumer Research, 31,* 26–42.

Aiken, K. D., & Boush, D. M. (2006). Trustmarks, objective source ratings, and implied investments in advertising: Investigating online trust and the context-specific nature of internet signals. *Journal of the Academy of Marketing Science, 34,* 308–323.

Alba, J. W., & Hutchinson, J. W. (2000). Knowledge calibration: What consumers know and what they think they know. *Journal of Consumer Research, 27,* 123–156.

Amsel, E., Bowden, T., Contrell, J., & Sullivan, J. (2005). Anticipating and avoiding regret as a model of adolescent decision making. In J. E. Jacobs & P. A. Klaczynski (Eds.), *The development of judgment and decision making in children and adolescents.* Mahwah, NJ: Erlbaum, 119–156.

Anderson, E., & Weitz, B. A. (1992). The use of pledges to build and sustain commitment in distribution channels. *Journal of Marketing Research, 29,* 18–34.

Anderson, J. R. (1993). *Rules of the mind.* Hillsdale, NJ: Erlbaum.

Anolli, L., Balconi, M., & Ciceri, R. (2002). Deceptive communication theory (DeMit): A new model for the analysis of deceptive communication. In L. Anolli, R. Ciceri, & G. Riva (Eds). *Say not to say: New perspectives on miscommunication* (pp. 73–100). Amsterdam, Netherlands: IOS.

Arkes, H. R., Boehm, L. E., & Xu, G. (1991). Determinants of judged validity. *Journal of Experimental Psychology: General, 121,* 446–458.

Arnett, J. J. (2004). *Emerging adulthood: The winding road from the late teens through the twenties.* New York: Oxford University Press.

Aspinwall, L. G., & Taylor, S. E. (1997). A stitch in time: Self-regulation and proactive coping. *Psychological Bulletin, 121,* 417–436.

Baldwin, D. (2005). Discerning intentions: Characterizing the cognitive system at play. In B. D. Homer & C. S. Tamis-Lemonda (Eds.), *The development of social cognition and communication* (pp. 117–144). Mahwah NJ: Erlbaum.

Bandura, A. (1997). *Self-efficacy: The exercise of control.* New York: W. H. Freeman.

Barnett, S. M., & Ceci, S. J. (2002). When and where do we apply what we learn? A taxonomy for far transfer. *Psychological Bulletin, 128,* 612–637.

Barone, M. J. (1999). How and when factual ad claims mislead consumers: Examining the deceptive consequences of copy x copy interactions for partial comparative advertisements. *Journal of Marketing Research, 36,* 58–74.

Barone, M. J., Manning, K. C., & Miniard, P. W. (2004). Consumer response to retailers' use of partially comparative pricing. *Journal of Marketing, 68,* 37–47.

Bartholomew, A., & O'Donahue, S. (2003). Everything under control: A child's eye view of advertising. *Journal of Marketing Management, 19,* 433–457.

Baumeister, R. F., & Heatherton, T. F. (1996). Self-regulation failure: An overview. *Psychological Inquiry, 7,* 1–15.

Bearden, W. O., Hardesty, D. M., & Rose, R. L. (2001). Consumer self-confidence: Refinements in conceptualization and measurement. *Journal of Consumer Research, 28,* 121–134.

Beebe, B. (2005). Search and persuasion in trademark law. *Michigan Law Review, 103,* 2020–2072.

Bell, J. B., & Whaley, B. (1991). *Cheating and deception.* Transaction Publishers: New Brunswick, NJ.

Berthoud-Papandroupoulou, I., & Kilcher, H. (2003). Is a false statement a lie or a truthful statement? Judgments and explanations of children 3 to 8. *Developmental Science, 6,* 173–177.

Berti, A. E. (2005). Children's understanding of politics. In M. Barrett & E. Buchanan-Barrow (Eds.), *Children's understanding of society* (pp. 69–103). New York: Psychology Press.

Best, J. (2001). *Damned lies and statistics: Untangling numbers from the media, politicians, and activists.* Berkeley, CA: University of California Press.

Bettman, J. R., Luce, M. F., & Payne, J. W. (1998). Constructive consumer choice processes. *Journal of Consumer Research, 25,* 187–217.

Bither, S. W., & Wright, P. L. (1973). The self confidence—advertising response relationship: A function of situational distraction. *Journal of Marketing Research, 10,* 146–152.

Block, L. G., & Keller, P. A. (1995). When to accentuate the negative: The effects of perceived efficacy and message framing on intentions to perform a health-related behavior. *Journal of Marketing Research, 32,* 192–203.

Block, L. G., & Keller, P. A. (1998). Beyond protection motivation: An integrative theory of health appeals. *Journal of Applied Social Psychology, 28,* 1584–1608.

Bok, S. (1999). *Lying: Moral choices in public and private life.* New York: Pantheon.

Boush, D. M. (2001). Mediating advertising effects. In J. Bryant & J. A. Bryant (Eds.), *Television and the American family* (pp. 397–412). Mahwah, NJ: Erlbaum.

Boush, D. M., Friestad, M., & Rose, G. M. (1994). Adolescent skepticism toward TV advertising and knowledge of advertiser tactics. *Journal of Consumer Research, 21,* 165–175.

Breitmeyer, B. (1984). *Visual masking: An integrative approach.* Oxford: Oxford University Press.

Brinol, P., Rucker, D. D., Tormala, Z. L., & Petty, R. E. (2004). Individual differences in resistance to persuasion: The role of beliefs and meta-beliefs. In E. S. Knowles & J. A. Linn (Eds.), *Resistance and persuasion* (pp. 83–105). Mahwah, NJ: Erlbaum.

Broniarczyk, S. M., & Alba, J. W. (1994). The role of consumers' intuitions in inference making. *Journal of Consumer Research, 21,* 393–407.

Brown, C. L., & Krishna, A. (2004). The skeptical shopper: A metacognitive account for the effects of default options on choice. *Journal of Consumer Research, 31,* 529–539.

Brucks, M., Armstrong, G., and Goldberg, M. E. (1988). Children's use of cognitive defenses against television advertising: A cognitive response approach. *Journal of Consumer Research, 14,* 471–482.

Bruno, K. J., & Harris, R. J. (1980). The effect of repetition on the discrimination of asserted and implied claims in advertising. *Applied Psycholinguistics, 1,* 307–332.

Bugenthal, D. B. (2000). Acquisition of the algorithms of social life: A domain-based approach. *Psychological Bulletin, 126,* 187–219.

Buller, D. B., & Burgoon, J. K. (1994). Deception: Strategic and nonstrategic communication. In J. A. Daly & J. M. Wiemann (Eds.), *Strategic interpersonal communication* (pp. 191–223). Hillsdale, NJ: Erlbaum.

Buller, D. B., & Burgoon, J. K. (1996). Interpersonal deception theory. *Communication Theory, 6,* 203–242.

Buller, D. B., Strzyzewski, K. D., & Hunsaaker, F. G. (1991). Interpersonal deception: II. The inferiority of conventional participants as deception detectors. *Communication Monographs, 58,* 25–40.

Caffi, C. (1999). On mitigation. *Journal of Pragmatics, 31,* 881–909.

Campbell, J. (2001). *The liar's tale: A history of falsehood.* New York: Norton & Company.

Campbell, M. C. (1995). When attention-getting advertising tactics elicit consumer inferences of manipulative intent: the importance of balancing benefits and investments. *Journal of Consumer Psychology, 4,* 225–254.

Campbell, M. C., & Keller, K. L. (2003). Brand familiarity and advertising repetition effects. *Journal of Consumer Research, 30,* 292–304.

Campbell, M. C., & Kirmani, A. (2000). Consumers' use of persuasion knowledge: The effects of accessibility and cognitive capacity on perceptions of an influence agent. *Journal of Consumer Research, 27,* 69–83.

Campbell, M. C., & Kirmani, A. (2008). 'I know what you're doing and why you're doing it': The use of the persuasion knowledge model in consumer research. In P. Herr (Ed.), *The handbook of consumer psychology.* Mahwah, NJ: Erlbaum.

Carpendale, J., & Lewis, C. (2006). *How children develop social understanding.* Malden, MA: Blackwell.

Ceci, S. J., Markle, F., & Chae, J. (2005). Children's understanding of the law and legal processes. In M. Barrett & E. Buchanan-Barrow, (Eds.), *Children's understanding of society.* New York: Psychology Press.

Chaiken, S. (1987). The heuristic model of persuasion. In M. P. Zanna, J. M. Olson, and C. P. Herman. *Social Influence: The Ontario Symposium,* (Vol. 5, pp. 3–39). Hillsdale, NJ: Erlbaum.

Chaiken, S., Liberman, A., & Eagly, A. H. (1989). Heuristic and systematic information processing within and beyond the persuasion context. In J. A. Uleman & J. A. Bargh, (Eds.), *Unintended thought* (pp. 212–252). New York: Guilford.

Chiappe, D., Brown, A., Dow, B., Koonz, J., Rodriguez, M., & McCulloch, K. (2004). Cheaters are looked at longer and remembered better than cooperators in social exchange situations. *Evolutionary Psychology, 2,* 108–120.

Cialdini, R. B. (1999). Of tricks and tumors: Some little-recognized costs of dishonest use of effective social influence. *Psychology & Marketing, 16,* 91–98.

Cialdini, R. B. (2001). *Influence: Science and practice* (4th ed.). New York: Harper Collins.

Coates, J. (1988). Epistemic modality and spoken discourse. *Transactions of the Philological Society, 86,* 110–131.

Cohen, F., Lambert, D., Preston, C., Berry, N., Stewart, C., & Thomas, E. (2001). A framework for deception. Technical Baseline Report, United States Department of Defense.

Cook, K. S., Hardin, R., & Levi, M. (2005). *Cooperation without trust?* New York: Russell Sage Foundation.

Cotte, J., Coulter, R. A., & Moore, M. (2005). Enhancing or disrupting guilt: The role of ad credibility and perceived manipulative intent. *Journal of Business Research, 58,* 361–368.

Crawford, V. P. (2003). Lying for strategic advantage: Rational and boundedly rational misrepresentation of intentions. *American Economic Review, 93,* 133–149.

Cunningham, L. A. (2005). Finance theory and accounting fraud: fantastic futures versus conservative histories, *Boston College Law School Working Paper.*

Dal Cin, S., Zanna, M. P., & Fong, G. T. (2004). Narrative persuasion and overcoming resistance. In E. S. Knowles & J. A. Linn (Eds.), *Resistance and persuasion* (pp. 175–191). Mahwah, NJ: Erlbaum.

Darke, P., & Ritchie, R. J. B. (2007). The defensive consumer: Advertising deception, defensive processing, and distrust. *Journal of Marketing Research, 44*, 114–127.

Davis, B. P., & Knowles, E. S. (1999). A disrupt-then-reframe technique of social influence. *Journal of Personality and Social Psychology, 76*, 192–199.

DeCarlo, T. E. (2005). The effects of sales message and suspicion of ulterior motives on salesperson evaluation. *Journal of Consumer Psychology, 15*, 238–249.

DePaulo, B. M., Kashy, D. A., Kirkendol, S. E., Wyer, M. M., & Epstein, J. A. (1996). Lying in everyday life. *Journal of Personality and Social Psychology, 70*, 979–995.

DePaulo, B. M., Lindsay, J. J., Malone, B. E., Mulenbruck, L., Charlton, K., & Cooper, H. (2003). Cues to deception. *Psychological Bulletin, 129*, 74–99.

Depaulo, B. M., & Morris, W. L. (2004). Discerning lies from truth: Behavioral cues to deception and the indirect pathway of intuition. In P. A. Anders & L. A. Stromwall (Eds.), *The detection of deception in forensic contexts* (pp. 15–40). Cambridge, UK: Cambridge University Press.

DePaulo, B. M., Wetzel, C., Sternglanz, R. W., & Wilson, M. J. (2003). Verbal and nonverbal dynamics of privacy, secrecy and deceit. *Journal of Social Issues, 59*, 391–410.

Diehl, M., Semegon, A. B., & Schwartzer, R. (2006). Assessing attentional control in goal pursuit: A component of dispositional self-regulation. *Journal of Personality Assessment, 86*, 306–317.

Doney, P. M., & Cannon, J. P. (1997). An examination of the nature of trust in buyer-seller relationships. *Journal of Marketing, 61*(2), 35–51.

Eco, U. (1976). *A theory of semiotics*. Bloomington: Indiana University Press.

Ekman, P. (1992). *Telling lies: Clues to deceit in the market place, politics, and marriage* (2nd ed.). New York, NY: W. W. Norton.

Ekman, P., & Friesen, W. V. (1969). Nonverbal leakage and clues to deception. *Psychiatry, 32*, 88–106.

Escalas, J. E. (2007). Self-referencing and persuasion: Narrative transportation versus analytical elaboration. *Journal of Consumer Research, 33*, 421–429.

Escalas, J. E., & Luce, M. F. (2004). Understanding the effects of process-focused versus outcome-focused thought in response to advertising. *Journal of Consumer Research, 31*, 274–285.

Evans, J. R. (1980). A new approach to the study of consumerism. In J. R. Evans (Ed.), *Consumerism in the United States: An inter-industry analysis* (pp. 1–10). New York: Praeger.

Ettinger, D., & Philippe, J. (2007). A theory of deception. Working paper, Paris School of Economics.

Fein, S. (1996). Effects of suspicion on attributional thinking and the correspondence bias. *Journal of Personality & Social Psychology, 70*, 1164–1184.

Fein, S., Hilton, J. L., & Miller, D. T. (1990). Suspicion of ulterior motivation and correspondence bias. *Journal of Personality and Social Psychology, 58*, 753–764.

Fein, S., McCloskey, A. L., & Tomlinson, T. M. (1997). Can the jury disregard that information? The use of suspicion to reduce the prejudicial effects of retrial and inadmissible testimony. *Personality and Social Psychology Bulletin, 23*, 1215–1226.

Fennis, B. M., Das, E. H. H. J., Pruyn, A.Th. H. (2004). If you can't dazzle them with brilliance, baffle them with nonsense: Extending the impact of the Disrupt-then-Reframe technique of social influence. *Journal of Consumer Psychology, 14*, 280–290.

Fitzkee, D. (1945). *Magic by misdirection.* San Rafael, CA: Saint Rafael House.

Ford, G. T., & Calfee, J. E. (1986). Recent developments in FTC policy on deception. *Journal of Marketing, 50*, 82–103.

Frankfurt, H. G. (2005). *On bullshit.* Princeton, NJ: Princeton University Press.

Friestad, M., & Wright, P. (1994). The persuasion knowledge model: How people cope with persuasion attempts. *Journal of Consumer Research, 21*, 1–31.

Friestad, M., & Wright, P. (1995). Persuasion knowledge: Lay people's and researchers' beliefs about the psychology of advertising. *Journal of Consumer Research, 22*, 62–74.

Friestad, M., & Wright, P. (1999). Everyday persuasion knowledge. *Psychology & Marketing, 16*, 185–194.

Fukuyama, F. (1995). *Trust: The social virtues and the creation of prosperity.* London: Hamish Hamilton, Ltd.

Gaeth, G. J., & Heath, T. B. (1987). The cognitive processing of misleading advertising in young and old adults: Assessment and training. *Journal of Consumer Research, 14*(1), 43–54.

Galotti, Kathleen M. (2005). Setting goals and making plans: How children and adolescents frame their decisions. In J. E. Jacobs & P. A. Klaczynski (Eds.), *The development of judgment and decision making in children and adolescents* (pp. 303–326). Mahwah, NJ: Erlbaum.

Ganesan, S. (1994). Determinants of long-term orientation in buyer-seller relationships. *Journal of Marketing, 58*, 1–19.

Gardner, D. M. (1975). Deception in advertising: A conceptual approach. *Journal of Marketing, 39*, 40–46.

Gibbs, R. W. (2001). Intentions as emergent products of social interactions. In B. F. Malle, L. J. Moses, & D. A. Baldwin (Eds.), *Intentions and intentionality* (pp. 105–120), Cambridge MA: Bradford.

Gigerenzer, G. (2002). *Calculated risks: How to know when numbers deceive you.* New York: Simon & Schuster.

Gilbert, D. T. (1991). How mental systems believe. *American Psychologist, 46*, 107–119.

Gilbert, D. T. (2002). Inferential correction. In T. Gilovich, D. Griffin, & D. Kahneman (Eds.), *Heuristics and biases: The psychology of intuitive judgment* (pp. 167–184). Cambridge, England: Cambridge University Press.

Gilbert, D. T., Krull, D. S., & Malone, P. S. (1990). Unbelieving the unbelievable: Some problems in the rejection of false information. *Journal of Personality and Social Psychology, 59*, 601–613.

Gneezy, U. (2005). Deception: The role of consequences. *American Economic Review, 95*(1), 384–394.

Goffman, E. (1959). *The presentation of self in everyday life*. London: Penguin Books.

Goldberg, M. E., Gorn, G. J., Peracchio, L. A., & Bamossy, G. (2003). Understanding materialism among youth. *Journal of Consumer Psychology, 13*, 278–288.

Goldberg, M. E., Niedermeier, K. E., Bechtel, L. J., & Gorn, G. J. (2006) Heightening adolescent vigilance toward alcohol advertising to forestall alcohol use. *Journal of Public Policy & Marketing, 25*, 147–159.

Goodman, E. P. (2006). Stealth marketing and editorial integrity. *Texas Law Review, 85*, 83–157.

Grazioli, S. (2006). Where did they go wrong? An analysis of the failure of knowledgeable Internet consumers to detect deception over the Internet. *Group Decision and Negotiation, 13*, 149–172.

Grazioli, S., Jamal, K., & Johnson, P. E. (2006). A cognitive approach to fraud detection. *Journal of Forensic Accounting, 7*, 1–24.

Grazioli, S., & Jarvenpaa, S. (2000). Perils of internet fraud. *IEEE Transactions on Systems, Man, and Cybernetics, 30*(4), 395–410.

Grazioli, S., & Jarvenpaa, S. L. (2003). Deceived: Under target online. *Communications of the ACM, 46*(12), 196–204.

Grazioli, S., & Wang, A. (2001). Looking without seeing: Understanding unsophisticated consumers' success and failure to detect internet deception. *Proceedings of the 22nd International Congress on Information Systems*, 193–203.

Green, M. C., & Brock, T. C. (2002). In the mind's eye: Transportation-imagery model of narrative persuasion. In M. C. Green, J. J. Strange, & T. C. Brock (Eds.) *Narrative impact: Social and cognitive foundations* (pp. 315–341). Mahwah, NJ: Erlbaum.

Greene, J. O. (2003). Models of adult communication skill acquisition: Practice and the course of performance improvement. In J. O. Greene & B. R. Burleson (Eds.), *Handbook of communication and social interaction skills* (pp. 51–92). Mahwah NJ: Erlbaum.

Greene, J. O., & Burleson, B. R. (Eds.), (2003). *Handbook of communication and social interaction skills*. Mahwah, NJ: Erlbaum.

Gregan-Paxton, J., & John, D. R. (1997). Consumer learning by analogy: A model of internal knowledge transfer. *Journal of Consumer Research, 24*, 266–284.

Gregory, W. L., Cialdini, R. B., & Carpenter, K. M. (1982). Self-relevant scenarios as mediators of likelihood estimates and compliance: Does imagining makes it so? *Journal of Personality and Social Psychology, 43*, 89–99.

Grice, H. P. (1975). Logic and conversation. In P. Cole & J. L. Morgan (Eds.), *Syntax and semantics: Speech acts*, (Vol. 3, pp. 41–58). New York: Academic.

Guerin, B. (2003). Language as social strategy: A review and analytic framework for the social sciences. *Review of General Psychology, 7*, 251–298.

Hafner, K., & Lyon, M. (1996). *Where wizards stay up late: The origins of the internet*. New York: Simon & Schuster.

Hamilton, R. W. (2003). Why do people suggest what they do not want? Using context effects to influence others' choices. *Journal of Consumer Research, 29*, 492–506.

Hanson, J. D., & Kysar, D. A. (1999). Taking behavioralism seriously: The problem of marketing manipulation. *New York University Law Review, 74*, 630–749.

Harris, R. J. (1977). The comprehension of pragmatic implications in advertising. *Journal of Applied Psychology, 62*, 603–608.

Harris, R. J., & Monaco, G. E. (1978). Psychology of pragmatic implication: Information processing between the lines. *Journal of Experimental Psychology: General, 107*, 1–22.

Harris, R. J., Trusty, M. L., Bechtold, J. I., & Wasinger, L. (1989). Memory for implied versus directly stated advertising claims. *Psychology & Marketing, 6*, 87–96.

Hasher, L., Goldstein. D., & Toppino, T. (1977). Frequency and conference of referential validity. *Journal of Verbal Learning and Verbal Behavior, 16*, 107–112.

Hawkins, S. A., & Hoch, S. J. (1992). Low-involvement learning: Memory without evaluation. *Journal of Consumer Research, 19*, 212–225.

Higgins, E. T. (1997). Beyond pleasure and pain. *American Psychologist, 52*, 1280–1300.

Higgins, E. T. (2000). Making a good decision: Value from fit. *American Psychologist, 55*, 1217–1233.

Hobbs, R. (1998). The seven great debates in the media literacy movement. *Journal of Communication, 48*, 16–32.

Holmes, J. (1990). Hedges and boosters in women's and men's speech. *Language and Communication, 10*, 185–205.

Huber, J., & McCann, J. W. (1982). The impact of inferential beliefs on product evaluations. *Journal of Marketing Research, 19*, 324–333.

Internet World Stats. http://www.internetworldstats.com/stats.htm (accessed May 1, 2007).

Jaccard, J., & Wood, G. (1988). The effects of incomplete information on the formation of attitudes toward behavioral alternatives. *Journal of Personality & Social Psychology, 54*, 580–591.

Jacoby, J. (2001). The psychological foundations of trademark law: Secondary meaning, genericism, fame, confusion and dilution. *Trademark Reporter, 91*, 1013–1089.

Jacoby, J., & Hoyer, W. D. (1987). *The comprehension and miscomprehension of print communications*. Rahway, NJ: Erlbaum.

Jain, S. P., & Posavac, S. S. (2004). Valenced comparisons. *Journal of Marketing Research, 41*, 46–58.

Johar, G. V., & Roggeveen, A. L. (2007). Changing false beliefs from repeated advertising: The role of claim refutation alignment. *Journal of Consumer Psychology, 17,* 118–127.

Johar, G. V., & Simmons, C. J. (2000). The use of concurrent disclosures to correct invalid inferences. *Journal of Consumer Research, 26,* 307–322.

John, D. R. (1999). Consumer socialization of children: A retrospective look at twenty-five years of research. *Journal of Consumer Research, 26,* 183–213.

Johnson, P. E., Grazioli, S., & Jamal, K. (1993). Fraud detection: Intentionality and deception in cognition. *Accounting, Organizations and Society, 18,* 467–488.

Johnson, P. E., Grazioli, S., Jamal, K., & Berryman, R. G. (2001). Detecting deception: Adversarial problem solving in a low base rate world. *Cognitive Science, 25*(3), 355–392.

Johnson, R. D. (1987). Making judgments when information is missing: Inferences, biases, and framing effects. *Acta Psychologica, 66,* 69–82.

Johnson, R. D. (1989). Making decisions with incomplete information: The first complete test of the inference model. In T. K. Srull (Ed.), *Advances in consumer research* (Vol. 16, pp. 522–528). Provo, UT: Association for Consumer Research.

Kahneman, D., Slovic, P., & Tversky, A. (1982). *Judgment under uncertainty: Heuristics and biases.* New York: Cambridge University Press.

Kamins, M. A., & Marks, L. J. (1987). Advertising puffery: The impact of using two-sided claims on product attitude and purchase intention. *Journal of Advertising, 16,* 6–15.

Kardes, F. R., Fennis, B. M., Hirt, E. R., Tormala, Z. L., & Bullington, B. (2007). The role of the need for cognitive closure in the effectiveness of the disrupt-then-reframe influence technique. *Journal of Consumer Research, 34,* 377–385.

Kardes, F. R., Posavac, S. S., & Cronley, M. L. (2004). Consumer Inference: A Review of Processes, Bases, and Judgment Contexts. *Journal of Consumer Psychology, 14,* 230–256.

Kardes, F. R., & Sanbonmatsu, D. M. (1993). Direction of comparison, expected feature correlation, and the set-size effect in preference judgment. *Journal of Consumer Psychology, 2,* 39–54.

Kardes, F. R., & Sanbonmatsu, D. M. (2003). Omission neglect: The importance of missing information. *Skeptical Inquirer, 27,* 42–46.

Keller, P. A., & McGill, A. L. (1994). Differences in the relative influence of product attributes under alternative processing conditions: Attribute importance versus attribute ease of imaginability. *Journal of Consumer Psychology, 3,* 29–49.

Keller, P. A., Lipkus, I. M., & Rimer, B. (2003). Affect, framing and persuasion. *Journal of Marketing Research, 40,* 54–64.

Kirmani, A. (1990). The effect of perceived advertising costs on brand perceptions. *Journal of Consumer Research, 17,* 160–171.

Kirmani, A. (1997). Advertising repetition as a signal of quality: If it's advertised so often, something must be wrong. *Journal of Advertising, 26,* 77–86.

Kirmani, A., & Campbell, M. C. (2004). Goal seeker and persuasion sentry: How consumer targets respond to interpersonal marketing persuasion. *Journal of Consumer Research, 31,* 573–582.

Kirmani, A., & Wright, P. (1989). Money talks: Perceived advertising expense and expected product quality. *Journal of Consumer Research, 16,* 344–353.

Kirmani, A., & Zhu, R. (2007). Vigilant against manipulation: The effect of regulatory focus on the use of persuasion knowledge. *Journal of Marketing Research, 44,* 688–701.

Kivetz, R., & Simonson, I. (2000). The effects of incomplete information on consumer choice. *Journal of Marketing Research, 37,* 427–448.

Klaczynski, P. A. (2005). Metacognition and cognitive variability: A dual-process model of decision making and its development. In J. E. Jacobs & P. A. Klaczynski (Eds.), *The development of judgment and decision making in children and adolescents* (pp. 39–76). Mahwah, NJ: Erlbaum.

Knowles, E. S., & Linn, J. A. (2004a). The importance of resistance to persuasion. In E. S. Knowles & J. A. Linn (Eds.), *Resistance and persuasion* (pp. 3–10). Mahwah, NJ: Erlbaum.

Knowles, E. S., & Linn, J. A. (2004b). Approach-avoidance model of persuasion: Alpha and omega strategies for change. In E. S. Knowles & J. A. Linn (Eds.), *Resistance and persuasion* (pp. 117–148). Mahwah, NJ: Erlbaum.

Koslow, S. (2000). Can the truth hurt? How honest and persuasive advertising can unintentionally lead to increased consumer skepticism. *Journal of Consumer Affairs, 34,* 245–269.

Kramer, R. M. (1994). The sinister attribution error: Paranoid cognition and collective distrust in organizations. *Motivation and Emotion. 18,* 199–230.

Kreps, D., Milgrom, P., Roberts, J., & Wilson, R. (1982). Rational cooperation in the finitely repeated prisoners' dilemma, *Journal of Economic Theory, 27,* 245–252.

Kreps, D., & Wilson, R. (1982). Reputation and imperfect information. *Journal of Economic Theory, 27,* 253–279.

Kricorian, K., Wright, P., & Friestad, M. (2007). Detecting persuasive intent and informative intent. Working paper, Lundquist College of Business, University of Oregon.

Kruglanski, A. W. (1989). *Lay epistemics and human knowledge.* New York: Plenum Press.

Kruglanski, A. W., & Webster, D. M. (1996). Motivated closing of the mind: "Seizing" and "freezing." *Psychological Review, 103,* 263–283.

Lee, A. Y., & Aaker, J. L. (2004). Bringing the frame into focus: The influence of regulatory fit on processing fluency and persuasion. *Journal of Personality and Social Psychology, 86,* 205–218.

Levin, I. P., Schneider, S. L., & Gaeth, G. J. (1998). All frames are not created equal: A typology and critical analysis of framing effects. *Organizational Behavior and Human Decision Processes, 76,* 1490.

Levine, T. R., & McCornack, S. A. (1991). The dark side of trust: Conceptualizing and measuring types of communicative suspicion. *Communication Quarterly*, 39, 325–339.

Levine, T. R., Park, H.S., & McCornack, S. A. (1999). Accuracy in detecting truths and lies: Documenting the "veracity effect." *Communication Monographs, 66*, 125–144.

Lewis, J. D., & Weigert, A. (1985). Trust as a social reality. *Social Forces, 63*(4), 967–985.

Luhmann, N. (1979). *Trust and power*. New York: John Wiley & Sons.

Luna, B., Garver, K. E., Urban, T. A., Lazar, N. A., & Sweeney, J. A. (2004). Maturation of cognitive processes from late childhood to adulthood. *Child Development, 75*, 1357–1372.

Main, K. J., Dahl, D. W., & Darke, P. R. (2007). Deliberative and automatic bases of suspicion: Empirical evidence of the sinister attribution error. *Journal of Consumer Psychology, 17*, 59–65.

Malle, B. F., Moses, L. J., & Baldwin, D. A. (2001). The significance of intentionality. In B. F. Malle, L. J. Moses, & D. A. Baldwin (Eds.), *Intentions and intentionality*. Cambridge MA: Bradford.

Martin, M. C. (1997). Children's understanding of the intent of advertising: A meta-analysis. *Journal of Public Policy and Marketing, 16*, 205–216.

Masip, J., Garrido, E., & Herrero, C. (2004). Defining deception. *Anales de Psicología, 20*, 147–171.

Mazursky, D., & Schul, Y. (2000). In the aftermath of invalidation: shaping judgment rules on learning that previous information was invalid. *Journal of Consumer Psychology, 9*, 213–222.

McAllister, D. J. (1995). Affect- and cognition-based trust as foundations for interpersonal cooperation in organizations, *Academy of Management Journal, 38*(1), 24–59.

McCornack, S. (1997). The generation of deceptive messages: Laying the groundwork for a viable theory of interpersonal deception. In J. O. Greene (Ed.), *Message production: Advances of communication theory* (pp. 91–126). Mahwah: Erlbaum.

McCornack, S. A. (1992). Information manipulation theory. *Communication Monographs, 59*, 1–16.

McCornack, S. A., & Parks, M. R. (1986). Deception detection and relationship development: The other side of trust. In M. L. McLaughlin (Ed.), *Communication Yearbook 9* (pp. 377–389). Beverly Hills, CA: Sage.

McGuire, W. J. (1968). Personality and susceptibility to social influence. In E. F. Borgatta & W. W. Lambert (Eds.), *Handbook of personality theory and research* (pp. 1130–1187). Chicago, IL: Rand McNally.

McQuarrie, E. F., & Mick, D. G. (1996). Figures of rhetoric in advertising language. *Journal of Consumer Research, 22*, 424–437.

McQuarrie, E. F., & Mick, D. G. (1999). Visual rhetoric in advertising: Text-interpretive, experimental, and reader-response analyses. *Journal of Consumer Research, 26*, 37–54.

Mears, D. P. (2002). The ubiquity, functions, and contexts of bullshitting. *Journal of Mundane Behavior, 3*(2), 21 pages. http://www.mundanebehavior.org/issues/v3n2/mears.htm, accessed January 21, 2008.

Menon, S., & Kahn, B. (2003). Corporate sponsorships of philanthropic activities: When do they impact perception of sponsor brand? *Journal of Consumer Psychology, 13,* 316–327.

Meyer, R. J. (1981). A model of multiattribute judgments under attribute uncertainty and information constraint. *Journal of Marketing Research, 18,* 428–441.

Michaels, D. (2008). *Doubt is their product: How industry's assault on science threatens your health.* Oxford, UK: Oxford University Press.

Mick, D. G. (2006). Meaning and mattering through transformative consumer research. Presidential Address to the Association for Consumer Research. In C. Pechmann & L. L. Price (Eds.), *Advances in consumer research.* Provo, UT: Association for Consumer Research.

Miller, G. R., & Stiff, J. B. (1988). *Deceptive communication.* Beverly Hills, CA: Sage.

Miller, K., Joseph, L., & Apker, J. (2000). Strategic ambiguity in the role development process. *Journal of Applied Communication Research, 28,* 193–214.

Mitnick, K. D., & Simon, W. (2002). *The art of deception: Controlling the human element of security.* Indianapolis, IN: Wiley Publishing.

Moore, E. S., & Lutz, R. J. (2000). Children, advertising, and product experiences: A multimethod inquiry. *Journal of Consumer Research, 27,* 31–48.

Moses, L. J., & Baldwin, D. A. (2005). What can the study of cognitive development reveal about children's ability to appreciate and cope with advertising? *Journal of Marketing & Public Policy, 24,* 186–201.

Moses, L. J., & Carlson, S. M. (2004). Self-regulation and children's theories of mind. In C. Lightfoot, C. Lallonde, & M. Chandler (Eds.), *Changing Conceptions of Psychological Life.* Mahwah NJ: Erlbaum, 127–146.

Muthukrishnan, A. V., & Ramaswami, S. (1999). Contextual effects on the revision of evaluative judgments: An extension of the omission-detection framework. *Journal of Consumer Research, 26,* 70–84.

Muraven, M., & Baumeister, R. F. (2000). Self-regulation and depletion of limited resources: Does self-control resemble a muscle? *Psychological Bulletin, 74,* 774–789.

Nader, R. (1965). *Unsafe at any speed: The designed-in dangers of the American automobile.* New York: Grossman.

Nelms, H. (1969). *Magic and showmanship: A handbook for conjurers.* New York: Dover.

Noordewier, T. G., John, G., & Nevin, J. R. (1990). Performance outcomes of purchasing arrangements in industrial buyer-vendor relationships. *Journal of Marketing, 54,* 80–94.

Norris, J. D. (1990). *Advertising and the transformation of American society, 1865–1920.* New York: Greenwood Press.

Obermiller, C., & Spangenberg, E. R. (1998). Development of a scale to measure consumer skepticism toward advertising. *Journal of Consumer Psychology, 7,* 159–186.

Pardes, Troy A. (2003). Blinded by the light: Information overload and its consequences for securities regulation, *Washington University Law Review Quarterly, 81,* 416–485.

Pechmann, C. (1992). Predicting when two-sided ads will be more effective than one sided ads: The role of correlation and correspondent inferences. *Journal of Marketing Research, 29,* 441–453.

Pechmann, C., & Knight, S. J. (2002). An experimental investigation of the joint effects of advertising and peers on adolescents' beliefs and intentions about cigarette consumption, *Journal of Consumer Research, 29,* 5–19.

Pechmann, C., Levine, L., Loughlin, S., & Leslie, F. (2005). Impulsive and self-conscious: Adolescents' vulnerability to advertising and persuasion. *Journal of Public Policy & Marketing, 24,* 202–221.

Pechmann, C., Zhao, G., Goldberg, M. E., & Reibling, E. T. (2003). What to convey in antismoking advertisements for adolescents: The use of protection motivation theory to identify effective message themes. *Journal of Marketing. 67,* 1–18.

Petty, R. E., Briñol, P., Tormala, Z. L., & Wegener, D. T. (2007). The role of metacognition in social judgment. In A.W. Kruglanski & E. T. Higgins (Eds.), *Social psychology: Handbook of basic principles* (2nd ed., pp. 254–284). New York, NY: Guilford Press.

Petty, R. E., & Brock, T.C. (1981). Thought disruption and persuasion. In R. E. Petty, T. M. Ostrom, & T. C. Brock (Eds.) *Cognitive responses in persuasion* (pp. 55–80). Hillsdale, NJ: Erlbaum.

Petty, R. E., & Krosnick, J. A. (1995). *Attitude strength: Antecedents and consequences.* Mahwah, NJ: Erlbaum.

Petty, R. E., & Wegener, D. T. (1998). Attitude change: Multiple roles for persuasion variables. In D. Gilbert, S. Fiske, & G. Lindzey (Eds.), *The handbook of social psychology* (4th ed., Vol. 1, pp. 323–390). New York: McGraw-Hill.

Petty, R. E., & Wegener, D. T. (1999). The elaboration likelihood model: Current status and controversies. In S. Chaiken & Y. Trope (Eds.), *Dual-process theories in social psychology* (pp. 41–72). New York: Guilford Press.

Pfau, M., Comption, J., Parker, K. A., Wittenberg, E. M., An, C., Ferguson, M., Horton, H., & Malyshev, Y. (2004). The traditional explanation for resistance versus attitude accessibility: Do they trigger distinct or overlapping processes of resistance? *Human Communication Research, 30,* 329–351.

Pham, M. T., & Higgins, E. T. (2005). Promotion and prevention in consumer decision-making: The state of the art and theoretical propositions. In S. Ratneshwar and D. G. Mick (Eds.), *Inside consumption: Consumer motives, goals, and desires* (pp. 8–43). New York: Routledge.

Pratkanis, A. R. (2008). Social influence analysis: An index of tactics. In A. R. Pratkanis (Ed.), *The science of social influence: Advances and future progress* (pp. 17–82). Philadelphia: Psychology Press.

Pratkanis, A. R., & Aronson, E. (2001). *Age of propaganda: The everyday use and abuse of persuasion.* New York: W.H. Freeman.

Pratkanis, A., & Shadel, D. (2005). *Weapons of fraud: A source book for fraud fighters.* Seattle, WA: AARP Washington.

Preston, I. L. (1975). *The great American blow-up: Puffery in advertising and selling.* Madison, WI: University of Wisconsin Press.

Preston, I. L. (1994). *The tangled web they weave: Truth, falsity, and advertisers.* Madison: University of Wisconsin Press.

Rand, P. (1993). *Design, form and chaos.* New Haven: Yale University Press.

Richards. J. I. (1990). *Deceptive advertising: Behavioral study of a legal concept.* Hillsdale, NJ: Erlbaum.

Richards, J. I., & Preston, I. L. (1992). Proving and disproving materiality of deceptive advertising claims. *Journal of Public Policy & Marketing, 11,* 45–56.

Ritson, M., & Elliott, R. (1999). The social uses of advertising. *Journal of Consumer Research, 26,* 260–277.

Robertson, T., & Rossiter, J. R. (1974). "Children and commercial persuasion: An attribution theory analysis. *Journal of Consumer Research, 1,* 13–20.

Roese, N. J. (1997). Counterfactual thinking. *Psychological Bulletin, 121,* 133–148.

Rogers, R. W. (1983). Cognitive and physiological process in fear appeals and attitude change: A revised theory of protection motivation. In J. Cacioppo & R. E. Petty (Eds.), *Social psychophysiology: A source book* (pp. 153–176). New York: Guilford Press.

Rose, N. (1999). *Governing the soul: The shaping of the private self* (2nd ed.). London: Free Association Books.

Rowe, N. C. (2007). Logical modeling of negative persuasion. *Persuasive Technology,* 105–108.

Rucker, D. D., Petty, R. E., & Brinol, P. (2008). What's in a frame anyway? A meta-cognitive analysis of the impact of one versus two sided messages. *Journal of Consumer Psychology, 18,* 137–149.

Russell, C. (2002). Investigating the effectiveness of product placements in television shows: The role of modality and plot connection congruence on brand memory and attitude. *Journal of Consumer Research, 29,* 306–318.

Russo, J. E., Metcalf, B. L., & Stephens, D. (1981). Identifying misleading advertising. *Journal of Consumer Research, 8,* 119–131.

Sagarin, B. J., Cialdini, R. B., Rice, W. E., & Serna, S. B. (2002). Dispelling the illusion of invulnerability: The motivations and mechanisms of resistance to persuasion. *Journal of Personality and Social Psychology, 83,* 526–541.

Sagarin, B. J., & Wood, S. E. (2007). Resistance to influence. In A. R. Pratkanis (Ed.), *The science of social influence: Advances and future progress* (pp. 321–340). New York, NY: Psychology Press.

Sanbonmatsu, D. M., Kardes, F. R., & Herr, P. M. (1992). The role of prior knowledge and missing information in multiattribute evaluation. *Organizational Behavior & Human Decision Processes, 51,* 76–91.

Sanbonmatsu, D. M., Kardes, F. R., Houghton, D. C., Ho, E. A., & Posavac, S. S. (2003). Overestimating the importance of the given information in multiattribute consumer judgment. *Journal of Consumer Psychology, 13,* 289–300.

Sanbonmatsu, D. M., Kardes, F. R., Posavac, S. S., & Houghton, D. C. (1997). Contextual influences on judgment based on limited information. *Organizational Behavior & Human Decision Processes, 69,* 251–264.

Sanbonmatsu, D. M., Kardes, F. R., & Sansone, C. (1991). Remembering less and inferring more: The effects of the timing of judgment on inferences about unknown attributes. *Journal of Personality & Social Psychology, 61,* 546–554.

Schul, Y., Burnstein, E., & Bardi, A. (1996). Dealing with deceptions that are difficult to detect: Encoding and judgment as a function of preparing to receive invalid information. *Journal of Experimental Social Psychology, 32,* 228–253.

Schul, Y., Mayo, R., & Burnstein, E. (2004). Encoding under trust and distrust: The spontaneous activation of incongruent cognitions. *Journal of Personality and Social Psychology, 86*(5), 668–679.

Schul, Y., Mayo, R., Burnstein, E., & Yahalom, N. (2007). How people cope with uncertainty due to chance or deception. *Journal of Experimental Social Psychology, 43*(1), 91–103.

Schurr, P. H., & Ozanne, J. L. (1985). Influences on exchange processes: Buyers' preconceptions of a seller's trustworthiness and bargaining toughness. *Journal of Consumer Research, 11,* 939–953.

Schwarz, N. (2004). Meta-cognitive experiences in consumer judgment and decision making. *Journal of Consumer Psychology, 14,* 332–348.

Scott, L. M. (1994). Images in advertising: The need for a theory of visual rhetoric, *Journal of Consumer Research, 21,* 252–273.

Sharpe, W. F. (2007). *Investors and markets: Portfolio choices, asset prices and investment advice.* Princeton NJ: Princeton University Press.

Shimp T. A. (1979). Social-psychological (Mis)representations in television advertising. *Journal of Consumer Affairs, 13,* 28–40.

Simmons, C. J., & Leonard, N. H. (1990). Inferences about missing attributes: Contingencies affecting use of alternative information sources. In M. Goldberg, G. Corn, & R. Pollay (Eds.), *Advances in consumer research* (Vol. 17, pp. 266–274). Provo, UT: Association for Consumer Research.

Simmons, C. J., & Lynch, J. G. (1991). Inference effects without inference making? Effects of missing information on discounting and use of presented information. *Journal of Consumer Research, 17,* 477–491.

Skurnik, I., Moskowitz, G. B., & Johnson, M. K. (2005). Biases in remembering true and false information: Illusions of truth and falseness. Unpublished Manuscript: University of Toronto.

Skurnik, I., Yoon, C., Park, D. C., Schwarz, N. (2005). How warnings about false claims become recommendations. *Journal of Consumer Research, 31,* 713–724.

Smetana, J. G., Campione-Barr, N., & Metzger, A. (2006). Adolescent development in interpersonal and societal contexts. *Annual Review of Psychology, 57,* 255–284.

Smith, H. M., & Betz, N. E. (2000). Development and validation of a scale of perceived social self-efficacy. *Journal of Career Assessment, 8,* 283–301.

Sowey, E. R. (2003). The getting of wisdom: Teaching statisticians to enhance their clients' numeracy. *The American Statistician, 57,* 89–93.

Speelman, C., & Kirsner, K. (2005). *Beyond the learning curve: The construction of mind.* Oxford: Oxford University Press.

Spence, M. (1973). Job market signaling. *Quarterly Journal of Economics, 87,* 355–374.

Sperber, D., & Wilson, D. (1986). *Relevance: Communication and cognition.* Oxford: Oxford University Press.

Sperber, D., & Wilson, D. (1995). *Relevance: Communication and cognition.* Oxford: Blackwell.

Stern, B. B. (1992). Crafty advertisers: Literary versus literal deceptiveness. *Journal of Public Policy and Marketing, 11,* 72–81.

Subrahmanyam, A. (2004). A cognitive theory of corporate disclosures. UCLA Anderson School Working Papers.

Szykman, L. R., Bloom, P. N., & Blazing, J. (2004). Does corporate sponsorship of a socially-oriented message make a difference? An investigation of the effects of sponsorship identity on responses to an anti-drinking and driving message. *Journal of Consumer Psychology, 14,* 13–20.

Taylor, S. E., Pham, L. B., Rivkin, I D., & Armor, D. A. (1998). Harnessing the imagination: Mental stimulation, self-regulation, and coping. *American Psychologist, 53*(4), 429–439.

Tobin, R. M., & Graziano, W. G. (2006). Development of regulatory processes through adolescence: A review of recent empirical studies. In D. K. Mroczek, & T. D. Little (Eds.), *Handbook of personality development* (pp. 263–284). Mahwah, NJ: Erlbaum.

Tormala, Z. L., & Petty, R. E. (2004). Resisting persuasion and attitude certainty: A meta-cognitive analysis. In E. S. Knowles & J. A. Linn (Eds.), *Resistance and persuasion* (pp. 65–83). Mahwah, NJ: Erlbaum, 65–83.

Tufte, E.R. (1997). *Visual explanation: images and quantities, evidence and narrative.* Cheshire, CT: Graphics Press.

Turnbull, W., & Saxton, K. L. (1997). Modal expressions as facework in refusals to comply with requests: I think I should say "no" right now. *Journal of Pragmatics, 27,* 145–181.

Vladeck, D. C. (2000). Truth and consequences: The perils of half-truths and unsubstantiated health claims for dietary supplements. *Journal of Public Policy and Marketing, 19*(1), 132–138.

Vohs, K. D. (2006). Self-regulatory resources power the reflective system: Evidence from five domains, *Journal of Consumer Psychology, 16*, 217–223.

Vohs, K. D., Baumeister, R. F., & Chin, J. (2007). Feeling duped: emotional, motivational, and cognitive aspects of being exploited by others. *Review of General Psychology, 11*, 127–141.

Ward, S., Wackman, D. B., & Wartella, E. (1977). *How children learn to buy.* Beverly Hills, CA: Sage Publications.

Webley, Paul (2005). Children's understanding of economics. In M. Barrett & E. Buchanan-Barrow (Eds.), *Children's understanding of society* (pp. 43–65). New York: Psychology Press.

Wegener, D. T., & Petty, R. E. (1997). The flexible correction model: The role of naïve theories in bias correction. In M. P. Zanna (Ed.). *Advances in Experimental Social Psychology, 29.* Mahwah, NJ: Erlbaum.

Wegener, D. T., Petty, R.E., Smoak, M.D., & Fabrigar, L.R. (2004). Multiple routes to resisting attitude change. In E. S. Knowles & J. A. Linn (Eds.), *Resistance and persuasion* (pp. 13–38). Mahwah, NJ: Erlbaum.

Wheeler, S. C., Brinol, P., & Hermann, A. D. (2007). Resistance to persuasion as self-regulation: Ego-depletion and its effects on attitude change processes. *Journal of Experimental Social Psychology, 43*(1), 150–156.

Wheeler, T. (2002). *Phototruth or photofiction? Ethics and media imagery in the digital age.* Rahway NJ: Erlbaum, 2002.

Williams, P., Fitzimons, G. J., & Block, L. G. (2004). When consumers do not recognize "benign" intention questions as persuasion attempts. *Journal of Consumer Research, 31*, 540–550.

Williamson, O. E. (1993). Calculativeness, trust, and economic organization. *Journal of Law & Economics, 36*, 453–487.

Wilson, S. R. (2002). *Seeking and resisting compliance: Why people say what they do when trying to influence others.* Thousand Oaks, CA: Sage.

Wilson, T. D., Centerbar, D. B., & Brekke, N. (2002). Mental contamination and the debiasing problem. In T. Gilovich, D. Griffin, & D. Kahneman (Eds.), *Heuristics and biases: The psychology of intuitive judgment* (pp. 185–200). Cambridge, England: Cambridge University Press.

Wright, P. (1973). The cognitive responses mediating the acceptance of advertising. *Journal of Marketing Research, 10*, 53–62.

Wright, P. (1975). Factors affecting cognitive resistance to advertising. *Journal of Consumer Research, 2*, 1–9.

Wright, P. (1981). Message-evoked thoughts: Persuasion research using thought verbalization. *Journal of Consumer Research, 7*, 151–175.

Wright, P. (2002). Marketplace metacognition and social intelligence. *Journal of Consumer Research, 28*, 677–682.

Wright, P., Friestad, M., & Boush, D. M. (2005). The development of marketplace persuasion knowledge in children, adolescents and young adults. *Journal of Marketing & Public Policy, 25*, 222–233.

Wyer, R. S., Jr., & Adaval, A. (2003). Message reception skills in social communication. In J. O. Greene & B. R. Burleson (Eds.), *Handbook of communication
and social interaction skills* (pp. 291–356). Mahwah, NJ: Erlbaum.

Wyer, R. S., Jr., & Radvansky, G.A. (1999). The comprehension and validation of
social information. *Psychological Review, 106,* 89–118.

Young, B. M. (1990). *Television advertising and children.* New York: Oxford
University Press.

Zaichkowsky, J. L. (2006). *The psychology behind trademark infringement and
counterfeiting.* Rahway, NJ: Erlbaum.

Zelazo, P. D., Astington, J. W., & Olson, D. R. (1999). *Developing theories of intention: Social understanding and self-control.* Mahwah, NJ: Erlbaum.

Zhou, L., Burgoon, J. K., Twitchell, D. P., Qin, T., & Nunamaker, J. F., Jr. (2004).
A comparison of classification methods for predicting deception in com-
puter-mediated communication. *Group Decision and Negotiation, 13,*
81–106.

Zuckerman, M., DePaulo, B. M., & Rosenthal, R. (1981). Verbal and nonverbal
communication of deception. In L. Berkowitz (Ed.), *Advances in experimental social psychology* (Vol. 14, pp. 1–59.) New York: Academic Press.

Author Index

A

Aaker, J., 37, 209, 218
Aaker, J. L., 37, 218
Adams, P. J., 66, 209
Adaval, A., 104, 226
Ahluwalia, R., 31, 116, 128, 209
Aiken, K. D., 199, 209
Alba, J. W., 35, 103, 209, 211
Amsel, E., 160, 209
An, C., 31, 221
Anderson, E., 144, 209
Anderson J. R., 144, 209
Anolli, L., 21, 26, 27, 43, 209
Apker, J., 66, 220
Arkes, H. R., 111, 210
Armor, D. A., 59, 60, 131, 132, 133, 224
Armstrong, G., 145, 148, 211
Arnett, J. J., 160, 210
Aronson, E., 206, 207, 222
Aspinwall, L. G., 131, 132, 133, 210
Astington, J. W., 104, 160, 226

B

Balconi, M., 21, 26, 27, 43, 209
Baldwin, D., 104, 154, 155, 156, 210
Baldwin, D. A., 104, 154, 155, 156,
    219, 220
Bamossy, G., 146, 215
Bandura, A., 136, 179, 210
Bardi, A., 96, 223
Barnett, S. M., 159, 210
Barone, M. J., 107, 115, 210
Bartholomew, A., 146, 210
Baumeister, R. F., 21, 37, 38, 135,
    210, 220, 225
Bearden, W. O., 139, 140, 210
Bechtel, L. J., 163, 175, 176, 177, 215
Bechtold, J. I., 163, 164, 165, 166, 216
Beebe, B., 193, 210
Bell, J. B., 43, 44, 210
Berry, N., 14, 15, 21, 39, 79, 80, 212
Berryman, R. G., 28, 126, 217
Berthoud-Papandroupoulou, I., 210

Berti, A. E., 146, 160, 210
Best, J., 71, 210
Bettman, J. R., 27, 62, 210
Betz, N. E., 138, 224
Bither, S. W., 137, 138, 210
Blazing, J., 115, 224
Block, L. G., 21, 36, 37, 64, 98, 115, 116, 179,
    211, 225
Bloom, P. N., 115, 224
Boehm, L. E., 111, 210
Bok, S., 211
Boush, D. M., xiii, xv, 34, 116, 145, 146, 147,
    148, 152, 199, 205, 209, 211, 225
Bowden, T., 160, 209
Breitmeyer, B., 46, 211
Brekke, N., 103, 225
Briñol, P., 21, 29, 31, 34, 35, 108,
    109, 129, 134, 211, 221, 222, 225
Brock, T. C., 45, 54, 128, 215, 221
Broniarczyk, S. M., 103, 211
Brown, A., 96, 212
Brown, C. L., 115, 211, 212
Brucks, M., 145, 148, 211
Bruno, K. J., 163, 165, 166, 211
Bugenthal, D. B., 156, 157, 211
Buller, D. B., 13, 21, 22, 23, 113, 119, 211
Bullington, B., 52, 67, 110, 111, 163,
    166, 167, 217
Burgoon, J. K., 13, 21, 22, 23, 113,
    119, 120, 211, 226
Burleson, B. R., 124, 215
Burnkrant, R. E., 31, 116, 128, 209
Burnstein, E., 96, 223

C

Caffi, C., 66, 211
Calfee, J. E., 214
Campbell, J. C., 204, 211
Campbell, M. C., 21, 38, 54, 105,
    107, 108, 116, 211, 212, 218
Campione-Barr, N., 16, 144, 160, 224
Cannon, J. P., 199, 213
Carlson, S. M., 154, 220
Carpendale, J., 154, 212

Carpenter, K. M., 60, 215
Ceci, S. J., 146, 159, 210, 212
Centerbar, D. B., 103, 225
Chae, J., 146, 159, 212
Chaiken, S., 21, 29, 35, 212, 221
Charlton, K., 22, 213
Chiappe, D., 96, 212
Chin, J., 21, 37, 38, 225
Cialdini, R. B., 21, 30, 31, 38, 49, 50, 51, 60, 137,
    163, 168, 169, 170, 172, 173, 174,
    175, 206, 212, 215, 222
Ciceri, R., 21, 26, 27, 43, 209
Coates, J., 66, 212
Cohen, F., 14, 15, 21, 39, 79, 80, 212
Compton, J., 31, 221
Contrell, J., 160, 209
Cook, K. S., 198, 212
Cooper, H., 22, 213
Cotte, J., 116, 212
Coulter, R. A., 116, 212
Crawford, V. P., 29, 212
Cronley, M. L., 56, 57, 102, 136, 217
Cunningham, L. A., 196, 212

D

Dahl, D. W., 100, 101, 219
Dal Cin, S., 54, 55, 213
Darke, P., 100, 101, 213, 219
Darke, P. R., 100, 101, 219
Das, E. H. H. J., 52, 110, 214
Davis, B. P., 176, 213
DeCarlo, T. E., 105, 213
DePaulo, B. M., 8, 12, 21, 22, 23, 65,
    119, 213, 226
Diehl, M., 139, 213
Doney, P. M., 199, 213
Dow, B., 96, 212

E

Eagly, A. H., 21, 29, 35, 212
Eco, U., 73, 153, 213
Ekman, P., 12, 21, 22, 23, 213
Elliott, R., 146, 222
Epstein, J. A., 8, 213
Escalas, J. E., 54, 60, 213
Ettinger, D., 21, 29, 213
Evans, J. R., 191, 213

F

Fabrigar, L.R., 31, 53, 135, 141, 225
Fein, S., 96, 99, 105, 213, 214

Fennis, B. M., 52, 67, 110, 111, 163, 166, 167,
    214, 217
Ferguson, M., 31, 221
Fitzimons, G. J., 115, 116, 225
Fitzkee, D., 46, 214
Fong, G. T., 54, 55, 213
Ford, G. T., 214
Frankfurt, H. G., 74, 75, 214
Friesen, W. V., 12, 21, 22, 23, 213
Friestad, M., xiii, xv, 14, 21, 32, 33,
    34, 38, 97, 100, 106, 114,
    115, 116, 117, 133, 145, 146,
    147, 148, 149, 151, 152,
    176, 193, 199, 205, 211,
    214, 218, 225
Fukuyama, F., 198, 214

G

Gaeth, G. J., 57, 62, 214, 219
Galotti, K. M., 160, 214
Ganesan, S., 199, 214
Gardner, D. M., 10, 214
Garver, K. E., 160, 219
Gavey, N., 66, 209
Gibbs, R. W., 104, 214
Gigerenzer, G., 70, 214
Gilbert, D. T., 103, 119, 214, 215, 221
Gneezy, U., 21, 29, 215
Goffman, E., 67, 74, 75, 76
Goldberg, M. E., 145, 146, 148,
    163, 175, 176, 177, 178,
    179, 180, 211, 215, 221
Goldstein. D., 111, 216
Goodman, E. P., 192, 215
Gorn, G. J., 146, 163, 175, 176, 177, 215
Graziano, W. G., 224
Grazioli, S., 21, 28, 43, 119, 126, 215, 217
Green, M. C., 54, 215
Greene, J. O., 124, 144, 215
Gregan-Paxton, J., 159, 215
Gregory, W. L., 60, 215
Grice, H. P., 24, 119, 215
Guerin, B., 65, 66, 67, 216

H

Hafner, K., 188, 216
Hamilton, R. W., 116, 214, 216
Hanson, J. D., 188, 197, 216
Hardesty, D. M., 139, 140, 210
Hardin, R., 198, 212
Harris, R. J., 67, 163, 164, 165, 166, 211, 216
Hasher, L., 111, 216

Hawkins, S. A., 111, 216
Heath, T. B., 57, 62, 214
Heatherton, T. F., 21, 37, 38, 135, 210
Hermann, A. D., 31, 134, 225
Herr, P. M., 103, 223
Higgins, E. T., 21, 35, 37, 60, 107, 216, 221
Hilton, J. L., 96, 99, 214
Hirt, E. R., 52, 67, 110, 111, 163, 166, 167, 217
Ho, E. A., 103, 223
Hobbs, R., 201, 216
Hoch, S. J., 111, 216
Holmes, J., 66, 216
Horton, H., 31, 221
Houghton, D. C., 103, 223
Hoyer, W. D., 10, 44, 216
Huber, J., 103, 216
Hunsaaker, F. G., 113, 119, 211
Hutchinson, J. W., 35, 103, 209

J

Jaccard, J., 103, 216
Jacoby, J., 10, 44, 216
Jain, S. P., 115, 216
Jamal, K., 21, 28, 43, 126, 215, 217
Jarvenpaa, S. L., 28, 215
Johar, G. V., 107, 111, 113, 137, 217
John, D. R., 146, 153, 159, 161, 199, 215, 217
John, G., 199, 220
Johnson, M. K., 113, 223
Johnson, P. E., 21, 28, 43, 126, 215, 217
Johnson, R. D., 103, 217
Joseph, L., 66, 220

K

Kahn, B., 115, 220
Kahneman, D., 62, 214, 217, 225
Kamins, M. A., 108, 217
Kardes, F. R., 52, 56, 57, 67, 102,
          103, 110, 111, 136,
          163, 166, 167, 217, 223
Kashy, D. A., 8, 213
Keller, K. L., 116, 212
Keller, P. A., 21, 36, 37, 60, 64, 98,
          115, 116, 179, 211, 212, 217
Kilcher, H., 210
Kirkendol, S. E., 8, 213
Kirmani, A., 105, 107, 108, 115,
          116, 212, 217, 218
Kirsner, K., 159, 224
Kivetz, R., 62, 218
Klaczynski, P. A., 160, 209, 214, 218
Knight, S. J., 146, 221

Knowles, E. S., 31, 32, 52, 53,
          110, 176, 211, 213, 218, 224, 225
Koonz, J., 96, 212
Koslow, S., 134, 218
Kramer, R. M., 101, 218
Kreps, D., 29, 218
Kricorian, K., 106, 218
Krishna, A., 115, 211
Krosnick, J. A., 128, 221
Kruglanski, A. W., 35, 99, 110, 111, 167, 218,
          221
Krull, D. S., 103, 119, 215
Kysar, D. A., 188, 197, 216

L

Lambert, D., 14, 15, 21, 39, 79, 80, 212
Lazar, N. A., 160, 219
Lee, A., 37, 209
Lee, A. Y., 37, 209, 218
Leonard, N. H., 103, 223
Leslie, F., 108, 146, 160, 161, 221
Levi, M., 198, 212
Levin, I. P., 62, 219
Levine, L., 160, 161, 221
Levine, T. R., 113, 118, 160, 218, 219, 221
Lewis, C., 154, 212
Lewis, J. D., 154, 198, 212, 219
Liberman, A., 21, 29, 35, 212
Lindsay, J. J., 22, 213
Linn, J. A., 31, 32, 52, 53, 110, 218
Lipkus, I. M., 217
Loughlin, S., 108, 146, 160, 161, 221
Luce, M. F., 27, 54, 60, 62, 210, 213
Luhmann, N., 198, 219
Luna, B., 160, 219
Lutz, R. J., 116, 145, 153, 220
Lynch, J. G., 103, 223
Lyon, M., 188, 216

M

Main, K. J., 100, 101, 219
Malle, B. F., 104, 214, 219
Malone, B. E., 22, 213
Malone, P. S., 103, 119, 215
Malyshev, Y., 31, 221
Manning, K. C., 107, 115, 210
Markle, F., 146, 159, 212
Marks, L. J., 108, 217
Martin, M. C., 97, 152, 153, 219
Mayo, R., 96, 223
Mazursky, D., 98, 100, 219
McAllister, D. J., 199, 219

McCann, J. W., 103, 216
McCloskey, A. L., 96, 99, 214
McCornack, S., 21, 22, 24, 25,
    26, 119, 219
McCornack, S. A., 113, 218, 219
McCulloch, K., 96, 212
McGill, A. L., 60, 217
McGuire, W. J., 127, 138, 219
McQuarrie, E. F., 73, 74, 219
Mears, D. P., 74, 75, 220
Menon, S., 115, 220
Metcalf, B. L., 166, 222
Metzger, A., 16, 144, 160, 224
Meyer, R. J., 103, 220
Michaels, D., 71, 72, 199, 200, 220
Mick, D. G., 3, 73, 74, 204, 219, 220, 221
Milgrom, P., 29, 218
Miller, D. T., 96, 99, 214
Miller, G. R., 11, 66, 99, 220
Miniard, P. W., 107, 115, 210
Mitnick, K. D., 79, 86, 88, 220
Monaco, G. E., 163, 165, 216
Moore, E. S., 116, 145, 153, 212, 220
Moore, M., 116, 212
Morris, W. L., 213
Moses, L. J., 104, 154, 155, 156, 214, 219, 220
Moskowitz, G. B., 113, 223
Mulenbruck, L., 22, 213
Muraven, M., 135, 220
Muthukrishnan, A. V., 103, 220

N

Nader, R., 191, 220
Nelms, H., 47, 220
Nevin, J. R., 199, 220
Niedermeier, K. E., 163, 175, 176, 177, 215
Noordewier, T. G., 199, 220
Norris, J. D., 190, 220
Nunamaker, J. F., Jr., 120, 226

O

Obermiller, C., 140, 221
O'Donahue, S., 146, 210
Olson, D. R., 104, 160, 226
Ozanne, J. L., 199, 223

P

Pardes, T. A., 197, 221
Park, D. C., 112, 224
Park, H.S., 113, 219
Parker, K. A., 31, 221

Parks, M. R., 21, 22, 24, 25, 26, 119, 219
Payne, J. W., 27, 62, 210
Pechmann, C., 108, 146, 160, 161, 163, 178,
    179, 180, 181, 221
Peracchio, L. A., 146, 215
Petty, R. E., 21, 29, 31, 34, 35, 45, 51,
    52, 53, 97, 103, 108, 109,
    110, 128, 129, 134, 135,
    141, 211, 221, 222, 224, 225
Pfau, M., 31, 221
Pham, L. B., 59, 60, 131, 132, 133, 224
Pham, M. T., 60, 107, 221, 224
Philippe, J., 21, 29, 213
Posavac, S. S., 56, 57, 102, 103, 115, 136, 216,
    217, 223
Pratkanis, A., 21, 30, 31, 49, 50, 51, 79, 88, 89,
    90, 182, 206, 207, 222
Preston, C., 14, 15, 21, 39, 79, 80, 212
Preston, I. L., 2, 9, 10, 14, 21, 67, 68, 212, 222
Pruyn, A.Th. H., 52, 110, 214

Q

Qin, T., 120, 226

R

Radvansky, G. A., 104, 226
Ramaswami, S., 103, 220
Rand, P., 47, 219, 222
Reibling, E. T., 163, 178, 179, 180, 221
Rice, W. E., 31, 137, 163, 168, 169,
    170, 172, 173, 174, 175, 222
Richards, J. I., 2, 9, 10, 222
Rimer, B., 217
Ritchie, R. J. B., 100, 101, 213
Ritson, M., 146, 222
Rivkin, I. D., 59, 60, 131, 132, 133, 224
Roberts, J., 29, 218
Robertson, T., 147, 148, 222
Rodriguez, M., 96, 212
Roese, N. J., 38, 222
Rogers, R. W., 21, 35, 37, 222
Roggeveen, A. L., 113, 217
Rose, G. M., 34, 116, 148, 152, 211
Rose, N., 67, 222
Rose, R. L., 139, 140, 210
Rosenthal, R., 22, 226
Rossiter, J. R., 147, 148, 222
Rowe, N. C., 56, 222
Rucker, D. D., 21, 29, 31, 34, 35, 108, 109, 129,
    134, 211, 222
Russell, C., 115, 222
Russo, J. E., 166, 222

S

Sagarin, B. J., 31, 137, 163, 168,
      169, 170, 172, 173, 174,
      175, 206, 207, 222
Sanbonmatsu, D. M., 103, 217, 223
Sansone, C., 103, 223
Saxton, K. L., 66, 224
Schneider, S. L., 62, 219
Schul, Y., 96, 97, 98, 100, 219, 223
Schurr, P. H., 199, 223
Schwartzer, R., 139, 213
Schwarz, N., 112, 223, 224
Scott, L. M., 73, 76, 223
Semegon, A. B., 139, 213
Serna, S. B., 31, 137, 163, 168, 169, 170, 172,
      173, 174, 175, 222
Shadel, D., 79, 88, 89, 90, 222
Sharpe, W. F., 28, 223
Shimp, T. A., 57, 223
Simmons, C. J., 103, 107, 217, 223
Simon, W., 79, 86, 88, 220
Simonson, I., 62, 218
Skurnik, I., 112, 113, 223, 224
Slovic, P., 62, 217
Smetana, J. G., 16, 144, 160, 224
Smith, H. M., 138, 224
Smoak, M.D., 31, 53, 135, 141, 225
Sowey, E. R., 70, 71, 224
Spangenberg, E. R., 140, 221
Speelman, C., 159, 224
Spence, M., 29, 224
Sperber, D., 25, 104, 224
Stephens, D., 166, 222
Stern, B. B., 73, 74, 224
Sternglanz, R. W., 12, 22, 213
Stewart, C., 14, 15, 21, 39, 79, 80, 212
Stiff, J. B., 11, 220
Strzyzewski, K. D., 113, 119, 211
Subrahmanyam, A., 197, 224
Sullivan, J., 160, 209
Sweeney, J. A., 160, 219
Szykman, L. R., 115, 224

T

Taylor, S. E., 59, 60, 131, 132, 133, 210, 224
Thomas, E., 14, 15, 21, 39, 79, 80, 212
Tobin, R. M., 224
Tomlinson, T. M., 96, 99, 214
Toppino, T., 111, 216
Tormala, Z. L., 21, 29, 31, 34, 35, 52, 67, 108,
      110, 111, 128, 129, 134, 163, 166,
      167, 211, 217, 221, 224

Towns, A., 66, 209
Trusty, M. L., 163, 164, 165, 166, 216
Tufte, E. R., 46, 47, 224
Turnbull, W., 66, 224
Tversky, A., 62, 217
Twitchell, D. P., 120, 226

U

Urban, T. A., 160, 219

V

Vladeck, D. C., 191, 224
Vohs, K. D., 21, 37, 38, 52, 135, 225

W

Wackman, D. B., 147, 225
Wang, A., 119, 215
Ward, S., 147, 225
Wartella, E., 147, 225
Wasinger, L., 163, 164, 165, 166, 216
Webley, P., 146, 153, 225
Webster, D. M., 110, 167, 218
Wegener, D. T., 21, 29, 31, 34, 35,
      51, 53, 97, 103, 129, 135,
      141, 221, 225
Weigert, A., 154, 198, 219
Weitz, B. A., 144, 209
Wetzel, C., 12, 22, 213
Whaley, B., 43, 44, 210
Wheeler, S. C., 31, 134, 225
Wheeler, T., 69, 70, 225
Williams, P., 115, 116, 225
Williamson, O. E., 198, 225
Wilson, D., 25, 104, 224
Wilson, M. J., 12, 22, 213
Wilson, R., 29, 218
Wilson, S. R., 225
Wilson, T. D., 103, 225
Wittenberg, E. M., 31, 221
Wood, G., 103, 216
Wood, S. E., 206, 207, 222
Wright, P., xiii, xv, 14, 21, 32, 33, 34, 35,
      38, 45, 97, 100, 106, 114,
      115, 116, 117, 128, 133, 137,
      138, 145, 146, 147, 148,
      149, 151, 152, 176, 193,
      205, 210, 211, 214,
      218, 225
Wright, P. L., 137, 138, 210
Wyer, M. M., 8, 213
Wyer, R. S. Jr., 104, 226

X

Xu, G., 111, 210

Y

Yahalom, N., 96, 223
Yoon, C., 112, 224
Young, B. M., 147, 148, 190, 226

Z

Zaichkowsky, J. L., 44, 226
Zanna, M. P., 54, 55, 213
Zelazo, P. D., 104, 160, 226
Zhao, G., 163, 178, 179, 180, 221
Zhou, L., 120, 226
Zhu, R., 107, 108, 218
Zuckerman, M., 22, 226

Subject Index

A

AARP. *See* American Association of Retired
    Persons (AARP)
Absurdism, 73
Acceptable use policy, 188
Adaptive deception protection, 207
Adolescent(s)
    advertising, 205
    coping with deceptive persuasion
        tactics, 175–176
    deception, 95
    executive function skills, 162
    MDP skills, 146
    persuasion, 205
    social interaction problems, 161
    social life domains, 156
Adolescent deception protection skills
    development, 143–162
    children's beliefs about television
        advertising, 146–148
    cross-context transfers, 156–159
    developmental psychology, 154–155
    domain specific skills, 156–159
    growing up targeted, 145
    marketplace deception-protection
        skills, 160–162
    persuasion knowledge development,
        149–153
    theory of mind, 154–155
Ad Skepticism Scale, 141
Adulthood deception protection skills
    development, 143–162
Advertising
    adolescents, 205
    authority tactics, 168
    children, 152–153
    coaching program effects, 170
    ethical practices, 170
    intentions, 152–153
    knowledge, 148, 152
    message deception, 147
    persuasion, 146
    processing, 150
    psychology, 116

    tactics in alcohol advertising, 177
    understanding, 153
Agent knowledge (AK), 33
Agent's motives truth effect, 112
AK. *See* Agent knowledge (AK)
Alcohol advertising
    ad tactics, 177
    coping strategies, 176–177
Aligned refutation product claims, 113
American Association of Retired Persons
    (AARP), 181
Anticipatory coping, 131
Art of Deception (Mitnick), 86
Assessed vulnerability approach, 171
Assurance seal, 119
Attention getting technology, 45, 46
Authority tactics, 50
    advertising, 168
Automatized inferencing tendencies
    exploitation, 67

B

BCP. *See* Bureau of Consumer
    Protection (BCP)
Biased framing, 63
Big con, 82–83
Bogeyman decoy, 61
Bookend distractions, 48
Bullshitting, 74–78
    marketing managers, 76
    marketplace tactics, 74–78
    salespeople, 76
Bureau of Consumer Protection
    (BCP), 193
    telemarketing, 194
Buyer-seller relationships, 199

C

Camouflage, 49
    marketplace deception tactics, 45–48
    tactics for deception, 41
Change-of-meaning process, 115
Charity fraud scams, 183

Children
    advertising intentions, 152–153
    advertising knowledge, 152
    beliefs about television advertising,
        146–148
    cognitive development, 155
    deception protection skills
        development, 146–148
    deception tactics, 158
    marketing pressure, 176
    marketplace, 158
    MDP skills, 157
    persuasion-related knowledge, 149
    persuasion-related skills, 149
    psychological baggage, 158
    social life domains, 156
Cigarette advertising coping, 178–180
Claim-belief interaction, 10
Claim-fact discrepancy, 10
Coaching program effects, 170
Cognitive cause-and-effect simulations, 60
Cognitive closure, 167
Cognitive development
    children, 155
    MDP skills, 144
    processes, 20
Cognitive processing, 84
Cognitive swamping, 53
College scholarship fraud, 195
Communication
    cooperative, 24
    copywriters deception, 81
    deception, 7
    deception protection skills, 124
    Gricean principles, 24
    marketing manipulative intent, 105
    mass deception, 188
    media, 206
    societal perspectives, 187–189
    stimuli deception, 83
    technology changes, 187–189
Concealment deception, 83
Consumer(s)
    attention deception, 40
    beliefs, 15
    cognitive closure, 167
    counter-deception skills, 124
    deception, 4, 99, 185, 187
    deceptive intent, 100
    deceptive persuasion, 131
    education programs, 19
    encoding, 100
    exploitation, 67
    false reality, 43

formation, 102
fraud, 4
inference, 102, 108
marketplace deception protection, 193, 194
omitted information, 103
post message attitudes, 109
problems, 187
processes, 108
product comparison, 103
protection, 17, 187, 191
psychologists persuasion, 116
research, 193, 194
researchers, 27
search sophistication, 193
self-protection, 139
self-regulatory skills, 124
sensitivity, 103
skills, 185
socialization skills, 161
television advertisements, 133
Consumer behavior
    deception, 3, 14
    deception protection, 189
    influence, 204
    persuasion, 204
    researchers, 117
Consumerism, 190
Consumer learning by analogy (CLA)
        model, 159
Contemporary developmental
        psychology, 154
Context bound deceptions, 13
Cooperative communication, 24
Coping
    appraisal PMT, 36
    deception persuasion, 1
    strategies, 97, 176–177
Corporate financial reports, 28
Corrupted persuasion tactics
    deception, 49
    marketplace deception tactics, 49–51
    resistance, 168–174
Counterarguing, 125, 128
Counter deception, 124
Credibility of media communication, 206
Critical deception insight, 151
Critical persuasion insight, 115
Cross checking, 69
Cross-context transfers, 156–159

D

DDT. See Deceptive disclosure tactics (DDT)
Deceit-minded marketers, 52

Deception
  accomplice, 12
  adolescence, 95
  advertising messages, 147
  alcohol advertising coping, 175–177
  authority tactics, 50, 172
  behaviors, 4
  camouflage tactics, 41
  commercial speech, 8
  communication, 7
  concealment, 83
  concepts, 6
  consumer, 40, 99
  consumer behavior, 3, 14
  consumer beliefs, 15
  consumer education programs, 19
  consumer researchers, 27
  contemporary developmental
      psychology, 154
  coping, 1
  coping development, 150
  coping skills, 143, 179
  coping strategy, 97
  core, 43
  corporate financial reports, 28
  corrupted persuasion tactics, 49
  cross checking, 69
  detection chances, 47
  economic consequences, 18
  economic knowledge, 148
  employees, 87, 197
  FDA, 200
  framings, 62–63
  FTC, 2, 11
  FTC Act, 9
  health care messages, 36
  impersonation, 174
  inside information, 90
  institution regulation, 19
  intent, 100
  intentional, 6
  Internet technology, 28
  interpersonal conversations, 22
  knowledge, 82
  landscaping methods, 90
  levels, 84
  lie-telling context, 23
  little lies, 8
  marketing behavior, 3
  marketing communication copywriters, 81
  marketing communication stimuli, 83
  marketing planners, 17
  marketing programs, 91
  marketplace definition, 7–8
  mass communication, 188
  methods for drug products, 72
  neutralizing skills, 125
  participants, 70
  persuasion, 1
  pictures, 74
  planning, 81
  pop culture, 203
  practices, 1, 14
  psychological effects, 152
  reality, 77
  resistance, 100
  risks, 93
  salespeople, 191
  self-protection rules, 171
  self-protective mindset, 99
  sequencing, 85
  social defenses, 66
  social trust, 18
  strategies, 65
  team, 80
  telemarketing, 87, 89
  telemarketing services, 65
  television advertising, 148
  tendencies, 118
  true self, 75
  truth monitoring, 67
  types, 5–6, 156
  validity tests, 77
  verbal skills, 138
  victims, 88
Deception detection
  coaching, 173
  deceptiveness coping prior
      research, 117–122
  designing teaching interventions, 175
  security systems, 15
Deception detective, 127
Deception marketers, 40, 92
  goals, 126
  marketing managers' deception
      decisions, 90–94
  professional deception planner mental
      model, 79–85
  social engineering, 86–87
  tactics, 98
  telescammer's mind, 88–89
  thinking, 79–94
Deception protection, 1, 36, 51, 123, 178
  beliefs, 163
  consumer activities, 189
  consumer problems, 187
  deceptive persuasion theoretical
      perspectives, 34

information, 192
knowledge, 30, 115
lessons, 171
risks, 134
Deception protection skills, 30, 39, 48,
        137, 163, 186
    adapting, 159
    cognitive development processes, 20
    communication skills, 124
    consumers, 185, 187
    development, 143–162
    MDP, 144
    social interaction, 124
Deception tactics, 34
    beliefs, 178
    children, 158
    framing, 62
    skills, 178
Deception theory
    deceptive persuasion theoretical
        perspectives, 22–28
    market economists, 29
Deceptive disclosure tactics (DDT), 42
Deceptive marketing, 16, 47, 163
    messages, 34–35, 131
Deceptive miscommunication theory
        (DeMiT), 26
Deceptiveness coping prior research, 95–122
    deception detection, 117–122
    heard-it-before truth effect, 111–113
    marketplace persuasion
        knowledge, 114–116
    message tactics, 102–110
    misleading interferences, 102–110
    omissions, 102–110
    suspicion, 96–99
    suspicion effects on subsequent
        persuasion attempts
        processing, 100–101
    uncertainty, 96–99
Deceptive Omega strategy, 54
Deceptive persuasion, 11, 13, 128
    adolescents cope, 175–176
    anatomy criteria, 39
    consumers, 131
    processes, 20
    tactics, 39, 175–176
Deceptive persuasion theoretical
        perspectives, 21–38
    aversion to being duped, 37–38
    deception protection, 34
    deception theory, 22–28
    dual-process persuasion models, 29

metacognition, 34
persuasion knowledge model, 32–33
persuasion resistance, 31
persuasion theory, 29–38
protection motivation theory, 35–36
regulatory focus theory, 35–36
social influence, 30
DeMiT. See Deceptive miscommunication
        theory (DeMiT)
Detection
    deceptive tactics, 174
    marketplace deception protection
        skills, 124–130
Developmental psychology, 154–155
Direct mail, 196
Disrupt-then-reframe (DTR)
    persuasion tactic, 130
    tactic, 110
Dissimulation tactic types, 44
Distraction, 45–48
Domain specific skills, 156–159
Doubt Is Their Product: How Industry's
        Assault on Science Threatens
        Your Health (Michaels), 72
Drug products, 72
DTR. See Disrupt-then-reframe (DTR)
Dual-intent message, 106
Dual-process persuasion models, 29
Dual-process theories, 29
Duped, 37–38

E

Economic consequences, 18
Economic knowledge, 148
Employee deception, 87, 197
Ethics
    marketplace deception, 15
    practices in advertising, 170
Event marketing, 145
Executive function skills, 162
Exploitation, 70–72

F

FBI. See Federal Bureau of Investigation
        (FBI) Internet Fraud
        Complaint Center
FDA. See Food and Drug Administration
        (FDA)
Federal Bureau of Investigation (FBI) Internet
        Fraud Complaint Center, 190
Federal Trade Act, 190

Federal Trade Commission (FTC), 193
  deception, 2
  marketing misrepresentations, 10
  staff members deception, 11
Federal Trade Commission (FTC) Act, 9
Financial services, 174
Flash flooding, 53
Food and Drug Administration (FDA), 200
Framings
  biased, 63
  deception tactics, 62–63
  loss-gain framing, 63
  marketplace deception tactics, 62–63
  persuasive, 109
  tactics, 62
  teaching, 174
  types, 63
Fraud, 126
FTC. *See* Federal Trade Commission (FTC)

G

General social confidence (GSC), 137
Giveaway clues, 24
Gricean principles, 24

H

Half-truths, 57
Hidden motives, 105

I

Illusion of falsity effect, 113
Image advertising, 179
Impersonation
  definition, 64
  marketplace deception tactics, 64
Implied claims coping, 164–175
Implied contrast, 68
Implied proof, 68
Implied significance, 68
Influence, 204
Inside information deception, 90
Institution regulation deception, 19
Integrated deception planning, 41
Intentional deception, 6
Internet
  marketing, 145
  spam, 195
  spyware, 195
  technology deception, 28
  trust, 199

Interpersonal conversations, 22
Interpersonal lies, 22

L

Landscaping
  methods, 90
  persuasion, 49
Learned deception-protective
  thinking, 31
Lie(s)
  context deception, 23
  deception, 8
  self-presentational perspective, 22
  telling, 23, 119
  vs. truth-telling, 119
Lie-bias state of mind, 120
Lie detection
  aspects, 120
  linguistic cues, 120
  skills, 121
Limited numeracy exploitation, 70–72
Loss-gain framing, 63

M

Malevolent distraction, 45
Manipulative intent, 105
Market economists, 29
Marketers
  confusion tactic, 111
  consumer inference, 102
  deception, 40, 92
  fraud, 126
  goals, 126
  misrepresentation, 44
  NFCC, 111
  strategies, 16
  tactics, 98
Marketing
  behavior, 3
  bullshit, 74–78
  campaigns, 42
  communication, 81, 83, 105
  FTC, 10
  managers, 76, 90–94
  messages, 95, 98
  misrepresentations, 10
  planners, 17
  pressure on children, 176
  programs, 91, 92
  tactics, 181
  tobacco firms, 179

Marketplace
  children, 158
  contexts, 106
  coping skills, 158
  interfaces confidence, 140
  knowledge, 115, 147
  persuasion, 32, 115, 147, 158
  persuasive intent, 106
  trust within societal
    perspectives, 197–200
Marketplace deception, 1–18
  context bound deceptions, 13
  deception agent's definition, 14
  defined, 6–7
  ethics, 15
  examination framework, 17–20
  legalistic definitions, 8–10
  modern marketplace deception, 3–16
  morality, 15
  persuasion, 11–12
  societal deception, 16
  society spectrums, 2
Marketplace deception protection
  (MDP), 53, 123, 129,
  135, 136, 143
  adolescents, 146
  belief components, 164
  children, 157
  cognitive development, 144
  components, 164
  consumer research, 193, 194
  deception skills, 144
  detection, 124–130
  development, 160, 162, 164, 201
  media literacy programs, 202
  neutralization, 124–130
  proactive coping skills, 131–132
  resistance, 124–130
  resource management skills, 133–135
  self-regulation, 139
  self regulatory resources, 123
  skills, 123–142
Marketplace deception protection
  self-efficacy (MDPSE), 136–142
Marketplace deception tactics, 39–58, 59–78
  automatized inferencing tendencies
    exploitation, 67
  camouflage, 45–48
  corrupted persuasion tactics, 49–51
  deceptive framings, 62–63
  distraction, 45–48
  exploitation, 70–72
  impersonation, 64
  limited numeracy exploitation, 70–72

  marketing bullshit, 74–78
  misleading language, 65–66
  omissions, 56–58
  persuasion tactics, 49–51
  research exploitation, 70–72
  rhetorical deception, 73
  run-around, 55
  simulation, 59–61
  statistical understanding
    exploitation, 70–72
  subverted persuasion tactics, 49–51
  suppressing deception-protection
    motivation and
    opportunity, 52–54
  types, 43–44
  verbal figures of speech, 73
  verbal misrepresentation, 68–69
  visual figures of speech, 73
  visual misrepresentation, 68–69
Masked stranger script, 184
Mass communication deception, 188
Mass media advertising, 169
MDP. See Marketplace deception
  protection (MDP)
MDSPE. See Marketplace deception
  protection self-efficacy
  (MDPSE)
Media communication credibility, 206
Media deception methods, 189
Media grammar, 202
Media literacy
  definition, 201
  programs, 202
Medicine advertising, 190
Messages
  cues, 107
  distribution, 42
  interpretation strategies, 25
  persuasive, 96, 101, 109
  processing, 107
  single-minded persuasion, 106
  tactics, 102–110
Metacognition
  confidence, 35
  deceptive persuasion theoretical
    perspectives, 34
Misleading interferences, 102–110
Misleading language, 65–66
Misleading statements, 66
Misunderstandings, 54
Modern marketplace deception, 3–16
Morality in marketplace deception, 15
Motivation within media communication, 206
Murk, uncertainty, and doubt (MUD), 200

N

Naive optimism, 25
Need for cognitive closure (NFCC), 110
   marketer's confusion tactic, 111
   types, 111
Negative consequences, 66
Neutralization, 124–130
Nondeceptive marketing, 90

O

Off the Hook program, 181–186
Omissions
   consumers' sensitivity, 103
   deceptiveness coping prior
      research, 102–110
   information, 56, 103
   information detection, 166–167
   marketplace deception tactics, 56–58
   neglect, 166

P

Page-jacking, 28
Partial truths, 176
Pattern-matching responses, 84
Persuasion
   adolescents, 205
   advertising, 117, 146
   agents, 71
   children, 149
   consumer behavior, 204
   consumer psychologists, 116
   coping skills, 179, 201
   development, 201
   information processing model, 127
   intent, 104, 106
   landscaping, 49
   marketplace deception, 11–12
   message, 96
   message framing, 109
   messages, 101
   motivated tactics, 116
   protection skills, 137
   psychologists, 203
   resistance, 31
   simulation, 60
   skills, 149
   social algorithms, 157
   thinking, 35
Persuasion knowledge (PK), 33
   children, 149
   development, 149–153

Persuasion knowledge model
   (PKM), 32, 114, 149
   deceptive persuasion theoretical
      perspectives, 32–33
   principles, 32–33
Persuasion tactics, 51
   identification development, 125
   marketplace deception tactics, 49–51
Persuasion theory, 21, 29–38
   aversion to being duped, 37–38
   dual-process persuasion models, 29
   metacognition and deception
      protection, 34
   persuasion knowledge model, 32–33
   persuasion resistance, 31
   protection motivation theory, 35–36
   regulatory focus theory, 35–36
   social influence, 30
Piagetian theory, 154
PK. See Persuasion knowledge (PK)
PKM. See Persuasion knowledge
      model (PKM)
PMT. See Protection motivation
      theory (PMT)
Point-of-sale displays, 153
Pop culture deception, 203
Post message attitudes, 109
Proactive coping, 131, 132
   development, 133
   marketplace deception protection
      skills, 131–132
Products
   claims, 113
   cognitive closure, 167
   comparison, 103
Product-to-product learning
      transfers, 160
Professional deception strategists, 79
Profits, Inc., 80
Promotion focus, 37
Protection motivation theory (PMT), 36
   coping appraisal, 36
   deceptive persuasion theoretical
      perspectives, 35–36
   threat appraisal, 36
Protection self confidence, 140
Protection self-efficacy, 136–142
Psychological baggage, 158
Pure Food and Drug Act, 190

R

Rare coin investments, 182
Razzle-dazzle, 48

Reality, 77
Refusal-skills ads, 180
Regulatory focus theory, 35–36
Representation, 9
Research exploitation, 70–72
Resistance, 124–130
    skill-based deception, 125
Resistance Preference Scale, 141
Resource management skills, 133–135
Rhetorical deception, 73
Risks, 93
Run-around strategy, 55

S

Salespeople
    bullshitting, 76
    deception, 191
Scammers, 89
Securities Exchange Commission
    (SEC), 196
Seeking and Resisting Compliance
    (Wilson), 32
Self-protection rules, 171
Self-protective mindset, 99
Self regulation, 139
    resources, 123
    skills, 124
Semiotics, 73
Servicescape, 60
Simulation
    definition, 60
    lures, 60
    marketplace deception
        tactics, 59–61
    persuasion, 60
Single-minded persuasion
    messages, 106
Skill-based deception resistance, 125
Social algorithms, 156
Social cognition theories, 21
Social consensus persuasion tactic, 51
Social defenses, 66
Social engineering
    deception-minded marketers
        thinking, 86–87
    deception techniques, 79
    tricks, 88
Social interaction
    adolescents, 161
    skills, 124
Social life domains, 156
Social persuasion, 12
Social trust, 18

Societal perspectives, 187–208
    communication technology
        changes, 187–189
    marketplace trust, 197–200
    regulatory protections, 190–196
    societal education, 201–208
    trust, 197–200
Society
    deception, 16
    education, 201–208
    spectrums, 2
Softening up tactics, 52
Sound science, 71
Statistical understanding
    exploitation, 70–72
Stealth marketing, 192
Subverted persuasion tactics, 49–51
Sugrophobia, 38
Suspicion, 96–99

T

Teaching marketplace deception
    protection skills prior
        research, 163–186
    cigarette advertising
        coping, 178–180
    corrupted persuasion tactics
        resistance, 168–174
    deceptive alcohol advertising
        coping, 175–177
    framing, 174
    implied claims coping, 164–175
    Off the Hook program, 181–186
    omitted information detection, 166–167
    telemarketing fraud participation
        reduction, 181–186
Technological deception methods, 189
Telemarketing
    BCP, 194
    deception, 87, 89
    fraud participation reduction, 181–186
    fraud scams, 163
    services, 65
Telemarketing Victim Call Center
    (TVCC), 182
Telescammers, 79
    mind, 88–89
Television advertising, 169
    consumers, 133
    deception, 148
Theory of mind (TOM), 154–155
Threat appraisal, 36
TK. See Topic knowledge (TK)

Tobacco firms, 179
Tobacco marketing, 181
TOM. *See* Theory of mind (TOM)
Topic knowledge (TK), 33
Transportation process, 54
Trust
    building impersonation tactics, 86
    buyer-seller relationships, 199
    definition, 198
    developmental factors, 199
    Internet, 199
    societal perspectives, 197–200
Truth
    agent's motives, 112
    bias, 95, 120
    effect, 112, 113
    monitoring, 67
    product claims, 113
    telling, 24, 46, 119
TVCC. *See* Telemarketing Victim
        Call Center (TVCC)
Two-sided appeals, 108

U

Uncertainty, 96–99
Undeceptive authority tactic, 172
Unprotected-persuasion cases, 135

V

Validity tests, 77
Verbal figures of speech, 73
Verbal lying, 68
Verbal misrepresentation, 68–69
Verbal skills, 138
Victims, 88
Visual deception, 70
Visual figures of speech, 73
Visual misrepresentation, 68–69

W

Weapons of Fraud (Shadel), 88
White lies, 8